THE REVOLUTIONS
OF 1848

THE REVOLUTIONS
OF 1848

Chapters from
Political and Social Upheaval

BY
WILLIAM L. LANGER

HARPER TORCHBOOKS
Harper & Row Publishers
New York, Evanston, San Francisco, London

This book appeared originally as chapters ten through fourteen in POLITICAL AND SOCIAL UPHEAVAL published in 1969 by Harper TORCHBOOKS.

THE REVOLUTIONS OF 1848

First TORCHBOOK edition published 1971.

LIBRARY OF CONGRESS CATALOGUE CARD NUMBER: 78–149362

STANDARD BOOK NUMBER: 06–131582–6

Chapter One

1848: THE SECOND REPUBLIC

I. THE EVE OF UPHEAVAL

IT HAS been perhaps too readily assumed that the revolutions which
broke over the Continent in 1848 reflected the rising power of the
middle class and its determination to force the recalcitrant governments to accept liberal reforms and constitutional government.
Tocqueville's great speech in the Chamber of Deputies on January 27,
1848, in which he warned of the danger of social as well as political
revolution, has been frequently quoted as prophetic. But a passage in
Tocqueville's *Recollections,* frequently overlooked, tends more or less
to deflate the importance of his address, for he remarks that in the
political melee of the time it was common practice to charge one's
opponents with endangering society. For that reason his warnings were
met with ironical sneers as well as with applause. Tocqueville admits,
furthermore, that he was not actually as alarmed as he claimed to be;
that in fact he did not expect so early or so formidable an uprising.
While perceiving the general factors making for revolution, he did not,
he confesses, foresee the accidents which were to precipitate it.[1]

Since it was the revolution in Paris on February 22, 1848, that set the
spark for the European conflagration, it is essential to understand its
causes and origins. In the first place, it should be remembered that in
France the well-to-do or upper middle class had gathered the fruits of
the July Revolution of 1830 and that the July Monarchy represented the
type of liberal government established in Britain in 1832 and aspired to
by the rising middle classes in other countries. There was from the
outset opposition to this regime on the part of intellectuals (writers,
artists, lawyers, doctors, educated workers), who regarded it as too
restricted and who in any case resented their exclusion from political life
for lack of sufficient income. Parenthetically, it might be remarked that

---

[1] J. P. Mayer, ed.: *The Recollections of Alexis de Tocqueville* (New York, 1959),
13–15; see also Edward T. Gargan: *Alexis de Tocqueville: the Critical Years, 1848–1851*
(Washington, 1955), 55 ff.

perhaps the most serious error committed by the governments of that time was the refusal to extend the franchise to this able, articulate and influential element of the population. Politically speaking, the opposition in France was nothing more than a parliamentary group, that is, a faction within the ruling class. Basically it objected to Guizot's monopoly of power and hoped to break his control by agitating for electoral reform. But even the more advanced wing of this "dynastic" opposition, the group around the newspaper *La Réforme,* though it advocated universal suffrage and some social legislation, was by no means revolutionary. Socialist writers, such as Louis Blanc, regarded revolution as premature and therefore doomed to failure resulting in a serious setback. All these men, from the parliamentary opponents of the regime, such as Thiers and Odilon Barrot, to the socialists, followed the career of Cobden and his Anti-Corn Law League. They hoped through propaganda and peaceful agitation to wear down the resistance to reform on the part of the government. The whole program of political banquets, also modeled on the British, was intended to open the way to a peaceful victory.[2]

In the Central European countries the professional and business classes were still striving to secure the type of political regime which already existed in France and Britain. The strength of the liberal movement varied from state to state, but the demand for the abolition of privilege and the introduction of constitutional government was common to all. Furthermore, the liberal program was everywhere a peaceful one, and everywhere it was beginning to bear fruit by 1848. In France most of the prominent deputies had joined the ranks of the opposition, and the National Guard, designed as the shield of the regime against revolution, was turning against it. It is hard to believe that the king and his prime minister could much longer have withstood the pressure from their opponents. In Germany the liberals of the Rhineland and Westphalia had become so insistent on reform that even the obstinate Prussian king was beginning to give way. Even in Vienna, the headquarters of reaction, many officials were in the ranks of the liberal opposition and in the court, too, there were advocates of reform. The dismissal of Metternich had by 1848 become a question

[2] Stanislas Mitard: *Les origines du radicalisme démocratique* (Paris, 1952), chap. iii; Alvin R. Calman: *Ledru-Rollin and the Second French Republic* (New York, 1922), 23 ff.; Leo R. Loubère: *Louis Blanc* (Evanston, 1960), 55 ff.; John J. Baughman: "The French Banquet Campaign of 1847–1848" (*Journal of Modern History,* XXXI. 1959, 1–15).

merely of time. As for Italy, the liberals there enjoyed the personal inspiration provided by Cobden's visit and Lord Minto's mission. They fully expected to realize their political program through peaceful agitation. The victory of the constitutional movement in the opening months of 1848 seemed to justify their expectations.[3]

There were, of course, genuinely revolutionary forces in Europe, as described in the foregoing chapters. But they were neither as numerous nor as well organized as the governments believed. The rulers, ever mindful of the French Revolution and the execution of Louis XVI, sat uneasily upon their thrones. They lived in chronic fear of secret societies and conspiracies aimed at themselves and at the whole political-social order. Actually the secret societies, even in Paris, were relatively weak in numbers and more or less paralyzed by dissension. They lacked leadership and clear programs. Their time had not yet come, as those clearheaded revolutionaries, Marx and Engels, were quick to realize. While trying to organize urban workers and unite them, they recognized that hopes of an early proletarian victory were illusory. They argued, therefore, that the correct strategy would be to support the *bourgeoisie* in its campaign to destroy the remnants of the feudal order, and thereafter to make war on it in its turn.

One is left then with the interesting problem of explaining how revolutions could break out in France and other countries and how they could triumph so easily. That the various governments had at their disposal the armed forces needed to suppress insurgency there can be no doubt. In France, for example, serious outbreaks had been beaten down on various occasions during the 1830's. And Czar Nicholas showed how, when confronted with seething discontent, one could escape revolution by using huge numbers of troops to snuff out opposition wherever it appeared and before it could attain dangerous proportions. By the application of ruthless measures he could even play the role of "gendarme of Europe."[4]

[3] Veit Valentin: *Geschichte der deutschen Revolution von 1848–1849* (Berlin, 1930), I, 400 ff., 416–417; Jacques Droz: *Les révolutions allemandes de 1848* (Paris, 1957), 71–83; Rudolf Stadelmann: *Soziale und politische Geschichte der Revolution von 1848* (Munich, 1948), 6 ff.; Heinrich von Srbik: *Metternich, der Staatsmann und der Mensch* (Munich, 1925), II, 259 ff.; Rudolf Kiszling: *Die Revolution im Kaisertum Oesterreich, 1848–1849* (Vienna, 1948–1952), I, 35.

[4] A. S. Nifontov: *Russland im Jahre 1848* (Berlin, 1954); Benjamin Goriely: "La Russie de Nicolas I en 1848" (in François Fetjö, ed.: *Le printemps des peuples,* Paris, 1948, 355–394); and especially John S. Curtis: *The Russian Army under Nicholas I* (Durham, 1965), chap. xi.

Other rulers, however, were more reluctant to have the troops shoot upon the populace and, what was more, they could not be sure that the troops would do so. The common soldiers of the new conscript armies could not be relied upon to fire upon their unarmed fellow citizens, as was shown in 1830 when two regiments of Marshal Marmont's forces defected in the very heart of Paris, and similar incidents took place in some of the disturbances in Germany. What this meant in effect was that the governments, while they had adequate military forces available, hesitated about using them, the more so as the new technique of barricade fighting, made possible by the paving blocks with which the streets were paved and the availability of other material for effective obstruction, greatly complicated the business of urban disorder.[5] One of the striking features of the revolutions of 1848 was the failure of the authorities to use the means of suppression which were at their disposal.

In retrospect it is hard to understand how the governments and the opposition elements could have been so purblind as to underestimate the dangers of truly popular insurrection. Much has already been said of the overcrowding of the cities, the unemployment and general misery of the lower classes. But all this must be underlined in speaking of the years 1846 and 1847, which were probably the worst of the entire century in terms of want and human suffering. For to the chronic hardships of the workers were added the tribulations resulting from crop failures, financial crisis and business depression. In the autumn of 1845 the potatoes, on which in many localities the lower classes depended for their food supply, suddenly turned black, became mushy and to a large extent inedible. It was an unknown disease, later identified as a fungus. In the following year the potato crop was again an almost complete failure. It was somewhat less disastrous in 1847, but again very poor in 1848. And to compound the food crisis, the grain crops, too, were below average in these years, so that the prices of wheat and rye quickly rose till they were double those of the preceding decade.[6]

[5] For greater detail, see the author's article "The Pattern of Urban Revolution in 1848" (in Evelyn M. Acomb and Marvin L. Brown, Jr., eds.: *French Society and Culture since the Old Regime,* New York, 1966, 90–118).

[6] T. P. O'Neill: "The Scientific Investigation of the Failure of the Potato Crop in Ireland, 1845–1846" (*Irish Historical Studies,* V, 1946, 123–138).

In Ireland, as might be expected, the potato famine led to one of the greatest tragedies of the century. Over 21,000 people died of actual starvation, while much larger numbers were taken off by hunger diseases such as typhus, dysentery and cholera, of which the latter occurred in violent epidemic form in 1849. It has been estimated that the "great hunger" claimed a million and a half victims, while another two hundred thousand fled annually on the typhus-stricken "plague ships," only to find a watery grave before reaching their destination. Travelers in Ireland saw corpses lying by the roadside and found the dead unburied in their deserted hovels. Everywhere strangers were besieged by starving, naked, desperate wretches (see Illustration 36). The 1851 Census reported that "the starving people lived upon the carcasses of diseased cattle, upon dogs, and dead horses, but principally upon the herbs of the field, nettle tops, wild mustard, and water-cresses. In some places dead bodies were found with grass in their mouths."[7]

During the famine England continued to import from Ireland large quantities of foodstuffs, even grain, which has led indignant critics to charge the London authorities with deliberately allowing the crisis to run its course in the hope of reducing the Irish population.[8] Although this charge is probably unwarranted, it is a fact that the British government was so deeply committed to the principles of private enterprise that it was most dilatory in taking relief action. At first it imported modest amounts of maize from America and sold them at low prices, and ultimately it set up a fairly extensive program of public works and introduced direct relief in the form of soup kitchens. But all these measures were taken without conviction. The prime minister, Lord John Russell, thought the idea of feeding a whole nation fantastic and was troubled about disturbing industry and trade by special grain

[7] Quoted in John E. Pomfret: *The Struggle for Land in Ireland, 1800–1923* (Princeton, 1930), 34. See also Lord Dufferin and G. F. Boyle: *Narrative of a Journey from Oxford to Skibereen* (London, 1847). The classic account of the famine is J. O'Rourke: *The History of the Irish Famine of 1847* (Dublin, 1875). There is a more recent, splendid co-operative study edited by R. D. Edwards and T. D. Williams: *The Great Famine* (Dublin, 1956), and a reliable, vividly written account by Cecil Woodham-Smith: *The Great Hunger* (London, 1962). On the horrors of the plague ships, see Arnold Shrier: *Ireland and the American Emigration* (Minneapolis, 1958), 157; and especially Oliver MacDonagh: *A Pattern of Government Growth, 1800–1860* (London, 1961).

[8] Francis Hackett: *The Story of the Irish Nation* (New York, 1922), 267 ff.; Edwards and Williams, *Great Famine*, viii–ix.

imports and public works. Charles E. Trevelyan, the official most directly responsible, was convinced that the situation must be left to "the operation of natural causes." The record of the government was certainly unedifying, but it was probably due more to "obtuseness, short-sightedness and ignorance" than downright heartlessness.[9]

On the Continent the crisis was only a little less disastrous than in Ireland. In Flanders many people were eating roots, grasses and carrion, and many others died of starvation and disease. By 1847 some 700,000 persons in Belgium were on public relief, while unknown numbers were succored by private charity. Thousands of wretched workers invaded the industral regions of northern France in search of work at almost any wage, only to be soon turned back over the frontier.[10]

In Germany the plight of the populations was such that the governments were obliged to import grain, open soup kitchens and provide employment through public works. Nonetheless serious food riots known as the "potato war" broke out in the spring of 1847 in Berlin and other cities (see Illustration 53). Barricades were thrown up and eventually troops had to be called out to quell the rioting. In Vienna, too, the workers attacked and plundered the foodshops before the government provided relief through the opening of soup kitchens.[11]

Unrest in France, too, produced food riots and attacks on grain transports, which in some localities had to be protected by troops. In Paris the price of bread rose by 50 per cent between 1845 and 1847, while the price of potatoes just about doubled.[12] Presently the situation

[9] Woodham-Smith: *Great Hunger,* chap. vii. Charles E. Trevelyan: *The Irish Crisis* (London, 1848) is practically an official defense. See further E. Strauss: *Irish Nationalism and British Democracy* (London, 1951), 85 ff.; Edwards and Williams: *Great Famine,* chap. iv.

[10] G. Jacquemyns: *Histoire de la crise économique des Flandres, 1845–1850* (Brussels, 1929), especially Books II and III; M. Défourny: "Histoire sociale" (in *Histoire de la Belgique contemporaine,* Brussels, 1928–1930, II, 258 ff.); Laurent Dechesne: *Histoire économique et sociale de la Belgique* (Paris, 1932), 418 ff.

[11] Sigmund Fleischmann: *Die Agrarkrise von 1845–1855* (Heidelberg, 1902); Jürgen Kuczynski: *Die Bewegung der deutschen Wirtschaft von 1800 bis 1946* (Berlin, 1947), 59 ff.; Theodore S. Hamerow: *Restoration, Revolution, Reaction* (Princeton, 1958), 77 ff.; and on Austria, Ernst von Zenker: *Die Wiener Revolution in ihren sozialen Voraussetzungen und Beziehungen* (Vienna, 1897), 96 ff.; Julius Marx: "Die Wirtschaftslage im deutschen Oesterreich vor dem Ausbruch der Revolution, 1848" (*Vierteljahrschrift für Sozial- und Wirtschaftsgeschichte,* XXXI, 1938, 242–282).

[12] Jeanne Singer-Kérel: *Le coût de la vie à Paris de 1840 à 1954* (Paris, 1961), 454, 462 ff.

was aggravated by a financial crisis and a business depression, which were much discussed but not fully understood.[13] The inevitable result was a rapid rise in the rate of unemployment. Thousands of workers, already faced with prohibitive food prices, had to rely on charity or public relief to keep body and soul together.[14]

Many writers, including Karl Marx, attributed the outbreak of revolution in 1848 to the misery and desperation of the masses.[15] This is true to a large extent, though the role and responsibility of the middle class should not be lost from view. Their demonstrations were often the occasion for the popular outbreaks. The banquet campaign of the French opposition illustrates the point perfectly. While the dining and speechmaking were the affair of those who could pay ten francs, huge numbers of non-diners gathered to listen to the denunciations of the government and the demands for reform. The opposition un-wittingly fanned the discontent of the masses without realizing the implications. Thiers was one of the few who objected to the banquet program, saying that he could see the red flag of the revolution under the banquet tables. But for the most part the government and the opposition were alike oblivious of the tremors already shaking society. As late as January, 1848, Louis Philippe is reported to have said to his Belgian relatives that he was so firmly in the saddle that "neither banquets of cold veal nor Bonaparte could unseat him."[16] And at the very same time the leaders of the dynastic opposition who were planning the monster Paris banquet actually called upon the populace

[13] Bertrand Gille: "Les crises vues par la presse économique et financière, 1815–1848" (*Revue d'histoire moderne*, XI, 1964, 5–30); T. J. Markovitch: "La crise de 1847–1848 dans les industries parisiennes" (*Revue d'histoire économique et sociale*, XLIII, 1965, 256–260).

[14] Henri Sée: *Histoire économique de la France* (Paris, 1951), II, 142 ff.; and the valuable studies collected by Ernest Labrousse, *Aspects de la crise et de la dépression de l'économie française, 1846–1851* (Paris, 1956), together with the lengthy review by Charles Pouthas in the *Revue d'histoire moderne et contemporaine*, IV, 1957, 309–316. See also Arthur L. Dunham: "Unrest in France in 1848" (*Journal of Economic History*, Suppl., VIII, 1948, 74–84); and on the situation in the northern industrial areas, the articles assembled in the *Revue du Nord* (XXXVIII, 1956).

[15] See Ernest Labrousse: "1848, 1830, 1789: comment naissent les révolutions" (*Actes du Congrès Historique du Centenaire de la Révolution de 1848*, Paris, 1948, 1–30); François Fejtö: "L'Europe à la veille des révolutions" (in his *Le printemps des peuples*, Paris, 1948, I, 25–126).

[16] Quoted by Brison D. Gooch: *Belgium and the February Revolution* (The Hague, 1963), 18.

to demonstrate, so as to make the function more impressive. Political myopia and stupidity could hardly be carried further.

2. FRANCE: THE FEBRUARY REVOLUTION

The French Revolution of 1848 was, like that of 1830, a matter of "three glorious days" of rioting and barricade fighting. It was the work of the opposition leaders, both inside the outside the Parliament, whose objective was to force Guizot from office and impose upon the king a cabinet that would put through political reforms. The occasion for the demonstrations was a monster banquet, to be held in Paris on February 22, 1848, with reduced rates to attract members of the lower middle class. The government, having first prohibited the project, agreed that it might be held in a well-to-do neighborhood, near the Champs Elysées, but only symbolically: that is, the banqueters were to disband at once on orders of the police and then test the legality of such assemblies in the courts. Many of the opposition leaders became soured on the whole enterprise, fearing it might have unwanted consequences, but a hard core of activists, such as Ledru-Rollin and others of the *Réforme* group, insisted on accepting the government's challenge. They called on the populace to assemble on the morning of February 22 at the Place de la Madeleine and invited the National Guard to join in a grand procession preceding the banquet. Deputies, National Guards in formation (though unarmed), students, and journalists were to march together up the Champs Elysées to the banqueting place. News of these arrangements, when it appeared in the newspapers, struck fears into the hearts of most of the opposition, who in a hastily convoked meeting, voted by a large majority to drop the whole business, parade, banquet and all. Even the most advanced newspapers now counseled the people to avoid trouble, to observe legality, and to deny the government a bloody success. Only a few, the poet Lamartine among them, stuck to the plan. He would march, declared Lamartine, though accompanied only by his shadow.[17]

Doubts as to the wisdom of the enterprise proved fully warranted.

[17] John J. Baughman: "The French Banquet Campaign of 1847–1848" (*Journal of Modern History*, XXXI, 1959, 1–15). On the February events, still the fullest study is that of Albert Crémieux: *La Révolution de février* (Paris, 1912). There are several more succinct and lively accounts, such as Maurice Soulié: *Les journées de février* (Paris, 1929); Jean Bruhat's book of the same title (Paris, 1948); and most recently the stimulating essay by Georges Duveau: *1848: the Making of a Revolution* (New York, 1967).

On the morning of February 22 a substantial crowd collected on the Place de la Madeleine, despite the cold and rainy weather. Presently a group of students appeared from the Left Bank and led a contingent to the Chamber of Deputies, where they were turned back by the police. Soon the crowds became unruly: street lamps were broken, omnibuses overturned, and efforts made to throw up barricades. However, the disturbances were desultory and sporadic. The police, occasionally supported by troops, seemed quite capable of dealing with the rioters and their barricades. In the evening the troops were ordered back to their barracks, which were scattered throughout the city. The king congratulated his ministers on their handling of the situation.[18]

It is little short of amazing that the situation should have been viewed with so much equanimity in court circles, for even though the crowds were as yet shouting only for the dismissal of Guizot and the adoption of reforms, the plight of the populace was certainly common knowledge and it could hardly have been supposed that the fracas would end with the pillage of gunshops and a few futile efforts to construct barricades. Furthermore, the Paris police, consisting chiefly of the Municipal Guard, was never intended to cope with larger disturbances. It numbered only about 3,500 men, mostly former soldiers, organized militarily in sixteen companies of infantry and five squadrons of cavalry. This Municipal Guard was renowned for its toughness and brutality, but its function, according to the prefect of police, was to prevent crime and forestall disturbances rather than to suppress them. Under the French system it was the National Guard, numbering in Paris about 80,000 and organized by legions (one for each of the twelve *arrondissements,* plus an elite cavalry legion), that was responsible primarily for protection of the regime. The National Guard was basically a bourgeois organization, hence meant to be the mainstay of the bourgeois monarchy. It had performed well in the early 1830's, but since 1840 had become more and more disaffected, so that by 1848 most of the legions were on the side of the opposition, not necessarily hostile to the monarchy, but certainly hostile to Guizot. The garrison troops, some 30,000 in number, were intended only for use in extreme situations, if called upon by the National Guard. In a nutshell, then, the

---

[18] Sébastien Charléty: *La Monarchie de Juillet* (Paris, 1921) is still one of the best accounts. The valuable police report for February 22 has now been published by Jean Tulard: *La préfecture de police sous la Monarchie de Juillet* (Paris, 1964), 168 ff.

police force, while excellent and devoted, was too small to handle a large-scale uprising. The troops were meant only for use as a reserve. All then depended on the National Guard, which was known to be discontented and unreliable. It is impossible to understand the optimism prevalent in government circles on the evening of February 22 without assuming that Louis Philippe expected that the Guard, when officially called out, would stand by the regime.[19]

On the morning of February 23, despite the foul weather, the crowds were larger than ever. The center of disturbance moved from the open avenues of the west to the old, congested, narrow streets of the center, where barricades could more easily be built. The mood of the people, too, had become more aggressive. To the shouts of "down with Guizot" and "long live reform" were now added denunciation of the king and the dynasty. The National Guard proved itself utterly ineffectual from the government standpoint. Even the legions from the wealthiest districts joined in the demand for reform. Those from the poorer sections were alarmingly radical. To quote an eminent French historian, the government, faced by a leaderless, amorphous riot, called up the National Guard and thereby created another, armed and official, riot. Naturally frightened by the almost total defection of the *bourgeoisie,* Louis Philippe in the early afternoon precipitately and unceremoniously dismissed Guizot.[20]

Had the king now called opposition leaders such as Thiers or Barrot to form a ministry, the situation might have been saved. But he disliked Thiers and detested the idea of reform. So matters remained in suspense while the disorders became more and more widespread and violent. Eyewitnesses are agreed that the Municipal Guard fought valiantly and well. But 3,500 men could hardly master the situation, the more so as the National Guardsmen openly fraternized with the rioters. As for the troops, they were badly shaken by the unwillingness

[19] On the police, Paul Pichon: *Histoire et organisation des services de police en France* (Issoudun, 1949), 88 ff., and especially Tulard: *La préfecture de police,* 61 ff. On the National Guard, the excellent monograph of Louis Girard: *La garde nationale, 1814–1871* (Paris, 1964); and on the troops, Jean Vidalenc: "L'armée française sous la Monarchie Constitutionelle" (*Information historique,* XI, 1949, 57–62).

[20] Charléty: *La Monarchie de Juillet,* 389. Crémieux: *La Révolution de février,* chap. iv, contains an analysis of the attitude of the various Guard legions. See also Girard: *La garde nationale,* 284 ff.; Adeline Daumard: *La bourgeoisie parisienne de 1815 à 1848* (Paris, 1963), 595 ff.

of the National Guard to play its assigned role. Without clear directives, army officers became discouraged and the troops demoralized.[21]

Events took a turn for the worse when, on the evening of February 23, a surging mob, accompanied by National Guards, collided with a detachment of troops on the Boulevard des Capucines (see Illustration 58). The troops, hard pressed, became panicky and opened fire, with the result that forty or fifty persons were left dead or wounded on the pavement. The populace, furious over this "massacre," paraded the dead through the town and spent the night in preparations to resist the government's alleged plan to slaughter the workers. To the wild sound of the tocsin, well over a million paving stones were torn up and over 4,000 trees felled to build the more than 1,500 barricades that by morning studded the city (see Illustration 59).[22]

When finally the king came to a decision, it was one that involved contradictory action. On the one hand he called on Thiers and Barrot to form a ministry, which was meant as a gesture of conciliation, and on the other he appointed General Bugeaud, the victor of the Algerian campaigns and a soldier itching to put "the rabble" in its place, to command both the troops and the National Guard, an obviously provocative move.[23] Both steps proved utterly futile. Thiers, who had greeted the downfall of Guizot with enthusiasm as ridding him of a hated opponent without jeopardizing the regime, found himself on the morning of February 24 swept along the streets by a menacing crowd and was, by the time he reached the Chamber of Deputies, so unnerved that he refused to take part in the debates and hurried back to his home by a roundabout route. His companion reported him as almost out of his wits, gesticulating, sobbing, uttering incoherent phrases.[24]

The fire-eating Bugeaud fared no better. He tried hard, on the morning of the 24th, to reopen communications between key points of the city, but failed, chiefly because of the almost complete defection of the National Guard and the demoralization of the troops, many of whom abandoned their weapons to the insurgents. By noon he was obliged to give up the attempt and proclaim a cease-fire. Louis Philippe made a last effort to rally at least some of the legions of the National

[21] P. Chalmin: "La crise morale de l'armée française" (in *L'armée et la Séconde République*, Paris, 1955, 27–76).
[22] Henri Guillemin: *La tragédie de quarante-huit* (Paris, 1948).
[23] Pierre de La Gorce: *Louis Philippe* (Paris, 1931), 403.
[24] Alexis de Tocqueville: *Recollections*, 60.

Guard and, having failed, decided to abdicate and flee the country. Only in disguise and secrecy was the royal family able to reach Le Havre and embark for England.

In the last analysis the bourgeois National Guard, organized solely to protect the dynasty and the regime, had become disgusted with both and had proved altogether unwilling to fight for it. Tocqueville quotes one guardsman as saying: "We don't want to get killed for people who have managed their business so badly." Not that the middle classes, either in or out of Parliament, had wanted a revolution. On the contrary, they feared disorders. But they had themselves aroused the populace with banquets and demonstrations, and appear to have thought, even in the February days, that they could manage the people once Guizot had been gotten rid of. The revolution was a remarkably bloodless one. On the government side there were only eighty dead, and on the popular side about 290. As revolutions go, this one proved mild because the resistance was so ineffectual.[25]

The tumult of February, 1848, ended with the insurgent assault on the Tuileries Palace, only minutes after the precipitate departure of the king and his family (see Illustration 43). Meeting with little resistance, the crowd overran the palace, threw the throne into the courtyard and wrecked the furnishings: "The common herd ironically wrapped themselves up in laces and cashmeres. Gold fringes were rolled around the sleeves of blouses. Hats with ostrich feathers adorned blacksmiths' heads, and ribbons of the Legion of Honor supplied waistbands for prostitutes" (Flaubert).

Meanwhile several members of the more moderate opposition (those of the newspaper *Le National*) had worked out a plan for a regency. Louis Philippe had abdicated in favor of his nine-year-old grandson, the Count of Paris, whose father had been killed in a carriage accident some years before. Since his uncle, the Duke of Nemours, was an archconservative and extremely unpopular, it was the idea of Barrot, the most recently appointed premier, that the boy's mother, Princess Hélène of Mecklenburg, who was attractive and well-liked, should

---

[25] For a vivid account of the final phase, see *Les barricades: scènes les plus saisissantes de la Révolution de 1848* (Paris, 1848). Gustave Flaubert: *L'éducation sentimentale* (1869) conveys a sense of complete confusion. The recently published observations of a Swiss eyewitness are particularly revealing: see "William de La Rive: un témoin génévois de la Révolution de 1848" (*Etudes*, XV, 1953, 143–163).

serve as regent. But this scheme, adopted with some enthusiasm by the deputies, was wrecked in almost no time. The crowds were shouting for a republic and were hardly in a mood to accept an arrangement so reminiscent of the deal of July, 1830. Furthermore, Lamartine had been won to the idea of a republic, on the theory that any other solution would mean renewed conflict and disastrous divisions. Having disappeared during the days of greatest crisis, the poet now emerged as the man called upon to lead "the people" along the road to a democratic republic, which in turn would unite all Frenchmen and usher in a new age of general welfare. In the critical days of late February, Lamartine of all men showed himself self-assured and courageous. He had helped to precipitate the troubles, and he was now to contribute substantially to the restoration of order.

It was about 1:30 P.M. on February 24 when the Duchess of Orleans arrived at the Chamber of Deputies with the heir to the throne and his younger brother. In the general hubbub she was unable to make herself heard, but Barrot spoke eloquently in favor of her regency until he was shouted down by a crowd of armed men—National Guards and workers—who invaded the hall. Ledru-Rollin, the confirmed republican, then made a windy speech calling for appointment of a provisional government, a demand supported by Lamartine. The latter, after a moving tribute to the courageous princess fighting for the rights of her son, proceeded to argue that what was needed was a government that could stop the flow of blood and forestall a civil war. The ultimate decision must be left to the country, to "that sublime mystery of universal sovereignty," but a provisional government was necessary to tide over. At this point a second and more ferocious invasion took place. Ruffians, coming from the sack of the Tuileries, brandished their guns and insulted the deputies, most of whom, including the president, fled for safety, leaving their seats to the newcomers. The duchess and her party, almost suffocated, barely managed to escape through a side corridor.[26]

Despite the pandemonium, Lamartine finally secured approval of a

---

[26] Crémieux: *La Révolution de février,* 373 ff. analyzes the often contradictory sources for this episode. See also Paul Bastide: *Doctrines et institutions politiques de la Séconde République* (Paris, 1945), I, 36 ff., 104 ff., and recent studies of the revolution such as Felix Ponteil: *1848* (Paris, 1937); Jean Dautry: *1848 et la Deuxième République* (2 ed., Paris, 1957); Emile Tersen: *Quarante-huit* (Paris, 1957); Georges Duveau: *1848* (New York, 1967).

provisional government, the membership of which was a distillation of numerous lists then in circulation. The president was an eighty-year-old revolutionary war horse, Dupont de l'Eure, who would serve as a figurehead. Lamartine, who was presently to become minister of foreign affairs, was to be the real leader. The others (Arago, Marie, Garnier-Pagès, Crémieux) were members of the moderate wing of the opposition, while Ledru-Rollin, a wealthy lawyer and eloquent republican agitator, represented the left wing. Late in the afternoon these harassed men set out on foot for the Hôtel de Ville, traditionally the focal point of Parisian affairs, where they had reason to fear lest the populace had already set up its own revolutionary government.

It was only with great difficulty that Lamartine and his associates could make their way through the throngs and into the building. Once inside, they were so beset with delegations that they had to move from one room to another in search of a spot for quiet deliberation. Presently a group, headed by Louis Blanc, arrived from the offices of *La Ré-forme,* the journal of the democratic, socialist group. Blanc demanded that members of his party be included in the government, and it was finally decided that Blanc, Flocon (editor of *La Réforme*) and a mechanic named Albert should be appointed secretaries to the provisional government. Though in the sequel they were to play a role equal to that of the regular members, this initial episode is instructive as revealing the reluctance of the moderate element to admit the more radical leaders to full standing.

During the hectic days that followed, the government was obliged, under popular pressure, to make a number of decisions, some of which at least went beyond what was palatable. Freedom of speech, assembly and association were proclaimed and the death penalty abolished in political cases. The troops, humiliated and disgruntled, were ordered withdrawn from the city and the detested Municipal Guard was dissolved. Caussidière, a prominent member of the revolutionary clubs, took over as chief of police and began to form a new Popular Guard (*garde du peuple*) drawn from recently released political prisoners. The government hastened, too, to order the recruitment of 24,000 volunteers between the ages of sixteen and thirty, to be organized as a National Mobile Guard (*garde nationale mobile*), two battalions for each *arrondissement,* the men to be paid 1.50 francs per day. By these measures it was hoped to re-establish an effective police force and at the same time take off the streets some of the restless, unemployed youngsters and ne'er-do-wells.[27]

The overriding issues, however, were those of the form of government and the "organization of labor." The crowds, milling about in front of the Hôtel de Ville, insisted on the proclamation of the republic, so as not again to be wheedled out of the fruits of their revolution. Most members of the provisional government had come to the conviction that any other form of government was for the time being impractical and likely to lead to further conflict. But Lamartine for one was unwilling to proclaim the republic out of hand. The whole country, he thought, was entitled to a voice in the matter. Time and again he harangued the crowd while his colleagues devised a formula saying that while the provisional government desired a republic, the final decision should be left to a nationwide vote, which should be taken as soon as possible. However, in the tumult and confusion Blanc and others gave the people to understand that the republic had in fact been proclaimed. There was little to be done about this, but Lamartine managed at least to talk the crowds out of adopting the red flag of the revolution in place of the tricolor. But here again something had to be done by way of compromise: members of the government agreed to wear a red rosette in their buttonholes and decreed that there should be a similar rosette at the peak of all flagstaffs.[28]

But the crowds wanted a social as well as a political republic. The "organization of labor" and the "right to work" were slogans on every tongue. The new regime must do something to ensure against unemployment, hunger and general misery, which were the chief grievances of the populace in these critical years. "Every trade, every industry was looking to the government to put a complete end to its miseries," says Flaubert. Around noon of February 25 an unknown young worker forced an entrance into the council chambers of the government and,

---

[27] P. Chalmin: "Une institution militaire de la Séconde République: la garde nationale mobile" (*Etudes d'histoire moderne et contemporaine*, II, 1948, 37–82); Max Jahns: *Das französische Heer* (Leipzig, 1873), 339 ff.

[28] Maurice Dommanget: *La Révolution de 1848 et le drapeau rouge* (Paris, 1948); J. S. Shapiro: "Lamartine: a Study of the Poetic Temperament in Politics" (*Political Science Quarterly*, XXXIV, 1919, 632–643); Ethel Harris: *Lamartine et le peuple* (Paris, 1932), Book III, chap. i; Henri Guillemin: *Lamartine en 1848* (Paris, 1948); André Becheyras: "Lamartine au pouvoir" (in *Esprit de 1848*, Paris, n.d., 41–76); Gordon Wright: "A Poet in Politics: Lamartine in 1848" (*History Today*, VIII, 1958, 616–627).

banging his rifle butt on the floor, exclaimed: "Citizens, the revolution was achieved twenty-four hours ago and the people is still waiting for results." Lamartine's attempt to reply was cut off with the words: "Enough of phrases, enough of poetry." The government was to proclaim the organization of labor within the hour. Lamartine refused, saying that he did not even know what was meant by the term. At this point Blanc saved the day by promising that the government would guarantee the workers employment and would give recognition to their associations. Thereupon the worker withdrew, never again to be heard from.[29]

Since Blanc and the workers were in control of the situation, it was impossible for other members of the government to gainsay his socialistic program. On February 26 it was decreed that national workshops (*ateliers nationaux*) should be opened in various sections of the city and that those admitted should be paid 2.00 francs a day when employed and 1.50 francs (later reduced) when not employed. Had Blanc had his way, these workshops would have been organized by trades and would have been producers' co-operatives such as he had long advocated. As it was, the national workshops had little in common with the social workshops (*ateliers sociaux*) beyond the resemblance in name. They were really nothing but a new version of the familiar *ateliers de charité*, or relief works in which the unemployed were put on grading or other unskilled jobs, without reference to trade. As for Blanc, the government, while rejecting his demand for a ministry of progress, appointed him chairman of a commission of labor, which became known as the Luxembourg Commission, from the palace where it held its sessions. Blanc quickly assembled representatives of different trades and, with their support, obliged the government on March 2 to decree the reduction of the workday in Paris to ten hours, and in the provinces to twelve. Needless to say, this regulation was not very scrupulously observed, since no provision was made for supervision or enforcement.[30]

[29] J. A. R. Marriott: *The Right to Work* (Oxford, 1919), lviii ff.; Donald C. McKay: *The National Workshops* (Cambridge, 1933), 10–11; Georges Lefranc: *Histoire du travail et des travailleurs* (Paris, 1957), 325 ff.

[30] Still valuable is the contemporary article by the economist Michel Chevalier: "Question des travailleurs: l'amélioration du sort des ouvriers; l'organisation du travail" (*Revue des deux mondes,* March 15, 1848, 1057–1086). See also Pierre Loustau: *Louis Blanc à la commission du Luxembourg* (Paris, 1908); Paul Keller: *Louis Blanc und die Revolution von 1848* (Zürich, 1926).

3. THE SECOND REPUBLIC

For several months after its proclamation the history of the Second Republic was one of stormy uncertainty. The provisional government, composed largely of men of moderate views, was more or less at the mercy of the populace, which meant the lesser middle class and the skilled artisans as well as the workers and paupers. For the time being Paris was without police protection of any kind. The Municipal Guard, which had done its duty all too well and had thereby incurred the undying hatred of the people, was at once dissolved, to be replaced gradually by the new *garde mobile*. The National Guard, whose part in the revolution had been crucial, was thrown open to all, so that by mid-March almost a hundred thousand were enrolled. It stands to reason that time would be required before these huge numbers could be integrated and the legions reformed and trained. As for the troops, they had been withdrawn from the city, utterly demoralized and disgruntled over their humiliating experience. In these circumstances the government had nowhere to look for support against the excesses of the population.

The situation, bad enough to begin with, was much aggravated by the onset of a severe financial and business crisis. The disorders of late February brought business to a standstill and provoked a panic. There were runs on the banks, bankruptcies and failures, so that the Bourse had to be closed. Government 5 per cent bonds fell from 116 on February 23 to 89 on March 7 and to 50 by April. With the economy paralyzed, it was inevitable that vast numbers of workers should find themselves idle. Where in 1847 about 335,000 had been employed in Paris, in 1848 there were only 147,000. An official investigation revealed that over 50 per cent of the work force was thrown out of work, and that production declined by about 53 per cent.[31] The government, faced by a rapidly mounting deficit, decided that the only alternative to national bankruptcy was the levy of a surtax of 45 centimes on every franc paid in direct taxes, exemptions to be made only at the discretion of the tax collector. By this device the unpropertied urban workers

---

[31] T. J. Markovitch: "La crise de 1847–1848 dans les industries parisiennes" (*Revue d'histoire économique et sociale*, XLIII, 1965, 256–260), which analyzes the voluminous inquiry of the Paris Chamber of Commerce. On the financial crisis, see also Jean Bouchary: "Economie et finances" (in Charles Moulin, ed.: *1848: le livre du centenaire*, Paris, 1948, 257–268).

would not be affected. The burden would fall on the landed classes, who did not for the moment present a threat to the regime or to society.[32]

The general acceptance of the republic not only by the middle class but by the aristocracy and the Catholic Church has often been commented on. There was indeed a closing of ranks to meet the threat of radical political and social revolution. For the new freedom removed all obstacles to the formation of radical clubs and the launching of radical newspapers. Within a few weeks there were 170 new journals and more than 200 clubs, in which popular leaders could expound the most advanced political and socialistic ideas. Thus Auguste Blanqui, the uncompromising revolutionist, founded the Central Republican Committee on the very day (February 28) of his release from prison. It soon had 3,000 members, with meetings every evening except Sunday. There Blanqui, in his prison rags, wearing black gloves, made a frightening appearance—dour, emaciated, fanatical, according to Victor Hugo "a gloomy apparition in which all the hatred born of all the miseries was incarnated."[33] One can understand how members of the middle class, once they had overcome their initial stupefaction, should have been agreeably surprised to find themselves still alive (Flaubert), but one can also understand their growing dread of the radical tide that confronted them.

Radical leaders kept harping on the theme that the people would not again allow the government to betray the principles of the revolution. There was to be not another bourgeois regime, but a political and social democracy. Furthermore, France was to resume its traditional role of champion of the rights of the people everywhere: it was to embark, if need be, on a crusade of liberty. Once freed of the yoke of tyranny, Europe could be reorganized as "the great European republic," a federation of free peoples transcending the narrow limits of

---

[32] See Rémi Gossez: "La resistance à l'impôt: les quarante-cinq centimes" (*Etudes*, I, 1953, 89–131); Ernest Labrousse: *Aspects de la crise et de la dépression de l'économie française, 1846–1851* (Paris, 1956).

[33] Charles Moulin: "Les clubs et la presse" (in *1848: le livre du centenaire*, 139–158); Suzanne Wassermann: *Les clubs de Barbès et de Blanqui* (Paris, 1913); Peter Amann: "The Changing Outlines of 1848" (*American Historical Review*, LXVIII, 1963, 938–952). Flaubert, in his *Education sentimentale*, gives a vivid account of a meeting of the Club of the Intellect, where everyone talked at once about altogether unrelated matters.

nationality: "In that holy, blessed day there will be no more wars of partition, of domination, of nationality, of influence."[34] Of course France, as the recognized leader of the new order, would see that a "just" settlement replaced the treaty of 1815, and a just settlement would mean the "natural" frontiers of the Rhine and the Alps. Thus French patriots, defying all logic, were eager to fight for the liberties of other peoples, but equally prepared to relieve them of part of their territory.[35]

Once again, then, the French Republic appeared as a threat to the peace of Europe. Czar Nicholas at once mobilized a large army to support any victim of French aggression. The Austrians prepared to fight in Italy, and the German states looked to Prussia to meet a possible assault on the Rhine. Most immediately threatened were the Belgians, who promptly appealed to the British for support. But Palmerston did not share the general alarm. He looked with scorn upon the new republic as the rule of forty or fifty thousand of the "scum of the faubourgs of Paris" and firmly believed that, if left to themselves, the French would soon restore the Orleans dynasty.[36] He therefore urged the other governments to avoid interference with France unless the latter actually embarked upon aggression.

Lamartine, Ledru-Rollin and Blanc had all, in the past, denounced Guizot's compliant foreign policy and had voiced hopes of sometime regaining France's "lost" territories. But Lamartine, now that he was responsible for France's security, proved himself a hardheaded realist. He at once made a bid for British friendship, so as to forestall attack by the Holy Alliance, and gave assurances with respect to Belgium and Spain, the areas of greatest British concern. Then on March 4 he published a directive to French diplomats, which was a masterpiece of contradiction. As a sop to French opinion he declared that in the eyes

---

[34] Garnier-Pagès, quoted by Pierre Quentin-Bauchart: *Lamartine et la politique étrangère de la Révolution de Février* (Paris, 1913), 26.

[35] Emile Tersen: *Le gouvernement provisoire et l'Europe* (Paris, 1948), 21; Quentin-Bauchart: *Lamartine,* 27: "They spoke less of the Rhine frontier and more of the deliverance of their oppressed brothers, but it was always the treaties of 1815 that they wanted to destroy." See also Paul Henry: *La France devant le monde* (Paris, 1945), 144 ff.

[36] Herbert Bell: *Lord Palmerston* (New York, 1936), I, chap. xix; Brison D. Gooch: *Belgium and the February Revolution* (The Hague, 1963), 27 ff.; Eugène de Guichen: *Les grandes questions européennes et la diplomatie des puissances sous la Seconde République* (Paris, 1925), I, 52 ff.

of the French Republic the treaties of 1815 were no longer valid. He then hastily added that as a practical matter the new regime would respect the *status quo*. France would not attack its neighbors, but would, if appealed to, come to the aid of oppressed peoples struggling for their freedom. In substance this long and windy document proclaimed a policy of peace, as Palmerston at once recognized. British opinion, as well as the foreign secretary, paid tribute to Lamartine, who was obviously a man of sense.

On the other hand, French opinion was far from satisfied. The provisional government, it seemed, was reverting to the pusillanimous policy of the past regime. Paris was full of foreigners, political exiles and workers, many of whom were members of the secret societies and now established clubs of their own. In addition, delegations began to arrive from "oppressed" peoples everywhere, soliciting support. There were English Chartists, Irish Nationalists, Belgians, Swiss, Poles, even Hungarians, Rumanians and Portuguese. Various members of the government received these delegations sympathetically, and put them off with promises of support in the event of active repression by their governments. "We love Poland, we love Italy, we love all oppressed peoples," said Lamartine to the Poles; "but we love France above all else and we are responsible for its destinies and perhaps for those of all Europe."[37]

The activists heard only as much as they wanted to hear. During March the Belgians, the Germans and the Savoyards all organized filibustering forces, confident that in a crisis the French government would come to their aid and meanwhile hoping to set the spark of revolution in their homelands. No doubt the French government was glad to be rid of these restless foreigners. Ledru-Rollin, the minister of the interior, gave them moral as well as modest financial support. But the foreign "legions" were poorly organized and ill-equipped. On crossing the frontiers they were quickly defeated. Beyond reviving the fears and suspicions of neighboring countries, they accomplished nothing. On the French side the radicals were profoundly disappointed. In every club and coffeehouse they had been busily rearranging the map of Europe and laying plans for the forthcoming crusade. They dreamed of landing in England, joining the Chartists, overthrowing the government and eventually liberating the Irish. Similar dreams were

[37] Henry: *La France devant le monde*, 150 ff.

indulged in with respect to Continental countries. Yet here was Lamartine and the government putting off foreign revolutionaries with fine words. In retrospect the workers' paper *L'atelier* in 1849 wrote that by refusing to liberate Poland, Italy, Hungary, the provisional government had given the tyrants of Europe a chance to recover their breath and at home had hastened the restoration of the conservative elements. Indeed, a whole century later the eminent socialist leader Léon Blum, though a confirmed pacifist, was to bemoan the failure of the government in 1848 to take the lead in a general revolution of the European peoples.[38]

The members of the provisional government were generally agreed that France could under no circumstances afford to become involved in foreign war, which would inevitably lead to radical dictatorship at home. On equally pressing domestic policies, however, opinion was divided. On March 2 the government had yielded to popular demand and decreed the introduction of universal manhood suffrage, which meant enlarging the electorate from 250,000 to 9,000,000. But even Ledru-Rollin, long the proponent of this system, now began to have doubts about suddenly calling upon the political scene millions of uneducated peasants and workers. In the hope of preparing a favorable outcome of the elections, which were fixed for April 9, he sent out special commissioners to replace the prefects. In late March several commissioners-general were appointed as "veritable proconsuls" for different regions. Despite opposition these commissioners worked hard and generally successfully to see that the right candidates were on the electoral lists and that influence and patronage were applied in the right places.[39]

Ledru-Rollin's misgivings about the possible outcome of early elections were fully shared by the radicals, who feared that the ignorant peasants and workers would be completely under the domination of employers, landlords and clergy, whose enthusiasm for the republic was thought to be superficial at best. Blanqui for one foresaw civil war

[38] Léon Blum: "La Révolution de Février" (*Revue socialiste*, n.s., No. 20, 1948, 321–336). In general see Georges Duveau: "Les relations internationales dans la pensée ouvrière, 1840–1865" (*Actes du Congrès Historique du Centenaire de la Révolution de 1848*, Paris, 1949, 277–283).

[39] P. Haury: "Les commissaires de Ledru-Rollin en 1848" (*La Révolution française*, LVII, 1909, 438–474); Calman: *Ledru-Rollin and the Second French Republic;* Felix Ponteil: *1848* (Paris, 1937), 34 ff.

between Paris and the provinces if the elections turned out to be reactionary. Since the forces of counterrevolution had been in control for
fifty years, it was not unreasonable to ask at least one year for the forces
of liberty.[40]

The growing antagonism between the moderates, who were a
majority in the provisional government, and the radicals, together with
the continuing economic crisis and the general instability, led to a series
of episodes comparable to the "days" of the great French Revolution.
The first of these, on March 16, had to do with the National Guard,
which had been opened to all on March 14, with provision for new
elections of the officers. The well-to-do elements, known as the *bonnets
à poil* from their fur caps, were outraged by the mass influx of the
lower classes and vagabonds. In formation, but unarmed, about
25,000 of them marched to the Hôtel de Ville to protest. The government was shocked, and Lamartine and other members roundly rebuked a delegation of the demonstrators, who thereupon disbanded.
The sole effect of the affair was to arouse the radicals, who were
planning a demonstration to press for social reforms. On March 17 a
huge crowd gathered to congratulate the government for resisting the
demands of the "reactionaries." Some 150,000 workers marched peace-
fully from the Place de la Concorde to the Hôtel de Ville, where the
popular "communist" Etienne Cabet headed a delegation petitioning
the government to postpone the elections by at least two months. The
authorities, highly gratified by the orderliness of the multitude, promised a decision within a week. Though all went off well, Lamartine
and his associates were shaken by the realization that they were at the
mercy of the populace. They were, said Lamartine in private, living on
a volcano, with no knowing when it might erupt.[41]

On March 26 the government decreed the postponement of the elections from April 9 to April 23, due evidently to the difficulty of
organizing so vast a poll in short order. Meanwhile the election of
National Guard officers took place on April 5 and turned out most
satisfactorily from the conservative or even moderate point of view.
The workers of Paris, it appeared, were still under the influence of the

[40] Neil Stewart: *Blanqui* (London, 1939), 102 ff.; Sylvain Molinier: *Blanqui* (Paris,
1948), 38.
[41] Girard: *La garde nationale,* 294 ff.; Henri Guillemin: *La tragédie de quarante-huit*
(Paris, 1948), 122 ff.; Duveau: *1848: the Making of a Revolution,* 81 ff.

upper classes. As Blanqui feared, they were not prepared to assume control. In any event, the National Guard, numbering now some 100,000 men, was to become once more a defense force at the command of the government. This was to be clearly shown by the events of April 16, the origins of which remain even more obscure than those of March 17. As background one must remember the increasing virulence of the propaganda war on both sides. The conservatives were floating every kind of charge and rumor about the plans of the "revolutionists," and made little secret of their intention of recalling the troops so as to ensure the preservation of order. The radicals, on their part, plastered the city with threatening placards and made their clubs forums for the most incendiary oratory. The Club of the Mountain, for example, announced that the people would boil the blood of the aristocrats in the cauldron of the revolution and make a stew that would sate the appetite of the famished proletarians.[42]

On April 14, respectable people were alarmed to read in the *Bulletin of the Republic,* a publication of the ministry of the interior, an article which, as it turned out later, was written by no less a person than the well-known novelist George Sand, who had been converted to social-ism and was now an ardent advocate of a new society. "Unless the elections bring the victory of social truth," she wrote, "there will be only one road to the safety of the people who built the barricades, and that will be to make its will known again and to postpone the decisions of a false national representation."[43]

There was some justification, then, for the fear that there was a radical plot in the making and that its objective was the removal of Lamartine and the moderates and the substitution of a committee of public safety for the objectionable provisional government. Blanc obligingly warned his colleagues that another great demonstration was planned for April 16, so precautions could be taken, and the radical leaders, including Blanqui, could be confidentially warned. As a result they tended to hold aloof at least in the initial stages. The demon-strators who, 40,000 strong, on April 16 marched from the Champs de Mars to the Hôtel de Ville found their procession hedged in on both sides by National Guards, while the new police, the *garde mobile,*

[42] Quoted by Moulin: "Les clubs et la presse."
[43] Albert Fournier: "George Sand en 1848" (*Europe,* XXVI, 1848, 140–150); André Maurois: *Lélia: the Life of George Sand* (New York, 1953), Part VII.

broke the crowd into sections. Shouts of "down with the communists" and "down with Cabet" began to be heard, and the demonstrators, for the most part leaderless, were soon faced with complete fiasco. Conservative newspapers crowed over their victory over the "barbarians" and rhapsodized over the "sublime élan" shown by the reconstituted National Guard.[44]

To celebrate this happy turn of events the government arranged a festival of fraternity for April 20. For hours the members stood in array at the Arc de Triomphe and presented new colors to the legions of the National Guard, as well as to five regiments of the army, which were now restored to their Paris barracks.

No less gratifying to the moderate elements was the outcome of the elections on Sunday, April 23, when fully 84 per cent of the electorate went to the polls. Ledru-Rollin's commissioners, it will be recalled, had done their utmost short of corruption to secure the election of "true" republicans, but on the other hand the conservatives, organized in the Republican Club for Freedom of the Elections, and the church hierarchy with its Committee for Defense of Religious Liberty had thrown their influence on the side of the traditional ruling classes. In many areas the bishops drew up lists of candidates for the priests to recommend to their flocks and in countless villages the priest joined the mayor in leading the procession to the polls. When one considers further that the small landholders and peasants suffered particularly from the imposition of the 45 per cent surtax, one can understand that the vote came out on the conservative side. Most of those elected belonged to the class of local notables. They would have been just as eligible for election under the highly restricted franchise of the July Monarchy. Indeed, 165 of them had sat in the Chamber of the previous regime. Almost half of them were local lawyers, while only about thirty could be classed as workers; actual peasants were completely absent.

Politically just about all the successful candidates described themselves as republicans, partly because for the time being no other regime was in prospect. It has generally been supposed that about half of them were moderate republicans, but recent studies suggest that this figure is exaggerated. There were evidently about 300 monarchists, mostly members of the dynastic opposition of the July Monarchy. On the other wing there were some seventy-five or eighty radicals and social-

[44] Guillemin: *La tragédie de quarante-huit,* 177.

ists. The "true" or confirmed republicans numbered not 500 but somewhat less than 300. In any event, the elections were a resounding victory for the moderate and conservative elements. Even in Paris only one radical leader, Armand Barbès, and twelve socialists were elected. Blanqui, Raspail and other radical leaders failed of election. In other words, even in Paris, the focus of the revolution, the workers and lower classes generally voted for the respectable, well-to-do candidates.[45]

The lines were now more clearly drawn than ever before. On the one side many of the new deputies might have said, with one of Flaubert's characters: "I had as much trouble as five hundred devils in making my fortune. And now people want to tell me that I'm not the master, that my money is not my own; in short, that property is theft. . . . Don't bother me with your Proudhon: I think I'd strangle him if he were here." On the other side were the radicals who, in one of their placards, warned the Assembly: "If you persist in defending the old social order, you will find our sections well organized and in the van on the day of reckoning."[46] No less an authority than Tocqueville, himself one of the deputies, tells us that everywhere the idea of an inevitable and imminent conflict was current.[47]

The members of the provisional government had all secured election to the new Assembly (see Illustration 60). Lamartine, who had so successfully held the fort during three critical months, was elected in ten departments and received 260,000 votes in the Seine. Ledru-Rollin polled 131,000 votes, but the more radical Blanc received only 120,000. Lamartine was generally looked upon as the man who could suppress the "socialists." He might have become provisional president had he so desired. But he had always taken a middle position and had been genuinely concerned with the plight of the common people. He now tried to mediate between the opposing wings and insisted that Ledru-Rollin be included in the new executive commission of five which was

[45] Alfred Cobban: "Administrative Pressure in the Election of the French Constituent Assembly, April, 1848" (*Bulletin of the Institute of Historical Research*, XXV, 1952, 133–159), and "The Influence of the Clergy and the 'Instituteurs primaires' in the Election of the French Constituent Assembly" (*English Historical Review*, LVII, 1942, 334–344); Rémond: *La Droite en France*, 87 ff.; Bastid: *Doctrines et institutions politiques de la Seconde République*, I, 176 ff. The analyses of Duveau: *1848*, 96 ff., and earlier writers should be corrected by the researches of George W. Fasel: "The French Election of April 23, 1848: Suggestions for a Revision" (*French Historical Studies*, V, 1968, 285–298).

[46] Quoted in Jean Dautry: *1848 et la Seconde République* (2 ed., Paris, 1957), 149.

[47] Tocqueville: *Recollections*, 107.

to replace the provisional government. His unwillingness to serve as the instrument of reaction naturally cost him much of his popularity among the deputies. When it came to the election of the new executive, Arago obtained 725 votes, Garnier-Pagès 715, Marie 702, Lamartine only 643 and Ledru-Rollin 458. Actually this body did little beyond appointing the ministers, who reported directly to the Assembly. The Assembly, in turn, operated through fifteen key committees.[48]

Since the majority of the Assembly was set on putting an end to the radicalism and socialism of Paris, it rejected out of hand Blanc's plea for the establishment of a ministry of labor and indeed gave short shrift to his commission of labor, which had been holding its sessions in the Luxembourg Palace and had long since become a thorn in the flesh of his bourgeois colleagues in the provisional government. Blanc, a dynamic idealist fertile in practicable ideas, had assembled several hundred employers and workers in something like an economic parliament. His commission received numerous petitions, aided in settling wage disputes and encouraged the organization of labor unions. Much time, understandably, was given to doctrinal debate on subjects such as the nationalization of the railroads, banks and major industries. From the profits, Blanc hoped, the government could then finance the producers' workshops which he had so much at heart. There was nothing subversive about this. Not even the workers called for a social revolution. What they asked was state action to guarantee work, a minimum age, insurance for old age, and so on. Even in the so-called "socialist" propaganda put out by the well-known writer Eugène Sue, there was talk only of a progressive income tax, nurseries for the children of working women, homes for the aged, free education, government insurance against fire, and the like. Nonetheless, the idea became firmly rooted that Blanc and his associates were intent on making over society along socialist lines.[49]

[48] Bastid: *Doctrines et institutions politiques,* I, 197 ff. On Lamartine's attitude, see his revealing letter to his niece, June 1, 1848, quoted in Edouard Vellay: "L'impopularité de Lamartine peu après l'ouverture de l'Assemblée Constituante" (*1848,* No. 188, 1951, 61–62).

[49] K. Bloch: *Geschichte der Kommission des Luxembourg* (Frankfurt, 1925); Jean Vidalenc: *Louis Blanc* (Paris, 1948); Leo R. Loubère: *Louis Blanc* (Evanston, 1960); Alexandre Zévaes: "La propagande socialiste dans la campagne en 1848" (*La Révolution de 1848,* XXXI, 75–94); Rémi Gossez: "L'organisation ouvrière à Paris sous la Seconde République" (*1848: Revue des révolutions contemporaines,* XLI, 1949, 31–45).

The antagonism between conservatives and radicals broke wide open on May 15, when, despite the efforts of Blanqui and Barbès to prevent a premature clash, huge crowds assembled on the Place de la Bastille and marched thence to the hall of the Assembly, a huge, hastily constructed wooden building within the courtyard of the Palais Bourbon. There the procession, largely unarmed, found a detachment of the National Guard, as well as the police and some regular troops. Since the officers of these forces had no particular directives and were uncertain of themselves, they gave no orders. The crowd easily brushed aside the National Guard, invaded the chamber and dropped from the galleries to the floor. Tocqueville, who was present, has left a vivid picture of the confusion that ensued as the invaders surged about while the deputies sat stone still, like the Roman senators awaiting the invasion of the Gauls. One radical leader, Raspail, read a petition calling for action on behalf of the Poles and for the formation of an army of liberation to be financed by a tax of a billion francs levied on the rich. Finally, after unconscionable delays, large contingents of the National Guard were called out. But by the time of their arrival, the crowd had for the most part disappeared, partly to escape the intolerable heat and partly to march to the Hôtel de Ville and set up a revolutionary government. Lamartine and Ledru-Rollin thereupon mounted horses and led a squadron of dragoons to the same destination. The demonstrators were easily dispersed and the upshot of the affair was that some 400 persons, including most of the radical leaders (Blanqui and Barbès had belatedly joined in the demonstration), were arrested and imprisoned. In March, 1849, the high court at Bourges sentenced them to life imprisonment. Blanc escaped indictment only by a narrow vote of the Assembly. Many of the radical clubs were closed down and more drastic legislation was enacted to forestall further risings. The first round of the conflict had been fought; the first victory of the conservatives had been won.

Once more, to celebrate so auspicious an event, a grand festival of concord was held on the Champs de Mars (May 21). Tocqueville tells us that some 200,000 bayonets flashed in the sun, but that the deputies were nevertheless so apprehensive of the populace that they came secretly armed with pistols, daggers and blackjacks. Nothing untoward happened as hour after hour the various guards and troops marched past the reviewing stand. But the bouquets of the sturdy young women

from the industrial *faubourgs,* says Tocqueville, fell on the assembled
deputies like hailstones, reminding the authorities that concord was
somewhat less than perfect.

4. THE JUNE DAYS

Although the primary purpose of the newly elected Assembly was to
draft a constitution for republican France, the deputies felt obliged to
deal first of all with the problem of the national workshops, in which
by June no less than 100,000 men were enrolled. The reader will recall
that these workshops had never been intended as a socialist experiment.
They were, in fact, not workshops at all, but merely a traditional
system of public relief in time of great unemployment (see Illustration
40). Initially the plans called for decentralized administration dealing
with perhaps 10,000 or 12,000 men. But the influx was so great that the
project had to be put under central direction. At the suggestion of the
director, a brilliant young engineer named Emile Thomas, the workers
were organized in paramilitary fashion, by squads, brigades and companies. They were a motley crew which included many skilled workers
and even professional men as well as ordinary day laborers. In the
acute economic crisis of the spring of 1848, the unemployment, by
official count, ran to 65 per cent in the construction trades, 72 per cent
in the furnishing trades, 58 per cent in hardware, 51 per cent in textiles
and clothing. Even artists were hard hit, as shown by the fact that the
eminent sculptor David d'Angers recommended many hungry drama-
tists, painters and designers for admission to the workshops.[50]

It was utterly impossible, at short order, to find useful work for so
many men. Actually, no more than 10,000 were employed at any one
time, mostly on grading jobs. Marie, the minister of public works,
proposed that a circumferential railway be built around Paris, and
Thomas suggested repavement of the roads running into the city.
These projects would have taken large numbers of workers out of the
center of the city, but they were all so expensive that the government,
financially hard pressed, could not seriously contemplate them.[51]

---

[50] Thomas' analysis of mid-May, 1848, is given in the appendix of Charles Schmidt:
Des ateliers nationaux aux barricades de juin (Paris, 1948). See also T. J. Markovitch:
"La crise de 1847–1848 dans les industries parisiennes" (*Revue d'histoire économique et
sociale,* XLIII, 1965, 256–260).

[51] Donald C. McKay: *The National Workshops* (Cambridge, 1933), 31; Schmidt: *Des
ateliers nationaux,* 22.

The government and the propertied classes were from the beginning beset with fear lest this huge conglomerate of hungry, desperate people be used by radical leaders for a new, social revolution. "These poor people," says Tocqueville, "were told that the wealth of the rich was in some way the produce of a theft practiced upon themselves." Since with only one franc a day they were on the very verge of subsistence, they constituted a real danger. For that reason Thomas had organized and disciplined them. Presently they were permitted also to enroll in the National Guard, where again they were under control. Nonetheless the new government was convinced that an end must be put to the workshop system, which was an intolerable drain on the exchequer as well as a social menace. The deputies, coming mostly from the provinces, shared the feeling prevalent among the peasants that, through the 45 per cent surtax, they were paying for the upkeep of the lazy ruffians of the capital.

Finally, after weeks of debate, it was decided on May 24 to close the workshops to new enrollment as the first step toward dropping from the rolls all those who had been resident in Paris less than six months and sending those aged eighteen to twenty-five into the army. Thomas, when he protested these decisions, was spirited away to distant Bordeaux under police escort.

Before long, thousands on thousands of unemployed workers, barred from the dole, were threatened with starvation, as shown by the numerous delegations begging for bread. The new director of the workshops foresaw France being engulfed in the misery of Ireland and warned the government that soon the flood would break the dykes.[52] One of the radical clubs began to campaign for a great popular banquet of the people in imitation of the earlier bourgeois banquets. At five sous (twenty-five centimes) some 30,000 subscribed and the movement became so formidable that the leaders themselves became alarmed. On June 10 it was decided to postpone the banquet to July 14, Bastille Day. But the project had stirred the lower classes, despite the fact that it had no specific objective or revolutionary intent. After its deferment workmen would gather in large numbers in the evening, knowing not where to turn. Presently these assemblies had to be

[52] See especially the evidence adduced by A. I. Molok: "Problèmes de l'insurrection de juin, 1848" (*Questions d'histoire*, II, 1954, 57–100).

broken up by the mounted police. The scene was then already set for the ensuing conflict.[53]

The majority in the assembly was more than ever convinced that there was on foot a widespread socialist conspiracy to establish a democratic and social republic. In preparation for defense the government therefore appointed as commander of the troops, the National Guard and the police (Mobile Guard) General Eugène Cavaignac, veteran of sixteen years of campaigning in Algeria and only recently named governor-general of that colony. Cavaignac's assignment was hardly an enviable one, for the 30,000 troops he had in and around Paris were still rather demoralized and not entirely reliable. The huge National Guard, too, was a questionable asset, for it was socially such a conglomerate that there was no knowing how much or what part of it could be counted on to fight the workers. His most effective force was the new Mobile Guard, 15,000 strong, well-drilled and tough.[54]

Hostilities began around noon on June 23, following vain protests by the workers against the government's decree dissolving the workshops. Barricades sprang up by the hundreds in the poorer sections of the city, and presently the entire area east of the present-day Boulevard Saint-Michel on the Left Bank and the Boulevards Sebastopol, Strasbourg and Barbès on the Right Bank was in the hands of some 50,000 insurgents. It must be emphasized that among the insurgents there were relatively few members of the workshops, whose dole the government promised to pay during the disturbances. The vast majority of the barricade fighters were destitute, unemployed workers who had been denied admission to the workshops and had no resources beyond charity. Most of them had come to Paris within the preceding year or two and were in a state of utter desperation, as shown by the doggedness of their resistance. Though a few of them may have been class-conscious fighters for a republic of the workers, most of them appear to have been utterly devoid of notions of political or social renovation.

---

[53] Peter Amann: "Prelude to Insurrection: the Banquet of the People" (*French Historical Studies*, I, 1960, 436–440), and "Du neuf on the 'Banquet of the People'" (*ibid.*, V, 1968, 344–350).

[54] General Doumenc: "L'armée et les journées de juin" (*Actes du Congrès du Centenaire de la Révolution de 1848*, 255–266); P. Chalmin: "Une institution militaire de la Séconde République: la garde nationale mobile" (*Etudes d'histoire moderne et contemporaine*, II, 1948, 37–82); Girard: *La garde nationale*, 309 ff.; Rémi Gossez: "Notes sur la composition et l'attitude de la troupe" (*Etudes*, XVIII, 1955, 77–110).

There is a real danger of reading into the June Days ideas which were to crystallize only much later.[55]

The June insurrection, in which not a single radical leader participated and which was therefore an unplanned, disorganized outbreak, never had much chance of success. It was able to secure control of a large part of the city simply because Cavaignac refused to take action until all his forces were ready and concentrated in three localities: at the National Assembly, at the Panthéon, and at the Place de la Concorde. An ominous development was the failure of the National Guard to respond in strength to the *rappel* of June 23. Many stayed in their own localities to protect their property. Only about 10,000 (10 per cent) reported for active duty. In these circumstances the government sent out an appeal to nearby *départements* to send contingents of their National Guards, and for the first time in French history the steamboat and railroad made the intervention of the provinces possible. On June 24 and 25 thousands of provincials, eager "to defend society against the threat of anarchic doctrines and to put an end to the intolerable dictation of the chronically insurgent Parisian workers" arrived in the capital. For the most part they were too late to share in the fighting, but they were used for guard duty and in general exercised a significant moral influence.[56]

On June 24 Cavaignac opened his offensive. His forces drove a wedge between the insurgents on the left and the right banks of the river and gradually closed in on the main centers of resistance, using artillery to blast the barricades. Much of the fighting was done by the Mobile Guard, the National Guardsmen participating to some extent on both sides, while the troops of the line were committed only where success seemed certain. By June 26 the workers had been driven back into the Faubourg Saint-Antoine, which, attacked from all sides, soon had to surrender (see Illustration 59). In four days of desperate fight-

---

[55] Marx, to be sure, saw the June Days as "a fight for the preservation or annihilation of the bourgeois order" (*The Class Struggles in France*). On the social diversity of the insurgency, see McKay: *The National Workshops*, 145 ff.; Emile Tersen: "Juin, 1848" (*La Pensée*, No. 19, 1948, 16–24); Rémi Gossez: "Diversités des antagonismes sociaux vers le milieu du XIXe siècle" (*Revue économique*, VII, 1956, 439–457); George Rudé: *The Crowd in the French Revolution* (Oxford, 1959), chap. xv.

[56] All told, about 100,000 provincials had arrived by July 1. See the archival study of Jean Vidalenc: "La province et les journées de juin" (*Etudes d'histoire moderne et contemporaine*, II, 1948, 83–144) and the remarks of Tocqueville (*Recollections*, 169, 182 ff.), many of whose friends hurried in from Normandy.

ing the insurgents had lost 400–500 men, while the attacking forces had
something like twice that number of dead. In terms of human life, the
worst, however, was still to come. The insurgents were hunted through
houses and alleys and some 3,000 were cut down in cold blood. Alexander Herzen, watching the slaughter, noted that Russian Cossacks
and Austrian Croat troops were meek as lambs compared to the
ferocious French guards. In addition to the slain, about 12,000 persons
were arrested, some of whom were released after four to six months,
while most were summarily deported to Algerian labor camps.[57]

Karl Marx was to describe the June Days as "the most colossal event
in the history of European civil wars," and they were indeed to occupy
a central place in socialist historical writing. As such, it would be hard
to exaggerate their importance. Yet in fact no socialist writer or leader
played any role in the insurrection, which was not in any sense a revolt
of a class-conscious industrial proletariat, but rather an uprising of
skilled as well as unskilled workers made desperate by hunger and
want. It is interesting chiefly as marking the culmination of a long-
term development. Population pressure and the social dislocations
occasioned by industrialization, reinforced by the crop failures of 1846
and 1847 and crowned by the sudden economic crisis provoked by the
February Revolution, had created such widespread unemployment that
no government, least of all the provisional government, could cope
with it over a longer period. The decision of the government to close
down the national workshops is understandable, but surely the transition should have been more gradual and some alternative solution
should have been sought. The abruptness of the action was, of course,
due to the great fear of social revolution. One might almost say that the
government, by its drastic action, seized the initiative and broke the
opposition of the workers before it could crystallize. The end result,
however, was to deepen class antagonisms and strengthen suspicions
and fears, making even gradual social reform ever more difficult. The
fruits of the June Days took the form not of democracy but of reaction.

[57] For Herzen's remark, see Edward H. Carr: *The Romantic Exiles* (London, 1933),
43, and for the repression Roger Ikor: *Insurrection ouvrière de juin, 1848* (Paris, 1936),
58; Schmidt: *Des ateliers nationaux,* 53 ff.

Chapter Two

UPHEAVAL IN CENTRAL EUROPE

I. THE REVOLUTION IN VIENNA

THE REVOLUTIONS in Central Europe, which were directly inspired by news of the easy success of the insurrection in Paris, to a large extent followed the pattern of their prototype. A flood of petitions and a series of demonstrations brought the common people upon the scene, with the inevitable result that the liberal middle class, once it had realized its program of constitutional government, was confronted by a radical movement which in certain places took on a distinct socialistic tinge. It stands to reason that in this area, where society was far less industrialized than further west, the forces of both liberalism and radicalism were less formidable than in France, and the chances of lasting success therefore greatly reduced. Besides, in Central Europe nationalism soon made its influence felt, so much so that eventually nationalist aspirations and claims overshadowed the issues of liberal government. In the entire Danube Basin the struggle of nationalities threatened the disintegration of the Hapsburg Monarchy, while in Germany proper the contrary drive toward unification became overriding. These crosscurrents created a situation so complex that the historian, able to speak of only one thing at a time, is at a loss for an acceptable pattern of discourse.

The impetus to revolution in the Hapsburg Empire was given by Louis Kossuth, who, in a passionate speech to the Hungarian Diet on March 3, 1848 declared that even though the peoples of the empire were loyal to the dynasty, the time had come to put an end to absolutism, to centralized bureaucratic government and indeed to all the repressive measures of the "Metternich System." All parts of the empire should be given representative institutions and the special position of the Kingdom of Hungary should be respected. Hungary must insist on complete autonomy under a responsible ministry.

It was this resounding address that raised excitement throughout the empire to fever pitch. The government, however, was too paralyzed to formulate an·effective policy. The emperor was feeble-minded and the council of state dominated by his uncle, the Archduke Louis, who, like the chancellor, Prince Metternich, was dead opposed to surrender under popular pressure. Metternich, now old and discouraged, recognized that the old regime was becoming impossible, but insisted that such changes as might be necessary should be made deliberately by the government, not by the people.[1]

Pressure of events, however, soon deprived the court of freedom of decision. On the morning of March 13, a bright spring day, the Estates of Lower Austria, an essentially feudal assembly in which, however, there were a number of liberal-minded aristocrats, were meeting in the Herrengasse to discuss a petition for reform to be presented to the emperor. Presently several thousand or more students from the university, who had suffered particularly under close police supervision and whose own petition had been rejected by the Court, arrived to persuade the Diet to adopt an advanced position. Crowds of bystanders assembled and there was much milling about in the narrow street. Excitement mounted as one student took it upon himself to read the full text of the Kossuth speech. Students began to invade the council chamber and presently the presiding officer of the Diet felt impelled to appeal to the Archduke Albert, commanding the garrison troops, to intervene and restore order.[2]

In Vienna, as in Paris, the preservation of public order devolved upon the paramilitary police (*Militär-Polizeiwache*), numbering about 1,200 men. The fact that the police on March 13 stood idly by during the disturbances was evidently due to the commander's view that large-scale riots were the business of the army. There was also a citizen's guard (*Bürgerwehr*) of 14,000 men recruited from the upper and middle *bourgeoisie* but, unlike the Paris National Guard, unarmed for the most part and used chiefly for parade purposes. In the last analysis, protection against civil disorders devolved upon the garrison troops,

[1] Heinrich Friedjung: *Oesterreich von 1848 bis 1860* (2 ed., Stuttgart, 1908), I, 17–18; Heinrich von Srbik: *Metternich, der Staatsmann und der Mensch* (Munich, 1925), II, 259 ff.; Constantin de Grunwald: *Metternich* (London, 1953), 286 ff.; Rudolf Kiszling: *Die Revolution im Kaisertum Oesterreich* (Vienna, 1948–1952), I, 35.

[2] For the background of the student agitation, see Julius Marx: "Polizei und Studenten" (*Jahrbuch des Vereins für Geschichte der Stadt Wien*, XIX–XX, 1963–1964, 218–250).

numbering about 15,000 men, who were quartered in barracks outside the ancient walls of the Inner City.[3]

The military forces at the disposal of the government were certainly sufficient to quell disturbances before they assumed the proportions of a revolution, but in Vienna as in Paris the authorities failed to issue specific orders. The archduke, left to his own devices, dispatched several squadrons of cavalry into the city, where they found it extremely difficult to operate because of the narrow, crowded streets. Presently missiles were thrown from the roofs and guns went off, no one knew just how or why. There were several dead, with resulting popular hostility. Before long, crowds of workers began to appear from the industrial suburbs. Only in the nick of time were the gates closed against them, whereupon they returned to their homes to engage in an orgy of machine breaking, incendiarism and looting.[4]

By late afternoon the disorder was such that a group of prominent citizens persuaded the lord mayor to call out the Citizen Guard and have the military withdraw from action. The archduke did in fact evacuate the Inner City and for several highly critical days the garrison troops stood idle on their parade ground outside the walls. The Citizen Guard, in turn, duplicated the role of the Paris National Guard: far from defending the regime, it deserted it. A deputation of guard officers proceeded to the palace and firmly demanded that Metternich be dismissed and the students armed, so that they might suppress the disorders among the workers. In the Imperial Council Metternich argued that the police and the troops could and should repress the disturbances. Too hasty dismissal of his chief minister had cost Louis Philippe his throne. The imperial house should not make the same mistake. Concessions to popular demands would lead no one knew where. The chancellor was supported vigorously by Prince Alfred von Windischgrätz, the governor of Bohemia, who on previous occasions

[3] Adolf Schmidl: *Wien und seine nächsten Umgebungen* (Vienna, 1847), 162–163; Karl Weiss: *Geschichte der Stadt Wien* (Vienna, 1872), II, 239 ff.; Viktor Bibl: *Die Wiener Polizei* (Vienna, 1927), 313; Hermann Oberhummer: *Die Wiener Polizei* (Vienna, 1937), I, 201 ff.

[4] Ernst Violand: *Die soziale Geschichte der Revolution in Oesterreich* (Leipzig, 1850), 69 ff.; Ernst von Zenker: *Die Wiener Revolution in ihren sozialen Voraussetzungen und Beziehungen* (Vienna, 1897), 112 ff.; Heinrich von Srbik: "Die Wiener Revolution . . . in sozialgeschichtlicher Beleuchtung" (*Schmollers Jahrbuch*, XLIII, 1919, 19–58); R. John Rath: *The Viennese Revolution of 1848* (Austin, 1957).

had suppressed outbreaks of workers in Prague and other cities. Energetic action, argued the prince, would soon end the insurrection. To dismiss Metternich would be nothing short of shameless cowardice. Nonetheless, the court eventually surrendered to popular pressure. In the evening Metternich was obliged to resign and flee in disguise across Germany to England. Meanwhile the students, having received permission to arm, secured several thousand muskets from the arsenal and formed patrols to ensure order.[5]

The success of the insurrection, which was entirely unplanned and unexpected, was due to the ineptitude of the government rather than to the strength of the opposition elements, among which only the students showed much grit and determination. The youths naturally rejoiced at their success, which put the government at their mercy. The court had to consent to the formation of a National Guard, which was to include a separate student corps, the Academic Legion. Though intended to comprise only 10,000 reliable citizens, the Guard soon numbered 30,000 and the Academic Legion another 7,000.[6]

The utmost dreams of the liberals were realized when the helpless government agreed to recognize civil rights, promised a constitution (March 15) and appointed a modern cabinet of well-known officials. Satisfaction with the fruits of the disorders was clearly indicated by the fact that fewer and fewer of the respectable people reported for service in the National Guard. By early April only about 7,200 showed real interest.[7] But the moderate liberal elements were soon to discover that they were now prisoners of more advanced, democratic forces, that is of the students, some 5,000 in number, who in turn were guided by a handful of instructors and junior staff members of the hospitals, such as Dr. Adolf Fischhof and Dr. Josef Goldmark. The students, furthermore, enjoyed the confidence of the workers in the suburbs, from whose midst many of them had come. During the spring of 1848 the popularity of the students was unlimited. Through a student committee they dominated the much larger Central Committee of Citizens, National Guards and Students, which more or less gave the law to the weak and confused government. Through never-ending demonstra-

---

[5] Srbik: *Metternich*, II, 280 ff.; Paul Müller: *Feldmarschall Fürst Windischgrätz* (Vienna, 1934), 66, 88–89.

[6] Paul Molisch: "Die Wiener akademische Legion" (*Archiv der oesterreichischen Geschichte*, CX, 1924, 1–207); Hugo Kerchnawe: *Die Ueberwindung der ersten Weltrevolution* (Innsbruck, 1932), 12, 17.

[7] Rath: *Viennese Revolution*, 123.

tions and the practice of "serenading" unpopular ministers or officials, the students invariably had their way. With no training in political science and but little acquaintance with western doctrines, they readily took their cue from a few radical leaders. Democratic clubs were opened and extremist newspapers founded that attacked not only the government but the aristocracy and church hierarchy.[8]

Pressures upon the government from the Magyars and the Czechs in addition to the outbreak of insurrection in Milan and the ensuing declaration of war by Piedmont help to explain the weakness of the authorities in dealing with the Viennese situation. Furthermore, developments in the rest of Germany made it imperative that Austria keep pace with the liberalism which was everywhere triumphant. On April 25, after hasty deliberation, the cabinet, under the influence of the liberal-minded Baron Franz von Pillersdorf, proclaimed a constitution generally modeled on the Belgian constitution of 1831, to apply only to those parts of the monarchy which were included in the Germanic Confederation, plus Galicia. There was to be a two-chamber Parliament for the German provinces and Bohemia, Moravia and Galicia. The upper chamber was to consist of imperial princes, landed aristocrats and higher clergy. The lower Chamber of Deputies was to be indirectly elected by qualified taxpayers.

Once again the moderate elements, though they had had no share in the making of the constitution, were quite content with its provisions. But the students and their radical supporters at once protested against limitation of the franchise to taxpayers. The government again yielded, agreeing that all should have the vote except laborers by the day and week, and domestic servants, all of whom were allegedly too dependent on others to exercise their right freely. Once more the students objected. On May 15 there were immense, threatening demonstrations, before which the government, still unwilling to use force, had to capitulate. It now accepted the demand for complete manhood suffrage, and for a single-chamber Parliament. Furthermore, it surrendered its last weapon by promising that in future military forces should not be brought into the city except when requested by the National Guard.[9]

[8] Hermann Meyer: *1848: Studien zur Geschichte der deutschen Revolution* (Darmstadt, 1949) as well as Rath: *Viennese Revolution,* chap. v, analyze the forces of radicalism and their leaders.

[9] The electoral issue is admirably analyzed by Peter Burian: *Die Nationalitäten in 'Cisleithanien' und das Wahlrecht der Märzrevolution, 1848–1849* (Graz, 1962), 29 ff.

So complete was now the domination of the radicals that the imperial court arranged for the flight of the emperor and his entourage to Innsbruck (May 17). News of this event caused consternation in moderate circles, where it was feared that the radicals would proclaim a republic. There was a revulsion of feeling against the students, who were blamed for the rampant radicalism. Hoping to capitalize on this turn of opinion, the government on May 25 decreed that the university be closed and the Academic Legion merged with the National Guard. But this heroic decision invited only further disaster. The populace backed the students and thousands of workers arrived from the suburbs to stiffen resistance to the government. For the first time barricades appeared in the streets and preparations were made to fight. Once again Pillersdorf quailed. On May 26 he gave in to all demands: there was to be a Committee of Citizens, National Guards and Students of Vienna for Preservation of the Rights of the People, in short a Committee of Safety. This committee, with a membership of 240, was presided over by Dr. Fischhof, who had been in the forefront of the radical student movement from the outset. It marked the complete triumph of radicalism in the capital, and the first serious effort to combat the prevailing unemployment which, as in Paris, had increased with the political instability. Something akin to the French national workshops was set up, with government pay for the needy. As in Paris, this experiment created new problems, which must be left for discussion in a later context.

2. THE THREAT OF DISRUPTION

The Hapsburg court probably regarded the uprising of the Vienna students and workers as less ominous than the pretensions of the various nationalities and more particularly the terrifying threat of a peasant insurrection as presaged by the Galician troubles of 1846. It will be remembered that by 1848 many Austrian landowners had convinced themselves that serfdom had seen its day and that it would be impossible to maintain it much longer in the face of rising discontent and class hatred. Under the circumstances, they argued, it would be better to take the initiative in its abolition so as to make the most favorable settlement possible. On March 20, therefore, the government decreed that forced labor (*robot*) and other feudal obligations should be abolished as of March 31, 1849, in Bohemia and Moravia. The landowners were to be indemnified by the government and the state in turn was to recoup through additional charges on the peasants. These concessions were extended to Styria, Carinthia, Carniola and Galicia during the following weeks. In Galicia, the most explosive area, the abolition of serfdom was made immediate.[10] By these preventive measures the government certainly exorcized one of the greatest threats to the existing society. The peasants, expecting to receive a much better settlement than was intended, lost interest in revolution and were more and more inclined actually to take sides against the restless townsmen.

In Hungary, where the agrarian problem was equally pressing, the Parliament at Pressburg, frightened by false rumors of a huge insurrection of serfs in the neighborhood of Budapest, voted the immediate abolition of serfdom (March 15).[11] But the great objective of the Magyar nationalists was elimination of the control of the Vienna government and establishment of Hungary as a completely independent state, united with Austria only through the person of the ruler. Kossuth's program of March 3 envisaged not only independence for the "Kingdom of Saint Stephen," but incorporation of Croatia-Slavonia, Transylvania and the so-called Military Frontier in the Kingdom of Hungary. This expanded and reformed Hungarian state was to be national and constitutional, completely self-governing, with a ministry responsible to Parliament. The latter was henceforth to meet not in Pressburg but in Budapest, the center of the Magyar world.

The lower chamber of the Hungarian Diet, the stronghold of the gentry, supported this program wholeheartedly, but the upper house, in which the magnates or great landowners and high clergy dominated, opposed such drastic innovations for fear of a serious clash with the Vienna Court. When news arrived of the insurrection in Vienna, the recalcitrant were soon forced into line. On March 15 a large delegation, including seventy-five parliamentarians as well as leaders such as Széchenyi and Kossuth, set out for Vienna on the Danube steamer *Bela*. The party was given an enthusiastic ovation by the Viennese populace, which idolized Kossuth as the personification of liberalism. At the Court long and heated discussions took place over several days. At issue particularly were the questions of future control over the Hungarian armed forces and disposition of the huge public debt. In the end the

---

[10] Jerome Blum: *Noble Landowners and Agriculture in Austria, 1815–1848* (Baltimore, 1948), 232 ff.

[11] György Spira: "La dernière génération des serfs de Hongrie" (*Annales*, XXIII, 1968, 353–367).

Court, fearful lest Hungary declare its independence and be lost to the dynasty, agreed to defer settlement of these vital matters and accepted the rest of the Hungarian demands.[12]

The Emperor Ferdinand, as king of Hungary, named Count Louis Batthyány, a liberal-minded magnate, to form a new cabinet. When completed, it included most of the leaders of the reform movement. Széchenyi became minister of communications and public works; Deák was given the ministry of justice, and Eötvös the ministry of public instruction. The more moderate reformers would have liked to exclude Kossuth, but fear of the public reaction induced them to give him, not the ministry of the interior, which he hoped for, but the troublesome ministry of finance.[13]

During the next three weeks the Hungarian Parliament approved some thirty "March Laws" which transformed the country from a feudal into a modern state of liberal stamp. These drastic changes were both political and social. Politically the king or the viceroy was to act only through the ministry, which was to be responsible to a Parliament meeting annually. The upper House of Magnates was to remain unchanged, but the lower Chamber of Deputies was henceforth to be elected by all males over the age of twenty, provided they were not in domestic service and possessed urban property worth 300 florins or landed property of at least ten acres. All religions were declared equal; preliminary censorship of the press was abolished; jury trials were instituted for press offenses; and a National Guard was established, to include all those who enjoyed the franchise. On the social side the exemption of the nobility from taxation was terminated; all feudal obligations and manorial jurisdictions were also ended, with provision for indemnification of the landowners by the state; church tithes were abolished without compensation, the state in future to provide the salaries of the clergy.[14]

---

[12] François Eckart: "La révolution de 1848 en Hongrie et la cour de Vienne" (*Actes du Congrès Historique du Centenaire de la Révolution de 1848*, Paris, 1948, 229–242); Julius Miskolczy: *Ungarn in der Habsburger Monarchie* (Vienna, 1959).

[13] According to the British agent, Joseph A. Blackwell, Kossuth "was regarded as an unavoidable fatality—a necessary evil by *all* his colleagues" (see the contemporary reports for March 19 and 22 in "England and the Hungarian Revolution," *South Eastern Affairs*, III, 91–132).

[14] These laws are well summarized in C. M. Knatchbull-Hugessen: *The Political Evolution of the Hungarian Nation* (London, 1908), II, 25 ff., and in Dominic G. Kosary: *A History of Hungary* (Cleveland, 1941), 221 ff.

The March Laws, in the words of one Hungarian historian, represented the victory of a nation liberating itself not only from a foreign bureaucracy but also from the selfish interests of its own ruling class.[15] But the self-sacrifice of the upper classes was not as wholehearted as might appear. If the nobility rallied to the Kossuth program, it was largely in panic and fear of a major peasant insurrection.[16] Rumor, which proved unfounded, had it that radicals in Budapest were about to rouse the peasantry for a grand assault on the manor houses. There was in fact a radical, republican movement in the capital, which on March 15 had rallied the populace and forced the city council as well as the commander of the troops to accept the Twelve Points, a program similar to that of Kossuth, to whom the radicals looked for leadership.

The leader of this radical movement was the poet Alexander Petőfi, who, at the age of twenty-five, had already won the hearts of the common people by his lyrics and had attracted attention even abroad. Petőfi, who had started life as a poor vagabond actor, had nevertheless educated himself. He had at least a reading knowledge of western languages and was well-acquainted with the poetry of Schiller, Byron, Shelley and contemporary French poets such as Hugo and Béranger. Fascinated by the history of the French Revolution, he idolized the republic and the republican leaders and eventually came to study even socialist writers such as Fourier. He was a man of the people and shared fully in their hatred of the privileged aristocracy. Indeed, he was a most thoroughgoing democrat and republican. In one of his best poems, *The Hungarian Noble* (1845), he had the aristocrat priding himself on his ignorance and idleness:

> Doing no work—that is life.
> I am idle, therefore I am alive.
> Work is for the peasant.
> I am a Hungarian noble.

[15] Heinrich Marczali: *Ungarische Verfassungsgeschichte* (Tübingen, 1910), 145.

[16] Erwin Szábo: "Aus den Parteien und Klassenkämpfen in der ungarischen Revolution von 1848" (*Archiv für die Geschichte des Sozialismus*, VIII, 1919, 258–307); Coloman Benda: "La question paysanne et la révolution hongroise en 1848" (*Etudes d'histoire moderne et contemporaine*, II, 1948, 231–242); Erzsebet Andićs: "Kossuth en lutte contre les ennemis des réformes et de la révolution" (*Studia historica*. XII, 1954, 1–169), 61 ff.

> What do I care about the country?
> The hundred troubles of the country?
> The troubles will soon pass off.
> I am a Hungarian noble.[17]

During the popular demonstration on March 15, Petöfi read his new *National Ode:*

> Up, Hungarian, your country is calling!
> Here is the time, now or never!
> Shall we be slaves or free?
> This is the question, answer—
> By the God of the Hungarians we swear,
> We swear to be slaves no more.[18]

The Twelve Points having been agreed upon, a delegation was sent to the Diet at Pressburg and received by Kossuth on March 17. The latter, however, displayed great caution, warning against any popular effort to coerce the Diet. Kossuth was clearly apprehensive lest the democratic-republican program estrange the nobility from the work of reform. The Diet was already much upset by the news of the Budapest rising and the radical program. It was the threat of radicalism that led the nobility to accept the reform program lock, stock and barrel after only the most cursory discussion.[19]

The Emperor Ferdinand, beset by countless difficulties, had no choice but to approve the March Laws (April 11). His entourage, however, was deeply troubled, not only by the laws, but by the efforts of the Hungarian government to incorporate Transylvania, Croatia and the Military Frontier (the eastern part of Croatia, organized as a military colony for protection of the empire against the Turks, and

[17] Quoted from D. Mervyn Jones: *Five Hungarian Writers* (Oxford, 1966), 262. See also Paul A. Löffler: *La vie d'Alexandre Petöfi* (Rodez, 1953); René Schwachhofen: *Bettelsack und Freiheit: Leben und Werk Alexander Petöfis* (Weimar, 1954), which is excellent.

[18] Jones: *Five Hungarian Writers*, 277.

[19] For the Budapest demonstration, see the excerpts from Petöfi's diary, available in German translation in Petöfi: *Prosäische Schriften* (Leipzig, 1895), 83 ff. There is a fairly good translation of the *National Ode* in *Sixty Poems by Alexander Petöfi*, translated by Eugenie B. Pierce and Emil Delmar. On the fears of the nobility, see Dominic Kosary: "L'aspect social de la révolution de 1848 en Hongrie" (*Actes du Congrès Historique du Centenaire*, 133-142), and György Spira: "L'alliance de Lajos Kossuth avec la gauche radicale et les masses populaires de la révolution hongroise de 1848-1849" (*Acta historica*, II, 1953, 49-150), 49 ff.

under direct jurisdiction of the Vienna government). Another serious problem was the attempt of the Hungarians to apply the taxes, customs and mines of the country to strictly Hungarian needs, and to secure control of the Hungarian regiments, of which only four were serving in Hungary, while six were in Italy and five in Austria and Bohemia.[20]

The dominant figure at the Court was now the Archduchess Sophia, a Bavarian princess married to the Archduke Francis Charles, a prince who was hardly better fitted to rule than his brother Ferdinand. Sophia was intelligent, strong-willed and courageous. Strictly conservative and clerical in her upbringing, she felt humiliated by the emperor's submission to the demands of "a mess of students," as well as by the many concessions that followed. She was determined to have the childless Ferdinand abdicate the throne as soon as possible in favor of her own eighteen-year-old son Francis Joseph. Prince Windischgrätz, Count Charles Stadion, the governor of Galicia, Archbishop Otmar Rauscher and a few other high officials, soon to be called the Camarilla, concurred entirely in this program. But military suppression of the revolution and the dynastic change would have to wait, for all available troops were needed in Italy. Meanwhile the Court would have to maneuver as best it could to stave off disintegration of the empire.[21]

It was the established practice of the Vienna government to combat the centrifugal forces of feudalism and nationalism by playing off one against the other. To counter Magyar pretensions it was decided to support the Croats, Serbs and Rumanians, all of them subject peoples of the Crown of Saint Stephen who were determined to resist the efforts of the Hungarian government to Magyarize them. On March 23, soon after the departure of the Hungarian delegation from Vienna, the emperor appointed as ban (governor) of Croatia Baron Joseph Jellachich (Jellačič), who was colonel of one of the frontier regiments and a friend of Louis Gaj, the leader of the Illyrian movement. A week later Gaj himself appeared in Vienna at the head of a large delegation requesting the union of Croatia, Dalmatia and Slavonia in one king-

[20] Gunther E. Rothenberg: "The Habsburg Army" (*Austrian History Yearbook*, III, Part I, 1967, 70–90).

[21] Little is known of the deliberations of the Camarilla, but see Heinrich Friedjung: *Oesterreich von 1848 bis 1860*, I, 13 ff.; Josef Redlich: *Emperor Francis Joseph of Austria* (New York, 1929), 11 ff.; Egon C. Corti: *Kindheit und erste Jugend Kaiser Franz Josephs I* (Vienna, 1950), 263 ff., which draws upon the archduchess' diaries.

dom, free of Hungarian control. The emperor, though he evaded definite commitments, indicated that the Croats could count on his support in their resistance to Hungarian pressures.[22]

The appointment of Jellachich came as a great blow to Kossuth, who had deluded himself into thinking that the new liberal institutions would counteract separatist, nationalist movements.[23] His disillusionment was complete when in early April Jellachich was made commander of all troops in Croatia and the Military Frontier, and when on April 19 he ordered all Croat officials to cease communication with the Hungarian government.

Kossuth's response, strongly supported by both liberal and radical elements, was to refuse the royal request for more Hungarian troops to be sent to the Italian theater of war. This move quickly brought the Vienna authorities to heel. On May 7 the Court reversed itself, called upon Jellachich to obey the orders of the viceroy of Hungary, appointed Marshal John Hrabovski to supersede Jellachich in command of the troops, and put all Croatian and Military Frontier forces under the Hungarian Ministry of War. Ten days later the Court, exposed to radical revolution in the capital, fled to Innsbruck. It was the moment of greatest crisis, so the imperial government yielded readily to the further proposals of a Hungarian delegation which arrived in Innsbruck. In return for the promise to provide more Hungarian troops for Italy, the Court gave assurances that it would discontinue support of the Croats. On June 10 Jellachich was deprived of all his offices and threatened with impeachment if he disobeyed.[24]

The court Camarilla was appalled by the emperor's repeated compliance and the Archduchess Sophia was now convinced that Ferdinand must be replaced as soon as possible. Jellachich was summoned to Innsbruck and probably encouraged to ignore the imperial orders. In any event, June 15 saw the Court's first important success: Windischgrätz' reduction of insurgent Prague through bombardment of the

[22] Kosary: History of Hungary, 226 ff.; M. Hartley: The Man who Saved Austria: the Life and Times of Baron Jellačić (London, 1912), 132 ff.; Ferdinand Hauptmann: "Banus Jellačić und Feldmarschall Fürst Windisch-Grätz" (Süd-Ost Forschungen, XV, 1956, 373–402).

[23] Zoltan I. Toth: "The Nationality Problem in Hungary in 1848–1849" (Acta historica, IV, 1955, 235–277).

[24] For a succinct review of these complicated happenings, see Gunther E. Rothenberg: "Jelačić, the Croatian Military Border and the Intervention against Hungary in 1848" (Austrian History Yearbook, I, 1965, 45–67).

city. This was the signal for an open reversal of Imperial policy. On June 19 Jellachich's deposition was revoked and no further secret made of the fact that the Court would again support the resistance of Croatians, Serbs and Rumanians to Hungarian rule. On May 13 a Serbian national congress had met at Karlowitz and declared the Serbs of the empire "politically free and autonomous under the House of Austria and the Crown of Hungary," at the same time voting closest co-operation with Croats, Slavonians and Dalmatians. Shortly after that the Rumanians of Transylvania had protested the action of the Magyar-dominated Diet in voting the union of Transylvania with Hungary. A national council had been set up under Abraham Jancu and the loyalty of the Transylvanian Rumanians to the Hapsburg dynasty reaffirmed.[25]

The duplicity of the Austrian court becomes somewhat more understandable when set in the framework of the war against Piedmont. Kossuth and other members of the Hungarian government made no secret of their sympathies for Italian aspirations and talked constantly of the need for recalling the Hungarian regiments serving outside the country. Beset by the revolt of the subject peoples, all Hungarian troops were needed at home. On July 11 Kossuth in a major speech called upon Parliament to declare the country in danger and authorize an army of 200,000 men for defense. While the Budapest government, therefore, displayed its hostility to the imperial Court, Jellachich proclaimed his loyalty to the dynasty and served as guarantor that the 40,000 Croatian and Frontier regiments in Italy would remain faithful.

An important turn in events came with Field Marshal Radetzky's resounding victory over the Italians at the Battle of Custoza (July 24), which led presently to the conclusion of an armistice in the Italian war. Croatian troops could now be released for reassignment to Jellachich. The Camarilla made up its mind that the time had come to put an end to the Hungarian threat to disrupt the empire. The Court returned to Vienna on August 12 and brushed aside last-minute efforts by Batthyány and Déak to arrive at an accommodation. On August 31 the

[25] G. Y. Develle: *La nouvelle Serbie* (Paris, 1918), 155 ff.; Hermann Wendel: *Der Kampf der Südslawen um Freiheit und Einheit* (Frankfurt, 1925), 229 ff.; L. S. Stavrianos: *Balkan Federation* (Northampton, 1942), 57 ff.; Dragoslav Stranjaković: "La collaboration des Croates et des Serbes en 1848–1849" (*Le monde slave*, n.s., XII, 1935, 394–404); Ladislas Makkai: *Histoire de Transylvanie* (Paris, 1946), 310 ff.; Mihail Roller: *Histoire de la Roumanie* (Bucharest, 1947).

March Laws, on which the new Hungarian regime rested, were declared incompatible with the Pragmatic Sanction of 1723 and destructive of the unity of the empire. A few days later Jellachich, who meanwhile had raised and organized a force of 50,000 men, began the invasion of Hungary. He crossed the Drave (September 11), hoping for the support of the Serbs for a rapid advance on Budapest. On the same day Batthyány, representative of the moderate element in Hungarian politics, resigned as premier and left Kossuth the undisputed leader in the conflict confronting the country.

3. THE AUSTRO-SLAVS

The counterpart of the Hungarian drive for independence was the effort of the Slavs of the empire to unite and attain equal status with the Germans and the Magyars in a federally organized state. The Czechs, as the most advanced of the Slavic peoples of the empire, naturally assumed the lead, making Prague the focal point of the movement. There, even before the outbreak of the revolution in Vienna, a spontaneous popular assembly had called for civil rights, the equality of the Czech and German languages, and even the "organization of labor." A committee, which was to draft an appropriate petition to the emperor, appealed to intellectual leaders such as Palacký and Havlícek, who produced the petition of March 22. Couched in submissive, moderate terms, it asked for the administrative union of Bohemia, Moravia and Austrian Silesia to form an autonomous state, roughly like the Hungarian state of the March Laws. On April 8 the hard-pressed Imperial Court granted most of these demands, though the question of the union of the three provinces was left for decision to the general Austrian Parliament which was to meet in early summer.

Thus far the Germans and Czechs of Bohemia had co-operated. The upper middle class (largely German intellectuals and businessmen) and the lesser middle class (mostly Czech shopkeepers and artisans) were united in the campaign for a liberal regime. The Germans, though dominant, appear to have been quite prepared to accept the Czech language as equal to the German and to have raised no objection to the projected union of the three historic lands. All were agreed that the feudal system must be ended. The rural population, half of which was landless and in great distress, was becoming menacingly restless. That feudal obligations and jurisdiction must be abolished was obvious even to the landowners. Palacký urged immediate action, so that the landowners might at least obtain compensation for the loss of their "property." There was real danger, he maintained, that the urban radicals might mobilize the peasants for a social revolution, which was the last thing the propertied classes wanted to see.[26]

The rift between the two nationalities was first revealed by an important episode in early April. At Frankfurt a commission (the *Vorparlament*) was preparing for the meeting of a German national assembly which was to work out the unification of the German states. Since Bohemia, Moravia and Silesia were included in the Germanic Confederation of 1815 and were always regarded by Germans as German territory, the Frankfurt commissioners invited Palacký to join them as a representative of the three provinces. To this invitation Palacký replied (April 11) in what was hardly less than a historical-political essay. He must decline the invitation, he said, because he was not a German, but a Czech devoted to his Czech nationality. The past connection of Bohemia with the Germanic Confederation, he continued, was "a mere dynastic tie" to which the Czech nation, that is, the Czech states, paid no attention. German nationalists, he charged, were undermining the Hapsburg Empire, but that empire was one "whose preservation, integrity, and consolidation is, and must be, a great and important matter not only for my own nation, but also for the whole of Europe, indeed for humanity and civilization itself." Only through that empire could the peoples of Eastern Europe be protected against Russian expansion and domination, "an infinite and inexpressible evil, a misfortune without measure or bound." None of the nationalities of the Danube Basin being strong enough to stand by itself, their union in one state was essential: "Assuredly, if the Austrian state had not existed for ages, it would have been a behest for us in the interests of Europe and indeed of humanity to endeavor to create it as soon as possible," he wrote in an oft-misquoted passage. He recommended that the Germans proceed to the unification of the German states and leave the peoples of the Hapsburg Monarchy to reorganize

[26] Arnost Klima: "Ein Beitrag zur Agrarfrage in der Revolution von 1848 in Böhmen" (*Studia historica*, No. 51, 1961, 15–26). The landowners, industrialists, merchants and intellectuals had been organized since 1833 in the Society for the Encouragement of the Industrial Spirit in Bohemia, which became more or less a political debating society. See Hans Raupach: *Der tschechische Frühnationalismus* (Haile, 1929), 57 ff., 109 ff. On Czech radicalism, see Berthold Bretholz: *Geschichte Böhmens und Mährens* (Reichenberg, 1924), IV, 75 ff.; and the suggestive Marxian study by I. I. Udalzow: *Aufzeichnungen über die Geschichte des nationalen und politischen Kampfes in Böhmen im Jahre 1848* (Berlin, 1953), 43 ff.

their empire on a federal basis, with full equality for all nationalities. Ultimately the German and Austrian Empires might enter upon a firm alliance, reinforced by a customs union.[27]

Palacký's famous letter amounted to a formulation of the doctrine known as Austro-Slavism, which hinged on the maintenance of the Hapsburg Empire in the interests at least of the Austrian Slavs, who, as nations, were too weak to hold their own in the modern world. It involved rejection of German efforts to incorporate any part of the empire (not only the Czech provinces but also the essentially German ones) in a new German Empire, and at the same time insistence on reorganization of the empire along federal lines, so that each nationality might be autonomous.[28]

An important step in the realization of this program would be the union of the Slavic peoples of the monarchy and an effort to put them on a par with the Germans and the Magyars. The idea was given impetus when in May the Vienna government ruled that the issue of elections to a German Parliament should be left to the provincial authorities. Thereupon the Bohemian Germans seceded from the National Committee which, since mid-April, had been the *de facto* government of Bohemia. The Czechs, on their side, did all they could to block the elections to the Frankfurt Parliament, so that in the end only the eighteen strictly German electoral districts (out of a total of sixty-eight) chose delegates.

After this first bout, the Czech leaders decided to convoke a Congress of the Slavs to counterbalance the Frankfurt Parliament and also the Magyar Parliament at Budapest. The rift between the Czechs and Slovaks was quickly bridged when, after the Hungarian government had rejected Slovak demands for self-government, the Slovak leaders fled to Prague and threw in their lot with the Czechs. It was Stúr in fact who drafted the invitation to the congress.[29]

[27] A full English translation may be found in the *Slavonic Review*, XXVI, 1948, 303–308.

[28] The doctrine is well analyzed in Otakar Odložilik: "A Czech Plan for a Danubian Confederation, 1848" (*Journal of Central European Affairs*, 1941, 253–274); Rudolf Wierer: "Palacký's staatspolitisches Programm" (*Zeitschrift für Ostforschung*, VI, 1957, 246–258).

[29] Albert Prazák: "Czechs and Slovaks in the Revolution of 1848" (*Slavonic Review*, V, 1927, 565–579), and "The Slavonic Congress of 1848 and the Slovaks" (*ibid.*, VII, 1928, 141–159); Daniel Rapant: "Slovak Politics in 1848–1849" (*ibid.*, XXVII, 1948–1949, 67–90, 381–403).

Palacký's intention was to invite only Slavs of the Austrian Empire, but some of the Galician Poles demanded that all Slav nations be invited, hoping no doubt that the entire Polish problem could then be put on the docket. In the end it was decided that non-Austrian Slavs might attend the congress, but only as guests, without vote. Actually only a few Prussian Poles and a few non-Austrian Serbs appeared, along with two Russians (one of them the great revolutionist Michael Bakunin). They were too few to act as a group. As individuals they were finally permitted to vote along with the Austrians, though Palacký made it clear that the sole issue before the congress was the future of the Austrian Slavs and the integrity of the Austrian empire.[30]

The Congress of the Slavs (or Slavic or Slavonic Congress, for short) opened its sessions in Prague on June 2. It was a typical midcentury assembly of middle-class intellectuals. There were only 35 aristocrats and 16 clerics among the 340 members. Most of the Austrian Slav leaders were present and gave the congress a distinctly moderate cast. Czechs and Slovaks were in the vast majority (237), while Poles and Ruthenians from Galicia numbered 61 and the South Slavs only 42. Each of the three sections, based on the foregoing classification, was to prepare a manifesto to the nations of Europe, establishing the claims of the Austrian Slavs; a petition to the emperor; and a plan for reorganization of the empire. There was evidently a good deal of heated debate, for by no means all the members were enamored of the Palacký program. The Poles disliked the Czechs and distrusted the Vienna government. They would have liked the co-operation of the Austrian Slavs in the struggle for Polish independence and in the effort to unite all Slavs on a democratic basis. Bakunin, who played an important part in the Polish-Ruthenian section, was utterly committed to the destruction of "the monstrous Austrian Empire" and considered Austro-Slavism pure utopia. The Slovaks, again, were reluctant to sever all connection with Hungary and were irked by Czech pretensions to leadership. The Poles, in contrast to the Slovaks and Croats, were well-disposed to the Magyars. And in addition to these divergent views there was the fundamental question whether the empire should be federalized on the

[30] Alfred Fischel: *Der Panslawismus bis zum Weltkrieg* (Stuttgart, 1919), 262 ff.; Lewis B. Namier: *1848: the Revolution of the Intellectuals* (London, 1944), 105; Henryk Batowski: "The Poles and their Fellow-Slavs in 1848" (*Slavonic and East European Review*, XXVII, 1949, 404–413).

basis of the historic lands (which was the Czech desire), or on the basis of ethnographic divisions.[31]

Failure to agree on so many points meant that in the end the congress produced little more than a vague, emotional manifesto to the nations of Europe, almost entirely the work of Palacký. The great historian reverted to his favorite thesis: the peace-loving Slavs who had been conquered and exploited by the warlike Germans were no longer willing to be victimized. They asked only liberty and equality for all nations as for all individuals. His manifesto called for justice to Poland, demanded that the Magyars cease their oppression of the Slavs, and expressed the hope that the Slavs still under Turkish rule might soon be given a chance to develop. After insisting on the federal reorganization of the Hapsburg Monarchy, it closed with a universal appeal:

We, the youngest but by no means the weakest people, in entering once more the political arena of Europe, propose that a general European Congress of Nations be summoned for the discussion of all international questions; being thoroughly convinced that free nations will more easily come to agreement than paid diplomats.[32]

When on June 12 the manifesto was approved by the congress, the sessions came to an end. Bakunin, writing some months later, described the meeting as "the resurrection of the Slavs," and declared that for them "it was the first day of a new life." Later commentators have described the congress as "the peak of the Slavonic renascence."[33] No doubt its effect was to enhance the national self-consciousness of Slavs everywhere and, despite all differences of interest and aim, make for mutual understanding and tolerance. In the last analysis the congress must be viewed as a product of the 1848 upheaval. The learned and high-minded intellectuals gathered there were genuinely moved by the

[31] Fischel: *Der Panslawismus*, 268 ff.; Hans Kohn: *Pan-Slavism* (Notre Dame, 1953), 72 ff.; and the excellent essay by Otakar Odložilik: "The Slavic Congress of 1848" (*Polish Review*, IV, 1959, 3–15). Some of the basic differences are discussed by Benoît P. Hepner: *Bakounine et le panslavisme révolutionnaire* (Paris, 1950), 253; see also Peter F. Sugar: "The Nature of the non-Germanic Societies under Habsburg Rule" (*Slavic Review*, XXII, 1963, 1–30).

[32] Full text in *Slavonic Review*, XXVI, 1948, 309–313; see also Namier: *1848*, 114; Josef Mačurek: "The Achievement of the Slavonic Congress" (*Slavonic Review*, XXVI, 1948, 329–340).

[33] Bakunin's remark is taken from the draft of his own appeal (see Josef Pfitzner: *Bakuninstudien*, Prague, 1932, 84). For the second question, see Mačurek: "Achievement of the Slavonic Congress."

ideals of liberty, equality and fraternity. They made a point of proclaiming their love and respect for all peoples. At the same time they
approached their immediate political problem in realistic fashion.
Austro-Slavism, as expounded by Palacký, was an excellent solution
for the problem of the Czechs, but it held less appeal for some of the
other Slavs. Before long the idealism of June was to give way to the
conflict of divergent aims and policies.

June 12, the day of the official end of the congress, was also the first
day of the insurrection in Prague which many historians regard as an
unfortunate episode and a severe blow to the notion of Slavic unity.
But the rising should be studied in its own right and not only in the
context of the congress. It was, in a sense, the counterpart of the
Vienna revolt of late May, an uprising of the unemployed and destitute, for which students provided a rudimentary leadership. It had no
specific plan nor program, and seems to have had no reference whatever to the nationalist issues which were being debated at the congress.
German and Czech students and workers acted in concert and were
opposed by the German and Czech upper classes without regard to
nationality.

In Prague as in Vienna there had been a proliferation of radical
literature during the spring of 1848, followed presently by strikes and
gatherings of workers. The peasants, too, were beginning to demonstrate opposition: they were refusing to wait a full year for abolition of
feudalism, were defaulting on their duties and threatening an agrarian
terror. Meanwhile Prince Windischgrätz, the governor, had returned to
his post on May 17. He had, in 1844, put down workers' revolts and
was all for applying military force to restore order in Vienna and other
centers of disturbance. In collaboration with the court Camarilla he
worked out a plan for combating urban insurrection: the strong points
of the city were to be occupied; the bayonet rather than the musket
was to be used in dispersing crowds; troops were to avoid involvement
in the narrow streets of the old cities; every effort was to be made to
keep open the main lines of communication; if necessary, artillery was
to be used to batter down barricades prior to their storming in bayonet
charges.[34]

By early June, Windischgrätz had concentrated all available forces
in the vicinity of Prague and had mounted artillery on the heights

[34] Hermann Kriebel: *Feldmarschall Fürst Windisch-Grätz* (Innsbruck, 1929), 13–14.

surrounding the city. The students, to whom his very name was anathema, demanded his recall and the cessation of military preparations. They even went so far as to ask for 2,000 muskets, so that they could preserve order. Naturally these demands were ignored by the governor. As a result, the closing of the congress was made the occasion for a great popular demonstration. Guns went off around the palace and Princess Windischgrätz, standing indiscreetly at a window, was shot dead. In almost no time hundreds of barricades went up all over the town. Several days of street fighting ensued, during which the insurgents made great efforts to instigate a peasant rising. Palacký and other leaders tried in vain to mediate. Windischgrätz, it seems, allowed the revolt to develop for some days so as to make the repression more complete. Eventually he withdrew his troops from the city and on June 16 began a systematic bombardment, despite the fact that the popular leaders had already indicated their readiness to capitulate.

Once the rising was suppressed, the local government or National Committee and the National Guard were dissolved and martial law established. There were numerous arrests and the foreign members of the congress were expelled. The revolutionary movement in Prague, basically a moderate movement, was thus snuffed out along with the radicalism of the students and workers. A flood of recriminations followed. The *bourgeoisie,* frightened by the specter of social upheaval, charged German and Magyar agents with having stirred up the populace. At the same time the Germans rejoiced at the suppression of the "anti-German" movement of the Czech nationalists and even debated the desirability of calling in Bavarian or Saxon troops to save the Bohemian Germans from a further "blood bath." Social as well as national lines were now sharply drawn.

Viewed in the framework of general Hapsburg history, the bombardment and reduction of Prague was an epoch-making event. It was the first "victory" of the conservatives over the revolutionaries, of the governments over the peoples. Windischgrätz had demonstrated that as long as the troops remained loyal, urban insurrections could be mastered. The popular movements had only ideas and ideals to support them. They could not hope to hold out against organized military power. That power none of the governments had been willing to apply in February and March. But by June they had recovered from their initial surprise and fright, or at least had begun to yield to the pressure of the military men, who, many of them, made no secret of their eagerness to give short shrift to the revolutionary "canaille." In doing just that, Windischgrätz had opened a new chapter in the story of the midcentury revolutions.[35]

4. ITALY: REVOLUTION AND WAR

The overriding concern of the Viennese government in the spring of 1848 was with Italy, where revolution had broken out in Milan, followed by Piedmontese intervention and war against Austria. The tension in Milan was already acute when news of the Vienna revolution arrived on March 17. The substantial liberal group, consisting of progressive nobles, merchants and bankers, was committed to the struggle for a constitution and dreamed of the expulsion of the Austrians and the organization of Italy as a national state along federal lines. But it hoped to attain its ends by propaganda and agitation, not by revolution.[36] It was rather the more radical, republican element that forced the pace and planned for a monster demonstration with a petition calling for freedom of the press, liquidation of the police force, formation of a civic guard, and convocation of a National Assembly.

On the morning of March 18 Count Gabrio Casati, the podestà or mayor, informed Count O'Donnell, the vice-governor, of the coming demonstration and, arguing that any show of military power would only enhance the unrest, persuaded him to request the commander of the garrison, General Radetzky, not to intervene unless expressly called upon to do so.[37] By noon on the same day about 10,000 people, some

---

[35] For a detailed history of the Prague insurrection, see the Marxist study of I. I. Udalzow: *Aufzeichnungen über die Geschichte des nationalen und politischen Kampfes in Böhmen im Jahre 1848* (Berlin, 1953), especially 122 ff.; but see also the "bourgeois" accounts of Bretholz: *Geschichte Böhmens*, IV, 100 ff.; and Namier: *1848*, 116 ff. On the military aspects, see Paul Müller: *Feldmarschall Fürst Windischgrätz* (Vienna, 1934), 112 ff.

[36] Gaetano Salvemini: *I partiti politici Milanese nel secolo XIX* (reprinted in his *Scritti sul Risorgimento*, Milan, 1961, 27–123); Walter Maturi: "Partiti politici e correnti di pensiero nel Risorgimento" (in *Nuove questioni di storia del Risorgimento e del unità d'Italia*, Milan, 1961, 39–130, especially 99 ff.).

[37] Joseph A. von Helfert: *Mailand und der lombardische Aufstand, März, 1848* (Frankfurt, 1856), 5 ff.; Cesare Spellanzon: *Storia del Risorgimento e dell'unità d'Italia* (Milan, 1936), III, 711; G. F. H. Berkeley and J. Berkeley: *Italy in the Making* (Cambridge, 1940), III, 81 ff.; and the critical analysis of Casati's activity in Alessandro Luzio: "L'apologia di O'Donnell" (in his *Studi critici*, Milan, 1937, 108 ff.).

armed with pistols, daggers or clubs, surged about the Broletto or city hall and all but forced Casati to lead a parade to the government palace to secure acceptance of the petition. When Casati arrived at the palace, two of the imperial guards had already been slain and the mob had begun to invade the building. O'Donnell, badly frightened, agreed to all the demands made upon him and followed the mob back to the Broletto as a hostage.[38]

Presently the narrow, winding streets of the old city bristled with barricades. The troops, who now belatedly intervened, were met with bottles, pans and other missiles thrown from the roofs. The crowd plundered the famous Uboldi collection of medieval armor and raided La Scala opera house for halberds, pikes and other weapons. During the night a central committee was formed to direct insurgent operations. Carlo Cattaneo, the eminent philosopher-economist and republican theorist, who at first had urged the folly of fighting while unarmed against the Austrian troops, became the guiding spirit of the committee. With only about 600 muskets the populace put up a ferocious fight, much more bloody than the Paris insurrection of the month before.

Radetzky, an octogenarian hero of the Napoleonic Wars and probably the ablest military man of his time, had long since foreseen trouble and had called for reinforcements, only to have his fears discounted in Vienna. As a result he had at his disposal only 13,000 men to preserve order in a city of 170,000, the rest of his forces being dispersed as garrisons in other towns.[39] Nonetheless he took up the fight, calling in 6,000 or 7,000 additional troops from neighboring towns. By the evening of March 18 he had retaken several key points, including the Broletto and the government palace. Violent fighting continued during the following days, until a heavy rain set in on the 20th. It then became increasingly difficult to hold and supply numerous scattered posts, so the troops were called back to the Castello, which many of them reached only through torrents of rain and showers of rocks, tiles and

[38] Antonio Monti: *Il 1848 e le cinque giornate di Milano* (Milan, 1948); Berkeley and Berkeley: *Italy in the Making,* III, 81 ff.; Spellanzon: *Storia del Risorgimento,* III, 711 ff.; Giorgio Candeloro: *Storia d'Italia moderna* (Milan, 1960), III, 165 ff.

[39] Feldmarschall Graf Radetzky: "Die Märztage des Jahres 1848 in Mailand" (*Oesterreichische Rundschau,* XIV, 1908, 339–348); Oskar von Arno: *Der Feldherr Radetzky* (Vienna, 1934), 54 ff.; Hugo Kerchnawe: *Radetzky* (Vienna, 1944), 62 ff.; Oscar Regele: *Feldmarschall Radetzky* (Vienna, 1957), 236 ff.

hot water poured from the rooftops. However, the Austrian forces still held the walls and gates of the old city and so prevented intercourse between the insurgents and the surrounding territory.

On March 22 Radetzky with heavy heart decided to evacuate the city. His troops, few in number, were weary and hungry, the country round about was seething with insurrection, and the threat of Piedmontese intervention might soon make withdrawal impossible. On March 23 the troops succeeded in making an orderly exit, "one of those sorry masterpieces of the art of war," to borrow Radetzky's own words. The "Five Days" of Milan were indeed among the most remarkable cases in history of successful street fighting.[40]

The Austrian troops, many of them barefoot and but scantily clad, reached Verona on April 1, having lost their munitions and other equipment on the way. They took refuge in the forts of the Quadrilateral: Peschiera and Mantua on the Mincio River and Verona and Legnago on the Adige, commanding the narrow passage between Lake Como and the Po River, and forming the boundary between Lombardy and Venetia. Both provinces were now in open revolt, for in Venice a popular rising had forced the Austrian troops to evacuate, after which the leaders, Daniele Manin, a prominent lawyer, and Niccolò Tommaseo, a well-known man of letters, had proclaimed the Republic of San Marco.[41]

Radetzky had lost upward of 11,000 men through the defection of Italian units in his army and isolation of a further 7,000 who were cut off in various places. All told he had hardly more than 35,000 men and with these he had now to face the prospect of attack by Piedmont and other Italian states supporting the Milanese revolution. The moderates in the Lombard capital had at once appealed to Charles Albert of Piedmont for support, not only against the Austrians, but against the

[40] Berkeley and Berkeley: *Italy in the Making,* III, 78. The literature on the Five Days is almost endless. On the Italian side, see Monti: *il 1848 e le cinque giornate,* Pietro Pieri: *Storia militare del Risorgimento* (Turin, 1962), 187 ff.; and the contemporary account of a Swiss officer, A. Le Masson, translated as *Military Events in Italy, 1848–1849* (London, 1851). On the Austrian side, General Karl von Schönhals' *Erinnerungen eines oesterreichischen Veteranen aus dem italienischen Kriege, 1848–1849* (Stuttgart, 1852) is something of a classic.

[41] Vincenzo Marchesi: *Storia documentata della rivoluzione e della difesa di Venezia negli anni 1848–1849* (Venice, 1913) is fundamental, but far less readable than George M. Trevelyan: *Manin and the Venetian Republic of 1848* (New York, 1923); Alessandro Levi: *La politica di Daniele Manin* (Milan, 1933), 9 ff.

violent, revolutionary elements in their own city. Perhaps if he had crossed the frontier at once, the king might have hampered the Austrian retreat or possibly have destroyed Radetzky's whole army, for he had a standing army of 45,000 men which could be raised to a strength of 60,000 in a short time. But Charles Albert, irresolute by nature, was kept from reaching a prompt decision by many and varied considerations.

In the first place, the king was deeply religious and conservative, much under the influence of the Jesuits. He still felt bound by the alliance concluded with Austria in 1831 to meet the threat of war with France. Although he had now turned against Austria and had more or less accepted the role assigned to him by Italian nationalists, his fears of revolution and of aggression by France had been reawakened by the February Revolution. Much as he would have liked to acquire Lombardy and if possible Venetia, he was most reluctant to aid and abet revolution in Milan, the more so as intervention might lead to renewed French claims to Savoy and Nice, or even to war. Furthermore, the British, Prussian and Russian ministers were all warning him against aggression as likely to result in a larger conflict. On the other hand, the pressure from liberals and nationalists was hardly to be resisted. On March 23 Count Cavour had published an unequivocal warning: "One way only lies open to the nation, to the government, to the king: war, war immediately and without delays."[42]

Later that day the decision for intervention was made, at a time when the insurrection in Milan was already successful and a provisional government had already been set up by Casati and his friends.[43] By March 26 the first Piedmontese troops reached Milan, while news of the expulsion of the Austrians evoked a storm of enthusiasm throughout the peninsula. Charles Albert, in the hope of discouraging French intervention, had announced that the Italians alone would liberate Italy: *Italia farà da se*. In the same spirit volunteers enrolled everywhere and popular pressure forced the various governments to contribute contingents of troops to the national war. The Tuscan

---

[42] William R. Thayer: *The Life and Times of Cavour* (Boston, 1911), I, 87; Amadeo Tosti: "L'età contemporanea" (in *Storia d'Italia,* Rome, 1958), 114.

[43] Salvemini: *I partiti politici Milanese,* 61 ff.; Adolfo Omodeo: *La leggenda di Carlo Alberto nella recente storiografia* (Turin, 1940), 93 ff.; and the standard biography of the king by Niccolò Rodolico: *Carlo Alberto negli anni 1843–1849* (Florence, 1943), 289 ff.

government dispatched 7,000 men (March 29), and the Duke of Parma a comparable number (April 9). Even the papal government fell in line: 7,000 regulars were sent to defend the Po frontier against any attempt by the Austrians to advance south. In addition 9,000 militia and volunteers were allowed to start for the north. Ferdinand of Naples, too, was obliged to participate by sending 14,000 men to the north by land and sea. Under the circumstances success seemed certain at an early date. Patriotic fervor ran high and everywhere the youth hoped to be in on the final triumph.[44]

At first all went well, for Radetzky remained inactive and thereby made it easy for Charles Albert to overrun Lombardy and reach the Mincio River (April 6). After winning the Battle of Goito (a minor engagement) the Italians crossed the river and invested Peschiera. But little more was done to exploit their temporary advantage. Military critics argue that if the Piedmontese had crossed to the south side of the Po and invaded Venetia, they might have cut the Austrian communications and deprived Radetzky of all hopes of reinforcement. Strong terms have been used in condemnation of the king for allowing himself to be torn this way and that by the conflicting counsels of his generals, none of whom had any real plans of campaign. In any event, several weeks were lost in argument.[45]

Political as well as military considerations help to explain Charles Albert's procrastination. He was hoping to acquire Lombardy and Venetia so as to establish a strong and prosperous North Italian kingdom. He was therefore troubled by the possibility that the Milan provisional government might set up an independent Lombard state and turn to the French Republic for support. He therefore regarded as urgent the "fusion" of Lombardy with Piedmont. This solution was entirely agreeable to most members of the Lombard provisional government, who as nobles and landowners felt uneasy about their revolutionary role and lived in fear lest radical elements in town and country

---

[44] General Mario Caracciolo di Ferolete: "Il contributo militare degli Stati Italiani" and General Cesare Cesari: "I voluntari," both in the General Staff official history *Il primo passo verso l'unità d'Italia, 1848–1849* (Rome, 1948).

[45] Rodolico: *Carlo Alberto*, 311 ff., defends the king. Among the critics, see Guido Porzio: *La guerra regia in Italia nel 1848–1849* (Rome, 1955), 24 ff., 47 ff., 64 ff.; Pieri: *Storia militare del Risorgimento*, chaps. vii and viii, and the same author's more extended treatment in "La guerra regia nella pianura padana" (in Ettore Rota, ed.: *Il 1848 nella storia italiana ed europea*, Milan, n.d., I, 169–479).

set off a social uprising. Dubious of their ability to maintain an independent Lombard state, they were in favor of union with Piedmont, which was conservative and monarchical. On the other hand the republican minority, led by Cattaneo, detested Charles Albert and despised the "backward" Piedmontese. Their ideal was in fact an independent Lombard republic, united with other Italian states on a federal basis like that of the Swiss Confederation or the American Union. "Italy," they maintained, "is physically and historically federalist."[46] As for defense against possible attack by Austria, the French Republic would undoubtedly lend assistance. Indeed, Cattaneo was in favor of calling in the French at once so as to clinch the victory over the Austrians.

Unfortunately for the republican minority, it was to meet with opposition even from that great republican theorist Joseph Mazzini, who on April 8 arrived in Milan and met with an enthusiastic popular reception. Mazzini regarded liberation from foreign rule as the matter of highest priority and had recently founded a National Italian Society in the effort to bring all factions together, "reserving till the day of victory measures that would enable the people to decide upon the form of government." Agreeing that Italy must do the job itself, he was bitterly opposed to French interference. He would support Charles Albert as long as the Piedmontese remained in the field.

In a famous meeting on April 30 Cattaneo made a supreme effort to convert Mazzini to his views. He argued that during the Five Days no one had come to the aid of the city, but that in the hour of victory Charles Albert, the man who in 1821 had betrayed the liberals and in 1834 had fired on the democrats, put in a prompt appearance: "I will be accused of irreverence," Cattaneo added, "but I swear that I would prefer to see the return of the Austrians rather than see a traitor as chief of Lombardy." Yet Mazzini remained unmoved. He would have nothing to do with plans to overturn the provisional government and call in the French. The meeting broke up in a huff and the republicans, politically speaking a distinct minority, could not recover from the blow dealt them by Mazzini's intransigence.[47]

---

[46] Bruno Brunello: *Il pensiero di Carlo Cattaneo* (Turin, 1925), 168 ff.

[47] The only full account of this meeting, written in 1852 at Cattaneo's request, was discovered and published by Antonio Monti: *Un dramma fra gli esuli* (Milan, 1921). For a good discussion of the problem of fusion, see Leopoldo Marchetti: "I moti di Milano e il problema della fusione col Piemonte" (in Roto: *Il 1848 nella storia italiana,*

The provisional government decided on May 12 to submit the question of fusion to a popular vote, which was taken on May 29. The fact that the voting was open may help to explain the outcome: 561,000 in favor of fusion and only 681 in opposition. Fusion with Piedmont was proclaimed on June 13 and was followed by similar action on the part of Parma (June 16), Modena (June 21) and the Republic of Venice (July 4). Manin and his associates were by no means enamored of the idea of fusion, but Venice was being blockaded by the Austrian fleet and was therefore obliged to look to Piedmont for aid.

Meanwhile the military situation worsened. The vision of a united effort by all Italian states faded away. In sending contingents to the north the various governments had acted under popular pressure. At bottom they disliked and feared Piedmont and had no desire whatever to assist Charles Albert to expand his kingdom. They made efforts, therefore, to induce the pope to take the lead in organizing an Italian League which would afford the individual states protection against the designs of others.

Pope Pius, for his part, was confronted with a painful dilemma. The papal cabinet, created under the new constitution to deal with temporal affairs, was headed by Count Recchi and consisted almost entirely of patriotic liberals, in close touch with Piedmontese nationalists. Supported by popular sentiment, the ministers urged His Holiness to declare war on Austria and participate actively in the campaign. Pius, who from the outset saw the conflict between his Italian patriotism and his responsibilities as head of an international church, saw no way of intervening in the national war except under cover of a League of Princes. He did what he could to bring such a league into being (see Illustration 56). But by mid-April it had become clear that Charles Albert, confident of victory, would not bind himself to share the spoils with others. [48]

II, 653–723); see also Franco Valsecchi: "L'intervention française et la solidarité révolutionnaire internationale dans la pensée des démocrates lombards en 1848" (*Actes du Congrès Historique du Centenaire*, 165–176); Brunello: *Il pensiero di Carlo Cattaneo*, 160 ff., 202; Mario Borsa: *Carlo Cattaneo* (Milan, 1945), 164 ff.; Gwilyn O. Griffith: *Mazzini* (New York, 1932), 185 ff.

[48] Pietro Pieri: "La missione di Mons. Corboli-Bussi in Lombardia e la crisi della politica italiana di Pio IX" (*Rivista di storia della Chiesa in Italia*, I, 1947, 38–84); Roger Aubert: *Le pontificat de Pie IX* (Paris, 1952), 27 ff.; Candeloro: *Storia d'Italia moderna*, III, 206 ff.

To complicate matters still further, the commander of the papal forces, General Giovanni Durando, was a Piedmontese officer who had as his adviser the ardent nationalist, Massimo d'Azeglio. Durando evidently had no intention of halting his advance at the Po, but was determined to invade Venetia and fight the enemy. On April 5 he issued an order of the day, written by D'Azeglio, which implied that the pope approved and indeed blessed the campaign "to exterminate the enemies of God and of Italy . . . . Such a war is not merely national, but highly Christian."[49] Pius, furious at Durando for presuming to proclaim a crusade against a Catholic power, at once rebuked him, but this did not prevent the general from crossing the Po (April 22). In Rome the ministers redoubled their efforts to secure a declaration of war, while the cardinals were equally energetic in opposing it. To terminate the argument the pope published an allocution to the College of Cardinals which was meant as an address to the entire Catholic world. He rejected the charge that by his reforms he had precipitated the revolutionary movements of 1848 and repudiated all thought of working for an Italian republic under his own presidency. As representative of God on earth he could not, he declared, make war, for, "according to the order of Our supreme Apostolate, We seek after and embrace all races, peoples and nations, with equal devotion of paternal love."

This famous allocution completed the disillusionment of the patriots, who had tried to make the pope the champion of Italian nationalism. He was now charged with betrayal of the national cause. His ministers resigned and disorder spread. Popular clubs and radical groups proliferated in Rome and agitation against priests, cardinals and even the Papacy became the order of the day. Then, to crown the pope's misfortune, the Austrian government on May 4 severed relations with the papal government.[50]

Ferdinand of Naples at once took heart from the pope's refusal to declare war. During April his situation had been extremely precarious,

[49] Berkeley and Berkeley, *Italy in the Making*, III, 164; Edward E. Y. Hales: *Pio Nono* (New York, 1954), 73.

[50] Friedrich Engel-Janosi: *Oesterreich und der Vatikan, 1846–1918* (Graz, 1958), 37 ff.; R. M. Johnston: *The Roman Theocracy and the Republic, 1846–1849* (New York, 1901), 357 ff.; Antonio Monti: *Pio IX nel Risorgimento italiano* (Bari, 1928), 97 ff.; Domenico Demarco: *Pio IX e la rivoluzione romana del 1848* (Modena, 1947), 71 ff.; Hales: *Pio Nono*, 76 ff.; D. Massé: *Pio IX e il gran tradimento del 1848* (Alba, 1948).

for Sicily, except for the citadel of Messina, had been lost to the insurgents and they had rejected all offers of autonomy. On April 13 they had declared the Sicilian throne vacant. On the mainland the government was wrestling with a financial crisis, with unemployment and general disorder. A radical minority, inspired by events in the north, demanded active intervention in the war against Austria and called for revision of the constitution which had been so recently granted. By mid-May the tension between the king and the radicals in the Parliament had reached the breaking point over the questions of the oath to the constitution and the right of the chamber to undertake revisions of the charter. Presently barricades appeared in the streets around the palace and fighting broke out between the royal troops and Swiss guards on the one hand and the radicals, supported by the National Guard and the people, on the other (see Illustration 63). After considerable loss of life, the insurrection was mastered on the evening of May 15.[51]

Ferdinand thus scored the first success of the governments against the forces of revolution. Yet he did not abolish the constitution. On the contrary, after driving the insurgent leaders from the city and dissolving the National Guard, he set a date for new elections and allowed a new Parliament to meet on July 1. It seems that the king in his policy had the support of the upper classes—the landowners and the businessmen—as well as of the landed middle class which was so characteristic of southern Italy. These propertied classes were much disturbed by the unrest, especially in the countryside. In certain places there were peasant outbreaks so serious that the landlords had to barricade themselves in their manor houses or seek refuge in the cities. At Cosenza the radicals in May set up a provisional government which was suppressed only through use of organized military forces.[52]

Relief from radical pressure enabled Ferdinand to recall the Neapolitan troops from the north, on the plea that they were needed for the reconquest of Sicily. General Guglielmo Pepe, veteran revolutionist and

[51] Domenico Demarco: *Il crollo del Regno delle Due Sicilie* (Naples, 1960), I, 152 ff.; Harold Acton: *The Last Bourbons of Naples* (New York, 1961), 228 ff. On the Sicilian revolution, see Federico Curato: *La rivoluzione siciliana del 1848–1849* (Milan, 1940).

[52] A. Williams Salomone: "The Liberal Experiment and the Italian Revolution of 1848" (*Journal of Central European Affairs,* IX, 1949, 267–288). On the agrarian unrest in the south, see Demarco: *Il crollo del Regno,* 157 ff.; Acton: *Last Bourbons of Naples,* 251 ff.; Pasquale Villani: *Mezzogiorno tra riforme e rivoluzione* (Bari, 1962), 75.

ardent patriot, followed Durando's example and disobeyed. About 1,000 men followed him in joining forces with the papal contingent, but the great majority returned to Naples, thus depriving Charles Albert of a substantial auxiliary force.[53]

Meanwhile Radetzky had received reinforcements of some 30,000 men who had managed to evade Durando's troops and pick their way through the foothills of the Alps to reach Verona. Charles Albert still failed to undertake major operations. He now deluded himself into thinking that he might acquire Lombardy and Venetia through diplomacy rather than war. The Austrian government, desperately beset by events in Vienna, in Bohemia and in Hungary, was approaching the verge of hopelessness, the more so as even the pope, through a special envoy, was begging the emperor to accept the inevitable and leave the Italian provinces to the Italians.[54] The French and British governments, too, were bringing pressure to bear in the same direction. Lamartine was genuinely sympathetic to Italian national aspirations, the more so as they promised to put an end to Austrian control and influence in the peninsula. Starting with the resolution not to countenance Austrian aggression against any Italian state, he soon reached the point of being ready to aid Piedmont to expel the Austrians, provided Lombardy and Venetia should then constitute one or two independent states. Their "fusion" with Piedmont would not be in France's interest, for it would result in the formation of a strong north Italian kingdom on France's frontier. Such a solution could be made palatable only through the cession to France of the Piedmontese provinces of Savoy and Nice, which would give France the "natural" frontier of the Alps in the southeast. Assuming that Charles Albert would not be able to defeat the Austrians without French aid, the French provisional government began to concentrate on the frontier a corps of observation (the "Army of the Alps"), which soon reached a strength of 60,000 men. At the same time the sale of large stocks of ammunition to the

[53] Giuseppe Paladino: "Il governo napoletano e la guerra de 1848" (*Nuova rivista storica*, III, 1919, 565–600; IV, 1920, 61–80, 341–372; V, 1921, 220–245); Rota: "L'antagonismo politico fra Torino e Napoli durante la guerra del 1848" (in his *Il 1848 nella storia italiana e europea*, I, 123–169).

[54] Monti: *Pio IX nel Risorgimento italiano*, 97 ff.; Engel-Janosi: *Oesterreich und der Vatikan*, 39, and *Die politische Korrespondenz der Päpste mit den oesterreichischen Kaisern, 1804–1918* (Vienna, 1964), 230 ff.

provisional government of Milan was authorized, and a special envoy sent to Turin to arrange for French intervention.[55]

Charles Albert was still convinced that the Italians could win on their own. He flatly refused to appeal to the French for aid, thinking the price exorbitant and fearing above all lest the presence of the French stimulate republicanism in Lombardy and elsewhere. He was reinforced in his attitude by Palmerston, who was greatly troubled by the threat of French action, the repercussions of which were hard to foresee. Convinced by Foreign Office representatives in Italy that the Italians were bound to succeed, he concluded that the sooner the Austrians were gotten out of Italy, the better it would be for all concerned. It made no difference to him whether Lombardy became an independent state or was united with Piedmont. The important thing was to forestall French intervention or a possible alliance of France with a Lombard republic. Not only in northern Italy but in Sicily also the British were exerting themselves to block the republican movement. Thus in Sicily they supported the candidacy of the duke of Genoa, younger son of Charles Albert, for the Sicilian throne, and actually succeeded in having him elected by the Palermo Assembly on July 10.[56]

As the threat of French intervention grew, the Austrian government sent to London Baron Karl Hummelauer to canvass the terms on which British diplomatic support might be obtained. In conversations with Palmerston (May 23-25), Hummelauer stressed the danger of French intervention and the impossibility for Austria to fight against France as well as Piedmont. In order to reach a settlement the Austrian government might be willing to agree to the establishment of a

[55] Paul Henry: "La France et les nationalités en 1848" (Revue historique, CLXXXVI, 1939, 48-77; CLXXXVIII, 1940, 234-258); César Vidal: "La France et la question italienne en 1848" (Etudes d'histoire moderne et contemporaine, II, 1948, 162-183); and the following studies by Ferdinand Boyer: "Lamartine et le Piémont" (Revue d'histoire diplomatique, LXIV, 1950, 37-57); "Les fournitures d'armes par le gouvernment français aux patriotes italiens en 1848 et 1849" (Rassegna storica del Risorgimento, XXXVII, 1950, 95-106); "Charles Albert et la Seconde République" (ibid., L, 1963, 463-512); "L'armée des Alpes en 1848" (Revue historique, CCXXIV, 1965).

[56] Ruggero Moscati: La diplomazia europea e il problema italiano nel 1848 (Florence, 1947), chap. ii; and the same author's more recent essay: "L'Europa e il problema italiano nel 1848-1849" (in F. Catalano, R. Moscati, and F. Valsecchi: L'Italia nel Risorgimento, Verona, 1964, 431-478); further, Gaetano Falzone: Il problema della Sicilia nel 1848 attraverso nuove fonti inediti (Palermo, 1951), which stresses French policy in Sicily.

self-governing Lombardo-Venetian kingdom under an Austrian archduke as viceroy. Parma and Modena might be added to this kingdom
so as to form a new north Italian state. Palmerston, however, argued
that the return of Lombardy to Austrian rule in any form would be
impossible. He proposed that Lombardy be ceded to Piedmont so as to
make a strong state on the French frontier, while Venetia might be
given autonomy within the Hapsburg Empire. Hummelauer, convinced that Austria must secure British mediation at any price, took
Palmerston's proposals *ad referendum,* only to learn a few days later
that the British cabinet, under the passionately Italophile Lord John
Russell, would agree to mediate only if Venetia as well as Lombardy
were abandoned by Austria.

On these same days the Lombard and Venetian leaders induced
Charles Albert to promise not to make peace as long as a single
Austrian soldier remained on Italian soil, and the French National
Assembly, recently elected, voted unanimously a resolution in favor of
the liberation of Italy (May 24). The French government, enraged by
Lombardy's vote for fusion with Piedmont, began to bring pressure on
Vienna to give up the Italian provinces on the understanding that they
should not be annexed to Piedmont. But the Vienna court could not
bring itself to accept the loss of more than Lombardy and that only
providing the problem of the public debt could be satisfactorily solved.
Venetia was to be given complete autonomy. A special envoy was sent
to Milan to negotiate with the Lombard authorities, while Radetzky
was instructed to take steps toward securing an armistice.[57]

Radetzky was furious at Vienna's defeatism and sent one of his
officers, Prince Felix zu Schwarzenberg, to argue the increasingly
favorable prospects of military success and plead for continuance of the
war. After much confabulation the Court abandoned the idea of
making cessions and arranged to send Radetzky yet another 20,000
men. Military operations now entered the concluding phase.[58] At
first the Piedmontese and Tuscans were able to block Radetzky's
attempted advance beyond the Mincio and scored a last success in the

[57] A. J. P. Taylor: *The Italian Problem in European Diplomacy, 1847–1849* (Manchester, 1934), 120 ff.; Moscati, "L'Europa e il problema italiano," 458 ff.; Ferdinand
Boyer: "Le problème de l'Italie du Nord entre la France et l'Autriche de fevrier à juillet,
1848" (*Rassegna storica del Risorgimento,* XLII, 1955, 206–217); and, on the Austrian
policy, Vittorio Barbieri: "I tentativi di mediazione anglo-francesi durante la guerra del
1848" (*ibid.,* XXVI, 1939, 683–726).

[58] Rudolf Kiszling: *Fürst Felix zu Schwarzenberg* (Graz, 1952), 34 ff.

reduction of Peschiera. But once again the Piedmontese king failed to follow up his successes, evidently hoping still that French threats and British pressure would induce the Austrians to abandon their Italian provinces. By early July, however, he was sufficiently disillusioned to be willing to settle for Lombardy, Parma and Modena, leaving Venetia to the emperor. But the Turin government, thinking less dynastically than the king, flatly refused to abjure its commitments and abandon Venetia, which had voted fusion with Piedmont, to its fate.

The Austrian government, staking everything on Radetzky's assurances, now resisted all efforts of the French and British to divest it of its Italian possessions. By the end of July Radetzky, provided now with superior forces and fire power, was ready for the decisive blow. On July 23 he attacked the long-strung Italian lines stretching from Rivoli in the north to Mantua in the south. Several days of fighting culminated in the Battle of Custoza (July 23–27), after which the defeated Italian forces were obliged to fall back to the Mincio. Presently they were in full retreat on Milan, in the outskirts of which city they suffered another defeat on August 4. Mazzini and other Lombard leaders were eager to defend the city, but the king and his high command were by this time demoralized, convinced as they were that further resistance was hopeless. Booed by the populace and denounced as a traitor by the Milanese leaders, Charles Albert was smuggled through the streets by night while his forces abandoned the city. They were followed by some 100,000 Lombards, who now sought refuge in Piedmont or Switzerland (see Illustration 37). Between the Lombards and the Piedmontese there was now nothing but bitterness. According to the former the Piedmontese had served only their own selfish ends, while according to the latter the Milanese had failed to make an appropriate contribution in men and supplies. There was more than a grain of truth in both charges.[59]

Consternation overcame the Italian governments on news of the disaster at Custoza. From both Turin and Milan envoys were dispatched to Paris to explore the possibilities of military aid. Charles Albert, still unwilling to pay the price for such aid, finally left the decision to his ministers. But the moment for action had passed. General Cavaignac, provisional head of the French government, and the new minister for foreign affairs, Jules Bastide, had learned from

[59] On the Milan crisis, see Pietro Silva: *Il 1848* (Rome, 1948), 138 ff.; Porzio: *La guerra regia*, 202 ff.; Pieri: *Storia militare*, 258 ff.

their agents in Italy that the Austrian armies were in great strength, numbering some 130,000 men. Since in any event it would take the French forces three weeks to cross the Alps, there was a real possibility that the Austrians might reach and occupy the passes before the French could get there. The French authorities were determined to intervene if the Austrians undertook an invasion of Piedmontese territory, but for the rest they fell back on the plans for joint mediation with Britain. On August 8 they proposed to London that mediation be offered on the basis of the Hummelauer memorandum of May 24, which envisaged the cession of Lombardy to Piedmont, autonomy for Venetia, and self-determination for Parma and Modena. But before anything could come of this project, Charles Albert had had his chief of staff, General Canera di Salasco, conclude an armistice for a six-week period. He seems to have hoped that within that period French and British pressure on Vienna would bring him Lombardy without his having to sacrifice Savoy. But the Austrian government temporized and evaded until on August 22 the Austrian foreign minister notified the French and British that Vienna would negotiate with Piedmont directly and that in any event Austria, having reconquered Lombardy, could no longer accept the Hummelauer memorandum as a basis for discussion.[60]

The Austrian reply was only the prelude to long and tedious negotiations which dragged on through the autumn of 1848 while the Austrian government was still too unsure of itself to speak categorically. But these discussions belong properly to the later phase of the Italian question. For the time being, the Battle of Custoza was decisive for Italian affairs and indeed for the entire development of the revolutionary situation in Europe. For Custoza had demonstrated even more conclusively than the reduction of Prague that so long as the governments could rely on their armies they could sooner or later master the forces of upheaval. They could in fact hope that in the work of repression they would enjoy the at least tacit support of the liberal middle class, which was not revolutionary to begin with and had quickly taken fright at the radicalism of the lower strata of the population, in the countryside as well as the towns.

Italian historians have long concerned themselves with the social structure of the 1848 revolution and more particularly with the ques-

[60] Taylor: *Italian Problem*, 137 ff., and the articles by Barbieri and Boyer cited in previous footnotes.

tion whether and to what extent the lower classes played a significant role. For the first phase of the revolution the answer is fairly clear.[61] The strongest element in the opposition was the liberal group, consisting of progressive nobles, the landed middle class and the banking and business class of the towns, together with professors at the universities, writers and other professional men. These people were most of them well-to-do. They were intent on reform while avoiding revolution. It was the much smaller, lower-middle-class element in the towns, many of whom were democrats and republicans, who in Milan provided the impetus for the huge popular demonstrations which introduced the revolution. The fighting on the barricades was done largely though not exclusively by workers—not factory workers, for the factory system was in its infancy, but artisans and journeymen suffering from unemployment, high food prices and generally low wages. Once the Austrians had been expelled, however, it was relatively easy for the respectable liberal classes to take over the provisional government and throw in their lot with Piedmont, if only as one way to avoid the growth of radicalism. As for the vast majority of the population, the peasantry, it was certainly moved by profound but ill-defined discontent. It is clear that the propertied classes, even radicals such as Cattaneo, were apprehensive of rural insurrection and were at times deterred in their activities by fear of stirring up forces which would or at least might end in social upheaval. In the early days of the Milan revolt, large numbers of peasants hurried to the city to enroll in the civic guard and aid in driving out the foreigner. But the provisional government, badly frightened by the prospect, refused them admittance to the guard and ordered them to return home. They were not even allowed to enter the gates.[62]

Actually, because of the predominant position of the liberals, the

[61] See, e.g., A. M. Ghisalberti: "Ancora sulla participazione populare al Risorgimento" (*Rassegna storica del Risorgimento*, XXXI–XXXIII, 1944–1946, 5–13); Niccolò Rodolico: "Atteggiamenti di gruppi sociali nel Risorgimento italiano" (*Accademia nazionale dei Lincei: Atti di convegni*, X ,1949, 351–363); Antonio Monti: "Guerra regia e guerra di populo nel Risorgimento" (in Ettore Rota, ed.: *Questioni di storia del Risorgimento*, Milan, 1951, 183–216); Palmiro Togliatti: "Le classi populari nel Risorgimento" (*Studi critici*, III, 1964); and most recently the excellent analysis by Franco Valsecchi: "Le classi populari e il Risorgimento" (*Cultura e scuola*, No. 15, 1965, 82–93).

[62] Valsecchi: "Le classi populari e il Risorgimento"; Denis Mack Smith: "The Italian Peasants and the Risorgimento" (in *Italia e Inghilterra nel Risorgimento*, London, 1954, 15–30); Albert Soboul: "Risorgimento et révolution bourgeoise" (*La pensée*, No. 95, 1961, 63–73).

revolutions of the spring of 1848 followed a normal course. The provisional governments were not seriously challenged or threatened. The really important feature was the war against Austria. This, it must be admitted, ended in complete fiasco, not only because the Piedmontese and their supporters had the bad luck to have a real military genius as their opponent, but because of the suspicions and rivalries between the Italian governments and above all because of the irresolution and military ineptitude of Charles Albert, to say nothing of the narrow selfishness of his aims. Having undertaken to expel the Austrians, he was afraid to act for fear of French intervention. He then turned to the British and French to mediate, a policy in which he was bound to fail if only because of the differences between those two powers as to what should be done with Lombardy once it had been abandoned by the Austrians. Radetzky solved this problem by squelching the defeatism of Vienna and then dealing the Piedmontese so decisive a blow that they were obliged to abandon the prize which they thought already in the bag. As for Mazzini's dream of the united Italians, who would be more than a match for an Austrian empire rent by conflicting forces, it turned out to be merely a pipe dream. In every Italian state there were patriots anxious to back Piedmont to the limit, but they were too few to impose their policy of intervention on the governments. Among the governments, one may safely conjecture, there were at least some that secretly rejoiced at Charles Albert's discomfiture.

Chapter Three

GERMANY: THE HEYDAY OF LIBERALISM

I. THE MARCH REVOLUTIONS

MARX and Engels, reflecting on the German situation in January, 1848, asked themselves whether the *bourgeoisie* of any country had ever been in a more splendid position to carry on its struggle against the existing government.[1] They were referring, of course, to the widespread distress and unrest and to the apparent failure of the liberals to take advantage of their opportunity. But these liberals—progressive officials, the upper stratum of the intellectuals and professional men, and especially the new business class—were as reluctant in Germany as they were else-where to provoke a revolution. Remembering the excesses of the 1793 Terror in France, they dreaded a major upheaval almost as much as did the princes and the aristocrats. Their hope was to attain their objective of constitutional government through peaceful organization and agitation along the lines of Cobden's Anti-Corn Law League. They might value popular unrest and demonstration as providential additional pressure on the governments, but they never intended any-thing remotely resembling the political or social overturn of the existing order.

Many of the German states experienced unwanted revolutions in the spring of 1848, the circumstances often varying widely from one locality to another. Perhaps most typical was the course of events in Baden, one of the most overpopulated parts of Germany, where distress among the people was chronic. There, too, parliamentary life was fairly well-developed and the forces of liberalism and even radicalism reason-ably well-organized. On receipt of the news of the February Revolu-tion, huge popular meetings took place at once in Mannheim and other cities. The demands of the people were for freedom of the press,

---

[1] Quoted by Karl Obermann: "Die Rolle der Volksmassen in Deutschland zu Beginn der Revolution von 1848" (*Geschichte in der Schule*, XI, 1958, 142–157), and "Die Volksbewegung in Deutschland von 1844 bis 1846" (*Zeitschrift für Geschichtswissen-schaft*, V, 1957, 503–525).

establishment of a citizen guard and other familiar liberal items. So formidable were the demonstrations that the government yielded at once. On March 2 a new cabinet, headed by the well-known liberal leaders Welcker and Bassermann, was installed. But before the liberal regime could get its footing, peasant outbreaks occurred, marked by attacks on Jewish moneylenders and especially on manor houses. Led by their elders the populations of whole villages hacked down the doors of their landlords, threw out the feudal records, forced the lords to sign away their traditional privileges, and plundered the forests. Troops had to be called out to restore a semblance of order.[2]

The pattern of development was much the same in other German states, for example, in Würtemberg, Hesse-Darmstadt, Saxony, Hanover, and the Hanseatic cities. Everywhere there were the same crowds, the same deputations, petitions and demonstrations, often accompanied by destruction of machines and in the countryside by sporadic outbreaks which in Würtemberg came to be a veritable peasant insurrection. In all these states the princes and governments were so terrified that they offered no resistance to popular demands. By mid-March, that is, even before the revolution in Vienna, most of the smaller German states had introduced responsible government and accorded civil liberties. The action of the masses in town and country had forced the procrastinating rulers to accept a solution which the changes of the foregoing decades had made all but inevitable.

In Bavaria the pressure for reform was curiously enmeshed with an old-fashioned court scandal. The aging king, Louis I, was infatuated with a young "Spanish" dancer, Lola Montez, who was actually the daughter of a British officer and a Creole mother. She was born, not in Andalusia, but in Ireland. All are agreed that she was an exceptionally beautiful creature, a young woman whose dark eyes, jet-black hair, and marvelous figure (invariably clothed in tight-fitting black velvet) left few men unmoved. But there was more to Lola than that. She had an alert mind and genuine wit, in fact, enough of a personality to have

2 Friedrich Lautenschläger: Die Agrarunruhen in den badischen Standes- und Grundherrschaften im Jahre 1848 (Heidelberg, 1915), chap. iii; Gunter Franz: "Die agrarische Bewegung im Jahre 1848" (Zeitschrift für Agrargeschichte und Agrarsoziologie, VII, 1959, 176–192); Franz Schnabel: "Das Land Baden in der Revolution von 1848–1849" (in Wilhelm Keil, ed.: Deutschland, 1848–1948, Stuttgart, 1948, 56–70); and the excellent account in Theodore S. Hamerow: Restoration, Revolution, Reaction (Princeton, 1958), chap. ix.

attracted Franz Liszt and Alexander Dumas, both of whom had been
her lovers. Liszt had introduced her to the circle of George Sand,
which was one of the most sophisticated and advanced in European
society. There Lola absorbed, from Lamennais and others, the principles of republicanism and socialism with which she attempted to
indoctrinate the Bavarian king.

Louis, so it seems, was captivated as much by her mind as by her
beauty. Soon after her arrival in Munich (October, 1846) he began to
turn to her for political advice. She soon became arrogant and
dictatorial. She publicly insulted ministers and insisted on the appointment of officials of her own choice. Nonetheless, the king adored her,
wrote her numberless romantic poems and eventually created her
countess of Landsberg. All the warnings of his ministers, of the high
clergy, even of the pope, fell on deaf ears. Presently the whole country
was outraged. In January and February of 1848, students staged
demonstrations against her and even launched an attack on her residence. The king ordered the university closed, but this move only
provoked more disturbances and led to clashes between the troops and
the populace. Finally the king, under heavy pressure from his ministers, asked Lola to leave. It was at this point that news arrived of the
revolution in Paris. Larger and larger crowds appeared on the streets,
singing the "Marseillaise" and calling for a republic. Soon barricades
appeared and the crowd attacked the arsenal. Louis was obliged to
yield to demands for freedom of the press and other concessions
(March 6). When, ten days later, it became known that Lola had
visited the city in disguise, the popular indignation was such that the
king had to banish his favorite from the country. For him this was the
final straw. An absolutist at heart, he could not envisage governing
under the new system. Besides, the loss of Lola was more than he could
bear. So on March 20 he abdicated the throne in favor of his son,
Maximilian II.[3]

[3] Erich Pottendorf: *Lola Montez* (Vienna, 1955) is devoted almost entirely to her
stirring eighteen months in Munich; Helen Holdredge: *The Woman in Black* (New
York, 1955), on the contrary, is particularly full on Lola's further career in America.
These rather colorful books should be supplemented by the sober professional accounts
of Michael Doberl: *Entwicklungsgeschichte Bayerns* (Munich, 1931), III, 135 ff.; Karl
Bosl and H. Schreibmüller: *Geschichte Bayerns* (Munich, 1955), II, 92 ff.; and especially
Egon C. Corti: *Ludwig I of Bavaria* (London, 1938), chaps. x, *et seq.*, which contributes
many new letters.

The Lola Montez affair had the effect of uniting all influential elements in Bavarian society in opposition to the king. The popular agitation against his favorite took on the character of political pressure and obliged the king to accept the principle of responsible government and indeed the entire liberal program. But the disorder and lawlessness was such in South Germany that the radicals were bound to take advantage of it. Led by Friedrich Hecker and Gustav Struve, they staged a meeting at Offenburg at which there was much talk of setting up clubs on the Jacobin model, organizing a committee of public safety and eventually proclaiming a German republic. Hecker did proclaim a republic at Konstanz (April 12), hoping for support of the peasantry and the defection of the troops, and trusting that a filibustering force of Germans, under the poet George Herwegh, would stage an invasion from Alsace. But the venture, which was poorly planned, led to much dissension among the leaders and ended in fiasco. On appeal from the grand duke of Baden, the federal Diet at Frankfurt sent Hessian and other troops which defeated Hecker's forces at Kandern (April 20). Hecker fled to Switzerland and the radical insurrection proved to be a mere flash in the pan. It was, nevertheless, indicative of the activist element in the revolution.[4]

But what mattered most was what happened in Prussia, the largest, most populous, and both economically and militarily the strongest of the non-Hapsburg states. The Rhineland, though still preponderantly agricultural, had already become an industrial center. It was a region where the transition to the factory system was causing much technological unemployment and where the economic crisis of 1846–1847 was making itself severely felt. In Cologne, for example, a third of the population was receiving relief at the beginning of 1848. Government officials were profoundly disturbed by the growing number of popular meetings and the appearance of radical newspapers.[5]

Of particular interest was the monster demonstration of March 3 in Cologne, engineered by Andreas Gottschalk and August von Willich, which spawned a petition going far beyond the usual radical program

---

[4] These events are treated in all the basic histories of the revolution, such as Veit Valentin: *Geschichte der deutschen Revolution* (Berlin, 1930), I, 240 ff.; Jacques Droz: *Les révolutions allemandes de 1848* (Paris, 1957), 158 ff.; Ernst R. Huber: *Deutsche Verfassungsgeschichte* (Stuttgart, 1957), II, 509 ff.

[5] Konrad Repgen: *Märzbewegung und Maiwahlen des Revolutionsjahr 1848 im Rheinland* (Bonn, 1955), chap. iv; Gerhard Becker: *Karl Marx und Friedrich Engels in Köln, 1848–1849* (Berlin, 1963), 12 ff.

and including such drastic demands as government by revolutionary committees, the protection of labor, and the satisfaction of human needs for all members of the population. Though the leaders were both members of the Communist League, there is no evidence that they were directly inspired by Marxist doctrine. It was only within the past few months that the Communist League had adopted the Marxian teaching and only a matter of weeks since the publication of the *Communist Manifesto*. Gottschalk and Willich were socialists on their own, whose radicalism was enough to frighten liberals as well as conservatives. Troops were called in, the meeting dispersed and the leaders arrested.[6] But both officials and businessmen promptly renewed their pressure on the king to concede the demands of the liberals. Frederick William stuck obstinately to his notions of paternalistic government until the demonstrations in Berlin itself became so formidable that, reluctantly and with some mental reservations, he decided to accept the principle of constitutional government and a responsible ministry.[7]

A group of radical intellectuals had existed in the capital at least since 1846, when Julius Berends and Friedrich Schmidt had appeared in the Artisans' Society. They gathered about the newspaper *Zeitungshalle,* which took its name from a reading room not far from the royal palace. These same men seem to have been instrumental in arranging the popular meetings in an entertainment park known as Unter den Zelten. On March 11, after the Berlin city council had rejected a popular petition, the crowds became aggressive, so that the council had to request the government to permit the formation of constabulary forces or security commissions to help preserve order without calling in the military.[8]

By this time it was almost too late to forestall an explosion. On

[6] Karl Obermann: *Die deutschen Arbeiter in der Revolution von 1848* (Berlin, 1950), 73 ff., is a standard Marxist account. On the non-Marxist side, see Rudolf Stadelmann: *Soziale und politische Geschichte der Revolution von 1848* (Munich, 1956), 70 ff.; and the excellent study by P. H. Noyes: *Organization and Revolution: Working-Class Associations in the German Revolutions of 1848–1849* (Princeton, 1966), 62 ff.

[7] Wilhelm Busch: *Die Berliner Märztage von 1848* (Munich, 1899), 4, 10; Ernst Kaeber: *Berlin 1848* (Berlin, 1948), chap. ii; Alfred Hermann: *Berliner Demokraten* (Berlin, 1948), 114 ff.

[8] Karl Haenchen: "Zur revolutionären Unterwühlung Berlins vor den Märztagen des Jahres 1848" (*Forschungen zur brandenburgischen und preussischen Geschichte,* LV, 1943, 83–114); Hermann Meyer: *1848: Studien zur Geschichte der deutschen Revolution* (Darmstadt, 1949), 61 ff.

March 13·cavalry forces charged the crowds and as usual showed
themselves brutal. The populace, which hated the troops for this very
reason, began to shout insults and hurl stones. Two days later huge
throngs surged about the royal palace and attacked the guards with
rocks and bottles. The crowds became more and more insistent that the
troops be withdrawn from the city. Only at this juncture did the
government authorize the formation of the security commissions.
Modeled on the British special constabulary, these commissions were to
consist of respectable citizens, such as guild masters, to be armed only
with truncheons and to wear white armbands for identification. At this
late hour these prosperous citizens were met by the populace only with
ridicule. Defeated in their efforts to restore order, they were presently
obliged to appeal to the military for protection.[9]

News of the victory of the revolution in Vienna naturally put
the situation in Berlin out of control completely. The king now began
to make concessions: he announced on March 18 that the press censorship would be abolished, the Diet would be convoked on April 2, a
constitution would be granted, and Prussia would assume the leadership in the effort to achieve German unity. The crowds responded
enthusiastically until they spotted the troops massed in the courtyard of
the palace, when they renewed their demands that the troops be
withdrawn. So great was the commotion that the king eventually
ordered General von Prittwitz to clear the palace square (see Illustration 64). The general and his cavalry escort were soon surrounded by
the crowd and had to be rescued by an infantry detachment. In the
process two musket shots rang out. No one was hurt, but the crowd
began to panic. Barricades began to appear as though by magic. By
evening severe fighting had broken out in many sections of the city.

The question has been much debated whether the Berlin uprising
was the work of foreign instigators. The king and his generals were
firmly convinced that French and Polish revolutionaries had come in
and stirred up the population. Though this charge can hardly be
substantiated from the available evidence, it is worth recalling that
Berlin like other big cities was experiencing a large and constant influx.

[9] Anon.: *Die Berliner Märztage, vom militärischen Standpunkte geschildert* (Berlin,
1850), 12 ff., is an official account. See further C. Nobiling: *Die Berliner Bürgerwehr,
1848* (Berlin, 1852), 55 ff.; Kaeber: *Berlin 1848*, 40 ff.; and Karl Haenchen: "Aus dem
Nachlass des Generals von Prittwitz" (*Forschungen zur brandenburgischen und
preussischen Geschichte*, XLV, 1933, 99–125).

Ten thousand workers are reported to have come to Berlin in 1847 and
many of these were desperate people in search of work. They may in
fact have contributed significantly to the insurrection. Furthermore, the
radicals of the *Zeitungshalle,* some of whom had contacts with foreign
revolutionary organizations, may well have provided leadership.
Berends and Bisky, for example, are known to have taken part in the
fighting.[10]

General Prittwitz commanded the garrison of about 15,000 troops
and a number of light guns. The rebels, on the other hand, lacked
weapons and munitions. They hurled paving stones from the roofs and
poured boiling water from the windows. Though the insurgents
fought ferociously, the military blew up the barricades by artillery fire,
after which the troops, as ruthless as their opponents, broke into the
houses, chased the insurgents up to the garrets and massacred those
whom it was inconvenient to drag off as captives. By midnight Prittwitz had secured control over the center of the city, but he had become
convinced, from the violence of the conflict, that to suppress the
uprising everywhere would be a long and costly undertaking. He
therefore advised the king to leave for Potsdam and withdraw the
troops from the city, which could then be blockaded and eventually
bombarded into submission. But the king, fully convinced that his
people had not spontaneously revolted against him, refused to abandon
the capital. Instead, he composed during the night a pathetic appeal *To
my dear Berliners* in which he offered to discuss the situation with
representatives of the people and evacuate the troops as soon as the
barricades were taken down. This document, which was tantamount to
surrender, has been called by one German historian "the swan song of
political romanticism and the patriarchal concept of government."[11]

What followed was utter confusion. The king, in a state of near
collapse, was beset on all sides by generals and city councilors, all with
their own ideas. Eager to close out the painful matter one way or

[10] Haenchen: "Zur revolutionären Unterwühlung Berlins"; Hermann: *Berliner
Demokraten,* 64.

[11] Erich Brandenburg: *Die Reichsgründung* (Leipzig, 1916), I, 195. Although on the
morning of March 19 the outcome of the fighting was at best a draw, most writers
consider that the eventual victory of the military was inevitable. On Prittwitz and his
plans, see Felix Rachfahl: *Deutschland, König Friedrich Wilhelm IV, und die Berliner
Märzrevolution* (Halle, 1901), 163, 172; Hermann: *Berliner Demokraten,* 125; Gordon
A. Craig: *The Politics of the Prussian Army* (Oxford, 1955), 93, 99.

another, Frederick William readily gave credence to unconfirmed rumors that the barricades were being dismantled. Brushing aside the protests of his brother William and the military men, he thereupon ordered the withdrawal of the troops to their barracks. Whether or not he then planned to leave for Potsdam is unimportant, for in the early afternoon a huge throng appeared before the palace accompanied by seven or eight wagons filled with the dead, wounds fully exposed. The king was obliged to appear on the balcony and salute the victims of the insurrection. Nothing, certainly, could have demonstrated more clearly the capitulation of the Prussian monarchy. It was indeed the deepest humiliation ever suffered by the Hohenzollern dynasty (see Illustration 65).

Frederick William completed his surrender by finally agreeing to the establishment of a Civic Guard (*Bürgerwehr*). Each district of the city was to supply a hundred men, drawn from among those who enjoyed full citizen rights. By evening this new force of 6,000 men was able to take over guard duties at the palace.[12] Thus the king placed himself entirely under the protection of his subjects. He was as defenseless, wrote the American minister on March 21, "as the poorest malefactor of the prisons." On March 22 Prince William, the leader of those who counseled suppression of the rebellion, fled to England to escape the public wrath.[13]

Careful analysis of the records of those who gave their lives in the Berlin barricade fighting leaves no shadow of doubt that it was an insurrection of the workers, by which must be understood artisans and journeymen in the traditional trades, since the number of factory workers was still insignificant. There were only about fifteen representatives of the educated class in a total of some 300 dead, and only thirty master craftsmen. The vast majority consisted of journeymen, among whom the cabinetmakers, tailors and shoemakers were most prominent.[14] Motivated chiefly by want and without a specific program of reform, the effect of their valor was to oblige the king to grant the

[12] C. Nobiling: *Die Berliner Bürgerwehr*, 1 ff.; O. Rimpler: *Die Berliner Bürgerwehr im Jahre 1848* (Brandenburg, 1883), 3 ff.

[13] Karl Haenchen: "Flucht und Rückkehr des Prinzen von Preussen im Jahre 1848" (*Historische Zeitschrift*, CLIV, 1936, 32–95).

[14] Ruth Hoppe and Jürgen Kuczynski: "Eine Berufs-bzw. auch Klassen und Schichtenanalyse der Märzgefallenen 1848 in Berlin" (*Jahrbuch für Wirtschaftsgeschichte*, 1964, Part IV, 200–276); Noyes: *Organization and Revolution*, 68 ff.

demands of the liberals. He adopted the national black-red-gold flag, promised to convoke an assembly to collaborate in the drafting of a constitution, announced that henceforth Prussia should be merged or fused with the new German national state, and, lastly, named a liberal cabinet under Ludolf Camphausen, in which David Hansemann was to serve as minister of finance. These eminent Rhineland businessmen were certainly ideal representatives of moderate liberalism.

The liberal press was at first lavish in its praise of the workers, who had served so well. Workers were taken into the clubs and programs were drafted for relief of the needy. On March 25 the city council set up a Deputation for Consideration of the Well-Being of the Working Classes and two days later the king promised to establish a ministry for trade, industry and public works which was to concern itself chiefly with the labor situation.[15] But propertied people were nonetheless uneasy about the demonstration of proletarian discontent. The American minister noted violent newspaper articles suggesting that the workers, having won the victory, were being excluded from the Civic Guard and so deprived of a rightful share in the new regime. Talk of this kind, he reported, had so frightened the propertied classes that many were leaving the city "from fear that a practical organization on the part of the communists has been effected." Even the ambassadors of foreign powers, he observed, were feeling uneasy whenever they appeared on the streets attended by liveried servants. On March 26 there was a monster assembly of workers which put forth demands for universal suffrage, a ministry of labor, a minimum wage and a ten-hour day.[16]

It was in this context that one of the king's friends, Josef Maria von Radowitz, urged him to court the support of the workers by an extensive program of social insurance and so obtain a counterweight to the forces of liberalism. These proposals were too much for the ultra-conservative court Camarilla, which was much more sympathetic to Otto von Bismarck's plans for a counterrevolution. Bismarck, a young Pomeranian Junker who was eventually to become Germany's Iron

[15] Noyes: *Organization and Revolution*, 71 ff.
[16] For the reports of Mr. A. J. Donelson, see *American Historical Review*, XXIII, 1918, 355–373. Further, Wilhelm Friedensburg: *Stefan Born und die Organisations-bestrebungen der Berliner Arbeiterschaft bis zum Berliner Arbeiterkongress* (Leipzig, 1923), 50 ff.; Obermann: *Die deutschen Arbeiter*, 89 ff., 100; Noyes: *Organization and Revolution*, 101 ff.

Chancellor, made his debut at this time with an attempt to organize the agrarian interests in support of the king's authority. He laid his plans before Princess Augusta, the wife of the refugee Prince William, but was refused her support (March 23). Neither the princess nor the king would envisage further civil strife, but the king at least was much inclined to look to conservative circles for counsel and support.[17]

Camphausen and the moderates aimed at a constitutional regime like that of the July Monarchy, but they were not in a position to resist the popular pressure for universal suffrage. They attempted, however, to minimize its effect by requiring a one-year residence for the franchise (thus excluding traveling journeymen and migrant workers) and by barring those who were on relief or served as domestics. The Diet (*Landtag*), which met on April 2, realized that these restrictions would not be tolerated and so reduced the residence requirement to six months and excluded only those on relief or convicted of crime. Even the Diet, however, rejected the idea of direct elections: voters were to choose members of electoral colleges who in turn would elect the deputies to Parliament. The efforts of the new, liberal regime to curtail the influence of the lower classes were unmistakable.[18]

Reflecting on the German revolution of 1848, Lenin bemoaned the fact that after March 18 the workers had not set up a revolutionary dictatorship. As it was, he remarked, they were left with nothing but "freedom to remain the party of extreme revolutionary opposition."[19] It seems clear, however, that the workers, having won the victory on the barricades, were by no means prepared to assume control of the government. They were probably more generally literate than the French or even the British workers, but they were quite unorganized and had nothing like united leadership. Friedrich Held and Gustav Schlöffel were popular, radical journalists, of whom the second has

[17] Erich Marcks: *Bismarck und die deutsche Revolution* (Stuttgart, 1939), and the extended critical review by Fritz Hartung: "Bismarck und die deutsche Revolution, 1848–1851" (*Die Welt als Geschichte*, VI, 1940, 167–178), as well as the same author's essay "Verantwortliche Regierung, Kabinette und Nebenregierung im konstitutionellen Preussen" (*Forschungen zur brandenburgischen und preussischen Geschichte*, XLIV, 1932, 1–45); G. Adolf Rein: "Bismarck's gegenrevolutionäre Aktion in den Märztagen 1848" (*Die Welt als Geschichte*, XIII, 1953, 246–262).

[18] Gerhard Schilfert: *Sieg und Niederlage des demokratischen Wahlrechts in der deutschen Revolution, 1848–1849* (Berlin, 1952), 49 ff.

[19] V. I. Lenin: "Two Tactics of Social Democracy in the Democratic Revolution" (1905), reprinted in his *Collected Works* (Moscow, 1962), IX, 17–140.

been described as "perhaps the only open advocate of violent class warfare and continuation of the revolution."[20] But their influence was limited. The workers were less interested in revolutionary theory than in securing better wages and shorter hours. There were numerous strikes in separate trades, most of which led to surrender by the timorous employers. These isolated efforts served to point up the need for better organization, and that was the chief aim of Stefan Born, who was to play the most prominent role in the German labor movement. Born, a journeyman typesetter only twenty-four years of age, had worked abroad and had become converted to Marxian Communism. He had arrived in Berlin on March 20 and had at once joined the radical *Zeitungshalle* group. He was instrumental in setting up a Central Committee of Workers (April 19), of which he became president, and in launching a genuine labor newspaper, *The People* (May 25). Born's basic objective was to organize the workers so that they might co-operate effectively in establishing a truly democratic regime and preparing the way for an eventual socialist state. He believed that disorder and revolution were more harmful than beneficial. Only through organization and peaceful political action could the workers attain their ends. So he never tired of warning the workers against the lure of fire-eating demagogues and against seduction by utopian schemers.

Born has at times been accused of betraying his Marxist origins, but he seems always to have adhered to the Marxist interpretation of history and indeed to the basic ideas of the *Communist Manifesto*. The point is that Born recognized the unpreparedness of the workers to assimilate highfalutin doctrine and in any case realized that their efforts would be futile unless organized. It has been well said of him that he put organization above program and that he emphasized the organization of laborers rather than the organization of labor.[21]

During the spring of 1848, workers' societies or clubs sprang up in many German cities, the one in Cologne being of particular interest because of the industrially advanced character of the city and because

[20] Noyes: *Organization and Revolution*, 108.
[21] The basic account of Eduard Bernstein: *Geschichte der Berliner Arbeiterbewegung* (Berlin, 1907) must be supplemented by intensive later studies such as Max Quarck: *Die erste deutsche Arbeiterbewegung* (Leipzig, 1924); Friedensburg: *Stefan Born*, 56 ff.; Obermann: *Die deutschen Arbeiter*, 107 ff., 118 ff.; Noyes: *Organization and Revolution*, 124 ff.

of the activity of Marx and Engels. Marx spent several weeks in Paris during March and there arranged to have the headquarters of the Communist League moved from London to the French capital. The notion that he took an active part in the debates of the Society for the Rights of Man appears to rest on a case of mistaken identity.[22] Marx devoted himself especially to the drafting of a program, *The Seventeen Demands of the Communist Party of Germany,* which was as much or more political than socialist. Its very first item called for a unified, indivisible German republic, while others included the arming of the people, the abolition of feudal dues without compensation to the owners, separation of church and state, free and equal education, and so on. This program was taken by the Paris Communists to various cities of Germany, where they attempted to found Communist cells. Those who, like Born in Berlin, devoted themselves to the organization of the workers for practical ends, came to play a significant role in the labor movement, while those who stuck more closely to the doctrines of Communism appear to have had but little success. Only a few labor leaders, such as Andreas Gottschalk in Cologne, were indifferent to political radicalism and indeed to socialist doctrine. Gottschalk was a benevolent doctor who knew the misery of the workers from personal experience. His objective was direct action by the workers to attain a workers' republic. His prestige in Cologne was unrivaled and the Workers' Society or union which he founded on April 13 had some 6,000 members in June. With its directorate of fifty, representing all the chief trades and industries of the city, it was a formidable organization which in general resisted merger with other groups.[23]

Marx arrived in Cologne on April 11, on the eve of the founding of Gottschalk's Workers' Society. Convinced as he was that a rising of the unorganized lower classes would be premature and that the soundest strategy for the workers was to support the radical elements of the *bourgeoisie* in winning control of the governments, Marx was intent

---

[22] S. Bernstein: "Marx in Paris, 1848" (*Science and Society,* III, 1939, 323–355; IV, 1940, 211–217); and especially Peter Amann: "Karl Marx: 'Quarante-huitard francais' " (*International Review of Social History,* VI (2), 1961, 249–255).

[23] Hans Stein: *Der Kölner Arbeiterverein, 1848–1849* (Cologne, 1921); Gerhard Becker: *Karl Marx und Friedrich Engels in Köln* (Berlin, 1963); Frolinde Balser: *Sozial-Demokratie, 1848/49—1863* (Stuttgart, 1962); Noyes: *Organization and Revolution,* 111 ff.; Werner Conze and Dieter Groh: *Die Arbeiterbewegung in der nationalen Bewegung* (Stuttgart, 1966), 33 ff.

above all on reviving the *Rhenish Gazette* and making it the organ for expression of his views. The problem was to find the needed funds and this proved difficult because even the radicals were suspicious of Communist designs. "They shy away from any discussion of social problems as from the pest," wrote Engels to Marx from Elberfeld; "the root of the matter is this, that even the radical bourgeois see in us their chief enemies of the future and therefore refuse to put any weapons into our hands that we would turn against them." In short, the radicals saw through Marx's game. In the end the Communist leaders had to put up their own money for the *New Rhenish Gazette,* which began to appear on June 1 and soon reached a circulation of 5,000 copies. By this time Marx had dissolved the Communist League (May), arguing that a secret organization was out of place under prevailing circumstances, but perhaps more in order to avoid conflict with Gottschalk. During the ensuing months Marx and his paper preached democracy more than socialism or communism. Indeed, he founded the Democratic Society (April 25) for co-operation with the radicals in the forthcoming elections. In July, when Gottschalk was arrested, Karl Schapper, a close collaborator of Marx, assumed the presidency of the Workers' Society and after Schapper's arrest (October) Marx himself took over.[24]

The later importance of Marx and Engels and their Communist doctrine has led, naturally, to much study of their activity in 1848 and certainly on the part of Marxist historians to some exaggeration of their contribution. German workers felt themselves close to the democratic elements of the lesser *bourgeoisie* and shared their hopes for a democratic republic. Some of their emerging leaders were members of the Communist League and even more of them were acquainted with the socialist doctrines of Weitling, Hess and the French theorists. But the

---

[24] Auguste Cornu: "Karl Marx et la révolution de 1848 en Allemagne" (*Europe,* XXVI, 1948, 238–252); Jean Meerfeld: "Der achtundvierziger Karl Marx" (in Wilhelm Keil, ed.: *Deutschland, 1848–1948,* Stuttgart, 1948, 89–99); Walter Schmidt: "Der Bund der Kommunisten und die Versuche einer Zentralisierung der deutschen Arbeitervereine im April und Mai, 1848" (*Zeitschrift für Geschichtswissenschaft,* IX, 1961, 577–614); Karl Obermann: "Ueber die Bedeuting der Tätigkeit von Friedrich Engels in Frühjahr und Sommer, 1848" (*ibid.,* IX, 1961, 28–47); August W. Fehling: *Karl Schapper und die Anfänge der Arbeiterbewegung* (Rostock, 1926), appendix; M. A. Kotschetkowa: "Die Tätigkeit von Marx und Engels in der Kölner Demokratischen Gesellschaft, April bis Oktober, 1848" (*Sowjetwissenschaft: Gesellschaftswissenschaftliche Beiträge,* 1960, Heft 11, 1155–1167).

strictly Marxist doctrine was of only recent date and evidently had but little impact. The contribution of the workers to the revolution must be sought, then, not in doctrine or organized action, but in the readiness of desperate men to mount the barricades and fight even against hopeless odds.[25]

This does not mean that the propertied classes were not deeply disturbed by the upsurge of artisan radicalism. After all, there had been for years endless discussion of the social question and the need for social reform. The liberals had not been unsympathetic to the plight of the workers, but they had expected to obtain reforms by peaceful methods. Never having envisaged the use of violence, they were appalled by the excesses to which the agitation for reform had led. More and more they recoiled from the implications of revolution until ultimately many of them found themselves in the conservative camp. To charge them with "betrayal of the revolution" is going too far, for they never intended revolution and can therefore hardly be blamed for shrinking from events which presaged a social as well as a political upheaval.

2. THE CHALLENGE OF POLAND

Europe in the spring of 1848 resounded not only with the tumult of revolution but also with threats of war. It seemed at first that Nicholas of Russia would draft the Prussians and Austrians for a crusade against the French Republic. The insurrections in Germany ruined any plans the czar may have had for such intervention, for his own armies could not be ready in less than several months and he could hardly expect support from the revolutionary governments of Germany. On the contrary, liberals and especially radicals were everywhere consumed with "flaming hatred of Russia," to quote a contemporary newspaper. They regarded liberty and tyranny as altogether incompatible and dreamed of setting up their own democratic republics. After destroying despotism they would eventually join all countries in a grand European republic which would once and for all dispose of the disputes

---

[25] This admittedly bourgeois evaluation is essentially the same as that of Karl Griewank: "Vulgärer Radikalismus und demokratische Bewegung in Berlin, 1842–1848" (*Forschungen zur brandenburgischen und preussischen Geschichte*, XXXVI, 1924, 14–38); Stadelmann: *Soziale und politische Geschichte*, chap. xi; Noyes: *Organization and Revolution*, 122; Conze and Groh: *Die Arbeiterbewegung*, 39 ff.

from which professional diplomats made their living. By many, war was regarded as inevitable, indeed, as highly desirable as a means of rallying all popular forces for the revolutionary task.[26]

Poland, of course, called for special consideration. What task could be more urgent than to undo the "crime" of 1772 and restore the "martyred" nation to independence and integrity? The pressure brought by Paris radicals on Lamartine was almost more than he could bear. Not that he lacked sympathy for the Poles, but he realized, in early March, that any effort to resurrect Poland would meet with the combined resistance of the three partitioning powers. He dared not even raise the issue of Russian Poland for fear of provoking war. There was, however, the possibility of working with the new liberal government of Prussia which emerged from the Berlin revolution.[27]

Prussia held the Grand Duchy of Posen (Poznan), which had been assigned to it in 1815 on the understanding that it should be given a large measure of autonomy. Though it was Polish territory and not included in the Germanic Confederation, Posen had a large German minority of some 700,000 souls. King Frederick William was well-disposed toward his Polish subjects and had, on his accession, introduced the use of the Polish language in the courts and schools. The minister for foreign affairs in the Camphausen cabinet, Baron von Arnim-Suckow, was prepared to go much further. On taking office he had at once used his influence to have the Polish insurgent leaders of 1846, Louis Mieroslawski and others, released from prison and presented to the king. Furthermore, he persuaded his colleagues to receive a deputation of Poles from Posen who asked for what amounted to autonomy. On March 24 the king reluctantly promised the Poles the "national reorganization" of the grand duchy under a commissioner aided by a board consisting of both Germans and Poles. Indeed, the Prussian government went so far as to permit droves of Polish refu-

---

[26] Eberhard Meyer: *Die aussenpolitischen Ideen der Achtundvierziger* (Berlin, 1938), 20 ff.; Lewis B. Namier: *1848: the Revolution of the Intellectuals* (London, 1944), 43 ff. On the rabid bellicosity of Marx and Engels, see Bertram D. Wolfe: "Nationalism and Internationalism in Marx and Engels" (*American Slavic and East European Review,* XVII, 403–417).

[27] Pierre Quentin-Bauchart: *Lamartine et la politique étrangère de la Révolution de février* (Paris, 1907); Eugène de Guichen: *Les grandes questions européennes et la diplomatie des puissances sous la Seconde République française* (Paris, 1925); Theodor Schiemann: *Geschichte Russlands unter Kaiser Nikolaus I* (Berlin, 1919), IV, 151 ff.; A. S. Nifontow: *Russland im Jahre 1848* (Berlin, 1954), 228 ff.

gees from France and Belgium to cross Germany to Posen, where Mieroslawski was organizing an incursion of Russian Poland.[28]

Arnim and other liberals were ready to give up Posen for the sake of restoring Poland. They realized that such a policy would mean war with Russia, but they actually desired such a conflict as a setting for establishing Prussian leadership in the unification of Germany and, more importantly, as forging an alliance with the western powers that would put an end, once and for all, to the pretensions of the Russian autocracy. On March 31 Arnim proposed to the French the conclusion of an alliance for the purpose of restoring Poland. This was going beyond suggestions which Lamartine had made, but he nevertheless promised Prussia armed support in the event of a Russian attack. The British, for their part, replied to unofficial soundings that they sympathized with Polish aspirations but felt that provocation of Russia should be avoided. Neither Britain nor France wanted to become involved in a major European war for the sake of Poland, the more so as Czar Nicholas was concentrating large forces on the Prussian and Austrian frontiers.[29]

While the French continued their efforts to induce the Prussians to give up Posen, events in the grand duchy itself soon made the question academic. The Poles soon took control of the local administration, whereupon the Germans began to organize resistance. Through pressure on the Berlin government they had the "reorganization" restricted to the purely Polish areas, which meant that a line of demarcation had

---

[28] Namier: *1848*, 57 ff., takes account of the Polish literature. On the German side, see Wolfgang Hallgarten: *Studien über die deutsche Polenfreundschaft in der Periode der Märzrevolution* (Munich, 1928); Wolfgang Kohte: "Deutsche Bewegung und preussische Politik im Posener Lande, 1846–1848" (*Deutsche wissenschaftliche Zeitschrift für Polen*, XXI, 1931, 1-216); Friedrich Schinkel: *Polen, Preussen und Deutschland* (Berlin, 1932); R. Hepke: *Die polnische Erhebung und die deutsche Gegenbewegung in Posen im Jahre 1848* (Posen, 1948). See also Stefan Kieniewicz: "The Social Visage of Poland in 1848" (*Slavonic and East European Review*, XXVII, 1948–1949, 91–105); Cyril E. Black: "Poznań and Europe in 1848" (*Journal of Central European Affairs*, VIII, 1948, 191–206).

[29] Erich Marcks: "Die europäischen Mächte und die 48-er Revolution" (*Historische Zeitschrift*, CXLII, 1930, 73–87); Friedrich Ley: "Frankreich und die deutsche Revolution, 1848–1849" (*Preussische Jahrbücher*, CCXIII, 1928, 199–216); Wislawa Knapowska: "La France, la Prusse et la question polonaise en 1848" (in *La Pologne au VIe Congrès Internationale des Sciences Historiques*, Warsaw, 1928, 147–166); Paul Henry: "Le gouvernement provisoire et la question polonaise en 1848" (*Revue historique*, CLXXVIII, 1936, 198–240), and *La France devant le monde* (Paris, 1945), 153 ff.

to be established. Meanwhile the Prussian commander, secretly encouraged by the king and court, began to suppress the Polish movement. Rather desperate fighting ensued, during which many of the Polish landlords sided with the Germans, blaming Mieroslawski and the revolutionaries for all the trouble. After Mieroslawski's defeat (May 9) the demarcation line was fixed so as to assign about two-thirds of the duchy (the mixed as well as the strictly German areas) to the German sphere. This part was then to be admitted to the Germanic Confederation and to send twelve deputies to the national Parliament at Frankfurt.

The French, encouraged by the Polonophilism of the Frankfurt radicals, protested against this "fourth partition" of Poland, but the debates in the Frankfurt Parliament (July 24–27) put the quietus on Polish hopes. While the radicals Robert Blum and Arnold Ruge pleaded the Polish cause, Wilhelm Jordan, from East Prussia, sounded a note of crass realism. The time had come, he argued, to renounce sentiment and concentrate on German rights: "It is time to wake up to a policy of healthy national egotism." It would be ridiculous to abandon Germany's mission in the East for the sake of "a few families who revel in court splendor and for a few charming mazurka dancers." At the end of the debate the vote was 342 to 31 in favor of recognizing the demarcation line and receiving the "German" part of the duchy into the new German Empire. The vote has been rightly taken as marking the triumph of political nationalism over the cosmopolitanism to which theretofore the liberals had been devoted.[30]

In Posen itself talk of reorganization became fainter and fainter until in 1851, when the tumult and shouting had died, the *status quo* was restored: the grand duchy remained a part of the Prussian Monarchy, and none of it was included in the revived Germanic Confederation. With the onset of reaction all thought of autonomy was abandoned. German officials resumed control and Polish nationalism was in eclipse.

In retrospect the pro-Polish policy of Count Arnim and Lamartine seems "risky and almost fantastic."[31] Yet it remains instructive evidence not only of the rabid popular hatred of Russian tyranny but also

[30] Roy Pascal: "The Frankfurt Parliament and the 'Drang nach Osten' " (*Journal of Modern History*, XVIII, 1946, 108–122).

[31] Erich Marcks: *Der Aufstieg des Reiches* (Stuttgart, 1936), I, 260 ff.

of the idealism of the period. Call it sentiment or romanticism if you will, yet one must pay tribute to the sense of justice which led the revolutionaries of 1848 to regard the righting of the wrong done the Poles as a matter of high priority, to be settled even at the expense of territorial sacrifices. It is important, too, as setting the stage for the period of realism that was to follow. The "reorganization" of Posen precipitated the conflict between German and Polish nationalism and provided the Prussian court and military a welcome opening for repression. Karl Marx, furious over the outcome of the debate in the Frankfurt Parliament, recognized at once that the "betrayal" of Poland was to be the first move in the offensive of the counterrevolution.

3. SCHLESWIG-HOLSTEIN: GERMAN AGAINST DANE

Even more ominous than the Polish question was the problem of Schleswig and Holstein, the German-speaking provinces of the Danish crown whose earlier, much involved history has been recounted in a previous chapter.[32] The local patriots, having challenged Copenhagen and been defeated, called upon the Germanic Confederation for help and thereby presented German nationalism with a supreme test. The problem was to be further aggravated by the fact that two major powers, Britain and Russia, had compelling interests in the maintenance of Denmark's integrity, since that state was the guardian of the Sound, the entrance and exit of the Baltic Sea. From the outset the future of Schleswig and Holstein was a European as well as a German-Danish problem.

German public opinion was all but unanimous in its demand that something be done to protect Germanism in the North and to demonstrate that German national interests were not to be trifled with, least of all by a minor power such as Denmark. King Frederick William of Prussia, though reluctant to countenance a revolutionary movement, felt obliged to champion the national cause, if only to recover the prestige he had lost during the Berlin insurrection. When, on April 12, 1848, the federal Diet at Frankfurt recognized the provisional government of the duchies at Kiel, voted to admit Schleswig to membership in the Germanic Confederation, and called upon the German governments to provide troops for action against the Danish king, Frederick William, like the rulers of Hanover and Brunswick, sent a contingent

[32] See above, Chapter VIII.

under General Friedrich von Wrangel which on April 23 crossed the boundary between the two duchies and began the invasion of Schleswig. Wrangel easily expelled the Danish forces and presently (May 2) carried the operations into Jutland, that is, the mainland part of the Danish Monarchy. In response the Danes blockaded the German coast and captured a number of German merchantmen. The Swedes, too, caught up in the revolutionary excitement, forced their king to appoint a liberal cabinet, which at once responded to Danish appeals by promising 15,000 men, provided either Britain or Russia should come to Denmark's support. In June some 4,500 Swedish-Norwegian troops did in fact land in Denmark.[33]

The impending defeat of Denmark and the consequent loss of the duchies at once brought Britain and Russia to the scene. Czar Nicholas, indignant over the Prussian king's support of a revolutionary movement, brought great pressure to bear in Berlin to have the German forces withdrawn from Danish territory. He even threatened to send Russian troops to force the evacuation of the Germans, if necessary. In Britain there was criticism of the Eider-Danes, the extreme Danish nationalists, but even more vigorous censure of German pretensions. The idea that any and all lands inhabited by Germans should belong to the projected German Empire raised suspicions of German designs on the Baltic provinces of Russia and revived fears of German claims to Alsace. Political nationalism threatened to undermine the entire public law of Europe. Benjamin Disraeli, in a famous speech of April 19, ridiculed German nationalism as "dreamy and dangerous nonsense" and warned that the German objective in the Schleswig-Holstein business was to acquire seaports and more particularly a suitable naval base. He called upon the British government to defend Denmark's possession of the duchies. Palmerston, for his part, had done his utmost to prevent the outbreak of war and was now intent on bringing hostilities to an end, if only to forestall intervention by Russia. He therefore at once offered to mediate.[34]

[33] Halvdan Koht: "Die Stellung Norwegens und Schwedens im deutsch-dänischen Konflikt" (*Videnskabs-Selskabets Skrifter, Hist.-Fil. Klasse*, Christiania, 1907), chap. i; A. Buscher: *Schweden-Norwegen und die schleswig-holsteinische Frage in den Jahren 1848–1863* (Greifswald, 1927).

[34] Alexander Scharff: *Die europäischen Grossmächte und die deutsche Revolution* (Leipzig, 1942), chap. iii, and "Europäische und gesamtdeutsche Zusammenhänge der schleswig-holsteinischen Erhebung" (in K. von Raumer and Theodor Schieder, eds.:

The Berlin government, under Russian pressure, ordered Wrangel to withdraw from Jutland (May 22) and accepted the British offer of mediation on the basis of a compromise: northern (that is, Danish-speaking) Schleswig to be incorporated with Denmark proper and the remainder to be united with Holstein in a new German state which, though a member of the Germanic Confederation, should remain connected with Denmark through a common sovereign. Unfortunately this proposal, which foreshadowed the settlement of 1919, was rejected both by the Danish king and by the provisional government of the duchies. Weeks of argumentation and bickering followed until eventually the Prussian government accepted Swedish mediation and signed an armistice at Malmö (August 26), to be valid for seven months. The agreement was clearly in Denmark's favor, for it would take the country through the winter, when blockade operations would be all but impossible. Furthermore, it provided for the evacuation of the duchies by the German forces and for the annulment of all acts of the Kiel government. The provisional government of the duchies was to be replaced by a joint Danish-German commission, the chairman of which was known to be pro-Danish.

Among German liberals the Malmö armistice was seen as a major defeat for national interests, and the Berlin government was therefore accused of treason to the national cause. The issue precipitated a severe crisis in the Frankfurt Parliament, as will appear presently. Yet the Prussian government could hardly have acted otherwise. It had the choice between signing the armistice or facing military intervention by Russia and Sweden, and perhaps even by Britain and France. Technically speaking, it should not have concluded the armistice without the concurrence of the Frankfurt authorities, for in the duchies Prussia and the other German states were acting only as agents of the Germanic Confederation. But the national Parliament was known to be rock-ribbed in its opposition to any compromise and would only have complicated matters through its obstruction. Yet the fact remained that Berlin had capitulated in behalf of all Germany and had thereby aroused the indignation and resentment of all nationalists, whether

Stufen und Wandlungen der deutschen Einheit, Stuttgart, 1943, 197–233); W. E. Mosse: *The European Powers and the German Question, 1848–1871* (Cambridge, 1958), 18 ff.; and the painfully detailed study of Holger Hjelholt: *British Mediation in the Danish-German Conflict 1848–1850* (*Historisk-Filosofiske Medellelser*, XLI, No. 1, Copenhagen, 1965).

liberal or radical. They refused to see and in the sequel were slow to learn that German problems were not exclusively the affair of the Germans. The organization of Germany rested on the international treaties of 1815, and it was to be expected that the signatories of those treaties would insist on having their say where their interests were concerned. In 1848 three major powers—Britain, Russia and France—were at one in rejecting the German claim to the duchies merely on the basis of language and race. More specifically, they denied the right of the Germanic Confederation to declare Schleswig a member without even consulting the king of Denmark, who, under the public law of Europe, was the undisputed possessor. Against the opposition of the united powers neither Berlin nor Frankfurt could hope to stand.

4. GERMAN UNITY: PROGRAMS AND PROBLEMS

By 1848 the question of German unity had been examined from every conceivable angle: political, economic, sentimental—and all means of attaining it had been critically scrutinized. So urgent had the matter become that several moves were made by official circles even before the insurrections in Vienna and Berlin had taken the problem out of the hands of the governments. Two Hessian aristocrats, the liberally minded brothers Heinrich and Max von Gagern, were particularly active. They had concluded that the Hapsburg Monarchy could hardly introduce representative government without running the risk of disintegration and that therefore Germany, if it was to be unified at all, must look to Prussia for leadership. But such leadership would be acceptable only on two conditions: one, that Prussia become a liberal, constitutional state; and two, that Prussia agree to its own dissolution. Each of its eight constituent provinces should become a separate state in the new Germany, so that no single power should be dominant. On February 28 Heinrich called for the election of a popular parliament to work out the new system. A week later the duke of Nassau sent Max on a tour of the German courts to propose the convocation of a national Parliament elected by the state legislatures, this national Parliament to serve as a lower house in conjunction with the existing federal Diet.

In the turmoil of early March the German princes hardly dared oppose the Gagern project, no doubt hoping that the king of Prussia would raise objection to sacrificing his state on the altar of German unity. As a matter of fact, however, Gagern arrived in Berlin just as the revolution triumphed and just as Frederick William in a public address promised to put himself at the head of the national movement and announced (with mental reservations, it seems) that henceforth Prussia should be merged with Germany. In conversation with the king, Gagern was to discover that Frederick William was indeed reluctant to envisage the partition of the monarchy, and furthermore that in the spirit of romantic loyalty he objected to the exclusion of Austria from the projected German national state. "Germany without the German provinces of Austria would be worse than a face without a nose," he declared.[35]

The king's friend, Radowitz, had already persuaded him to take the initiative in reforming the Germanic Confederation through agreement between the member governments. Radowitz had gone to Vienna and had induced Metternich to concur in a meeting of ministers at Dresden on March 25, where the problem could be explored. But this project was wrecked by the outbreak of revolutions. There remained only the possibility that the federal Diet at Frankfurt might itself do the job. It had already (on March 10) invited the German governments to send special emissaries (*Vertrauensmänner*) to Frankfurt for this purpose. Seventeen delegates, all prominent liberals, presently put in an appearance and, under the chairmanship of Heinrich von Gagern, threw themselves into the task. For a time there seemed at least a fair chance that the new liberal governments emerging from the revolutions might in this way forge the new German national state.

But nonofficial groups were soon to steal the show. As early as March 5, fifty-one notables, mostly liberal deputies from the South German parliaments, had met at Heidelberg to discuss the problem of unification. The Baden radicals, Friedrich Hecker and Gustav von Struve, had proposed that a democratic republic be proclaimed at once, but this was too much for the majority of those present and was at once defeated. Instead it was decided to convoke a preliminary Parliament (*Vorparlament*) at Frankfurt on March 31 to plan elections for a national Parliament.[36]

The members of the pre-Parliament were for the most part deputies

[35] Quoted by Heinrich von Srbik: *Deutsche Einheit* (Munich, 1935–1942), I, 326. See also Friedrich Meinecke: *Weltbürgertum und Nationalalstaat* (Munich, 1908); 301 ff.; George Kuntzel: *Heinrich von Gagern und der grossdeutsche Gedanke* (in *Gesammtdeutsche Vergangenheit: Festgabe für Heinrich Ritter von Srbik*, Munich, 1938, 266–275).

[36] For a succinct account, see Richard K. Ullmann and Sir Stephen King-Hall: *German Parliaments* (New York, 1954), 46 ff.

or former deputies of the South and West German states. The 141 Prussian representatives came chiefly from the liberal Rhineland and carried much weight, since only two Austrians took part. Though it had neither governmental nor popular mandate, the pre-Parliament brushed aside the program of the group of seventeen and also rejected Struve's proposal that it assume supreme power and proclaim a federal republic. It decided that the projected national Parliament should be elected by universal suffrage, the details to be left to the various state governments. East and West Prussia and the "German" part of Posen, as well as Schleswig, were also to be included though not members of the Germanic Confederation. Those parts of the Hapsburg Monarchy that were in the Confederation (that is, Bohemia, Moravia, Silesia, Slovenia, as well as the German-speaking provinces) were also to be included. Pending the meeting of the national Parliament, set for May 1, the pre-Parliament appointed a committee of fifty to deal with matters of federal concern in conjunction with the federal Diet.

In setting the regulations for the elections most of the governments not only ignored the pre-Parliament's recommendation of direct election of deputies but also restricted the concept of universal suffrage. For example, they required a six months' residence, thus shutting out from the vote the numerous itinerant workers. Furthermore, those on relief were almost everywhere denied the vote. In many states domestics, day laborers and apprentices were excluded from the franchise, as being not really independent. In the elections it seems that many abstained who were entitled to vote. In certain places abstentions ran to 30 per cent, due evidently to lack of interest in politics in areas where economic distress was great or else to desire to protest against the electoral restrictions.[37]

In the larger cities Democratic Societies had been hastily organized, mostly by radical groups, to formulate programs and nominate suitable candidates. But the time was short and the voters for the most part were left to their own devices, unless they followed the counsel of their priest or pastor. The lower classes, in so far as they voted at all, tended to choose electors who were often more radical than the deputies whom they in turn elected. In the industrial city of Düsseldorf, for instance, the electoral college consisted of artisans (one-third), inn-

[37] Gerhard Schilfert: *Sieg und Niederlage des demokratischen Wahlrechts in der deutschen Revolution* (Berlin, 1952), 122 ff.; Theodore S. Hamerow: "The Elections to the Frankfurt Parliament" (*Journal of Modern History*, XXXIII, 1961, 15–33).

keepers (one-fifth), merchants and factory owners (one-eighth) and lawyers (one-tenth).[38] The members of the so-called Frankfurt Parliament were for the most part men of influence and repute, either on the national or the local level. Out of over five hundred members there were only four journeymen and no common laborer. However, the upper classes were also poorly represented. There were only thirty-eight landlords, of whom only twenty-five were nobles. The number of merchants and industrialists was even smaller.

The phrase "Professors' Parliament," coined at the time, has stuck to the assembly ever since, much as the revolution in Germany has been stamped "the revolution of the intellectuals." Actually there were in the Parliament about fifty professors and sixty secondary-school teachers, but they were definitely outnumbered by the government officials, lawyers, clergymen and writers. It was not really a Professors' Parliament, though it is true that the vast majority of the members were well-educated and belonged to the liberal upper middle class. Certainly no popularly elected assembly has ever been intellectually more distinguished.[39]

The Frankfurt Parliament opened its sessions on May 18 in the Church of St. Paul, a circular structure well adapted to the purpose.[40] Heinrich von Gagern was chosen president, and before long political groupings (hardly organized parties) began to form and meet in various hostelries, from which they presently took their names. The majority of the deputies belonged to the center, being men of bourgeois origin devoted to the principles of political and economic liberalism and eager to achieve national unification, but in no sense revolutionary. Many of them were, in fact, much disturbed by the threat of political and social upheaval. For this reason, if for no other, they wanted to avoid conflict with the governments, with which they hoped to cooperate in remaking Germany. They have often been accused, espe-

[38] Konrad Repgen: *Märzbewegung und Maiwahlen des Revolutionsjahres 1848 im Rheinland* (Bonn, 1955), 227, 305 ff.

[39] Efforts to classify the members by social standing have produced only divergent estimates. See Karl Demeter: "Die soziale Schichtung des deutschen Parlaments seit 1848" (*Vierteljahrschrift für Sozial- und Wirtschaftsgeschichte*, XXXIX, n.d., 1–29); Paul Albrecht: *Die volkswirtschaftlichen und sozialen Fragen in der Frankfurter Nationalversammlung* (Halle, 1914), 5 ff.; Droz: *Les révolutions allemandes*, 270; Huber: *Deutsche Verfassungsgeschichte*, 610 ff.; Schilfert: *Sieg und Niederlage*, 402 ff.

[40] This historic church was largely destroyed during the Second World War, but was rebuilt in expectation that it would become the seat of the post-war German Parliament. The present interior arrangement is quite different from what it was in 1848.

cially by Marxist writers, of having "betrayed" the revolution and having turned to support the reaction. It should be remembered, however, that the revolution was not of their making, nor even desired by them. Of the Parliament it has been well said that it was a revolutionary assembly of which the membership was preponderantly non-revolutionary.[41]

To the left of center were a number of radicals, mostly lawyers and writers, poorly paid and without much prestige, who were described at the time as the *ecclesia militans* of the fourth estate.[42] These men were radicals in the political sense, men out of patience with the existing institutions and desirous of really popular government, with a German national state on a centralized, democratic, republican base. Although closely related to the artisans and skilled workers, the radicals concentrated on political reform and left the workers more or less to find their own salvation.

Not only Marxist but also liberal historians have criticized the Frankfurt Parliament for its indecision, not to say its pusillanimity. Marx maintained that it should at once have declared its full sovereignty and acted dictatorially. Veit Valentin, author of the standard history of the 1848 revolution, attributed the failure of the Parliament to its unwillingness to employ revolutionary methods and its inability to recognize the requirements of the new democracy. An even more recent writer, Wilhelm Mommsen, has charged the leaders of the Parliament with wanting to close out the revolution before it had really gotten under way, and was convinced that thereby the liberal cause was already lost when the Parliament assembled.[43]

Marx, who had counted on supporting the bourgeois revolution as

---

[41] Gustav Radbruch: "Die frankfurter Grundrechte" (in Wilhelm Keil, ed.: *Deutschland, 1848–1948*, Stuttgart, 1948, 80–88); see also Reinhart Kosseleck, in Werner Conze, ed.: *Staat und Gesellschaft im deutschen Vormärz* (Stuttgart, 1962), 77 ff.; Veit Valentin: "La date de 1848 dans l'histoire de l'Allemagne" (*Société d'histoire moderne*, séance de March 1, 1936); Friedrich Meinecke: *1848: eine Säkulärbetrachtung* (Bonn, 1948), 12 ff., 22; Karl Griewank: "Ursachen und Folgen des Scheiterns der deutschen Revolution von 1848" (*Historische Zeitschrift*, CLXX, 1950, 495–523).

[42] Lenore O'Boyle: "The Democratic Left in Germany, 1848" (*Journal of Modern History*, XXXIII, 1961, 374–383); Wilhelm Abel: "Der Pauperismus in Deutschland" (in *Wirtschaft, Geschichte und Wirtschaftsgeschichte, Festschrift für Friedrich Lütge*, Stuttgart, 1966, 284–298).

[43] Auguste Cornu: "Karl Marx et la révolution de 1848 en Allemagne" (*Europe*, XXVI, 1948, 238–252); Lenin: "Two Tactics of Social Democracy in the Democratic Revolution" (in *Collected Works*, IX); Valentin: *Die deutsche Revolution*; Mommsen: *Grösse und Versagen des deutschen Bürgertums* (Stuttgart, 1949), 217–218.

the prelude to the rising of the proletariat against the capitalist system, was naturally disappointed when he discovered that the *bourgeoisie* had no intention of fighting the governments to the death. But the criticism of the liberal historians is harder to understand, for the Parliament did in fact at once assume the sole right to draft a federal constitution and presently decreed that this constitution should be binding on all German states. Furthermore, it applied itself at once to the establishment of a provisional federal executive. Due to the fact that the Czechs of Bohemia and Moravia had refused to take part in the elections, the Hapsburg Monarchy, which was entitled to 190 seats, actually had only 120 deputies, while Prussia had 198. For this reason the sentiment of the moderates favored Prussian leadership or at least an executive directory of three, yet the Parliament eventually yielded to the radical demand for a single head and on June 28 chose Archduke John as vicar-general (*Reichsverweser*). John, though an uncle of the Austrian emperor, was a man well known for his progressive views. Having accepted the Frankfurt appointment, he at once named Prince Leiningen, a half-brother of Queen Victoria of Great Britain and a confirmed liberal, to head the federal cabinet.

These were undeniably important strides in the direction of federal control, taken while the governments were still paralyzed and prevented by radical pressures from offering active resistance. But the efforts of the Frankfurt Parliament were soon to meet ominous setbacks abroad as well as at home. The attempt to secure full control of foreign affairs failed when both Britain and France declined to receive fully accredited ambassadors and protested formally against the Parliament's action in the Schleswig affair. The attitude of these powers, initially well-disposed toward the aspirations of German nationalism, underwent drastic changes as the territorial implications of German unification began to emerge. Only the United States continued to be wholly sympathetic, offering to exchange ministers. Other powers preferred to wait and see.[44]

On the domestic front the issue was control over the armed forces. Liberals and radicals were at one in their hatred of standing armies,

---

[44] See footnote 34 above, and in addition Hans Precht: *Englands Stellung zur deutschen Einheit, 1848–1850* (Berlin, 1925); Günther Gillesen: *Lord Palmerston und die Einigung Deutschlands* (Hamburg, 1961), 32 ff.; Paul Henry: *La France devant le monde* (Paris, 1945), 153 ff.

regarded by them as instruments of repression. Their ideal was a militia on the Swiss model, but as a first step the Frankfurt government on July 16 called on the armies of all states to adopt the national colors and take an oath of allegiance to the Archduke John as commander-in-chief. Many of the lesser states complied, but both Prussia and Austria refused. In Prussia the king was already involved in dispute with his own Parliament over control of the forces. Since his army was the one really powerful German force, he fancied himself as the ultimate commander-in-chief. In any event, the Frankfurt government had no way of enforcing its decree and had to accept defeat. It was the first serious contest between nationalism and state particularism and its outcome was soon to becloud other efforts at popular control.[45]

The Frankfurt Parliament spent the early weeks of its existence in receiving countless deputations and petitions, and in working out its organization. Committees (twenty-four in all) were set up to draft a statement of fundamental rights, to study constitutional problems, to handle foreign affairs, and so on. One of the most important committees was the Economic Committee, which, in addition to questions of trade and industry, had responsibility also for the problems of labor. For some time the debates of the Parliament centered on basic rights (*Grundrechte*). Indeed, the Parliament has been charged with spending so much valuable time on learned discussion of principles that by the time it arrived at the problem of federal organization the governments had already recovered sufficiently to obstruct the popular will. It should be remembered, however, that prevention of a return to the Metternich system was a matter of great and immediate importance and also that it was necessary to arrive at uniform principles in order to counteract the forces of particularism. Allowing for the expansive rhetoric of the period, the debates reveal not only eloquence and learning but the kind of hardheaded reasoning with which professors are rarely credited.[46]

Considering its nature and membership, it was only to be expected

---

[45] Gerhard Ritter: *Staatskunst und Kriegshandwerk* (Munich, 1954), I, 148 ff.; Gordon A. Craig: *The Politics of the Prussian Army* (Oxford, 1955), 111 ff.; Huber: *Deutsche Verfassungsgeschichte*, II, 647 ff.

[46] Radbruch: "Die Frankfurter Grundrechte," and the analytical study of Herbert A. Strauss: *Staat, Bürger, Mensch: die Debatten der deutschen Nationalversammlung über die Grundrechte* (Aarau, 1947).

that the Parliament should hold to the principles of liberalism. Its treatment of the agrarian problem is a   good example. During the spring of 1848 several governments, confronted with peasant disturbances, had decreed the abolition of all feudal dues, usually with provision for compensation to the owners of servitudes resting on the land. The Parliament took much the same line. It declared all patrimonial rights at an end, abolished without compensation feudal obligations of the peasantry (including the hated hunting and forest rights), but decreed that dues connected with the land should be commuted into money payments. The details were left largely to the state governments.[47]

Equally important, in the light of later developments, was the question of industrial labor, more particularly the plight of craftsmen and artisans working at the traditional trades and suffering greatly from technological unemployment and the growing competition of machine production. These were the people who, in their desperation, had fought on the barricades and who now staked their hopes on the radical democratic program. They were not, in general, Communists or even socialists. It is true that Karl Marx, through his *New Rhenish Gazette,* was exercising increasing influence, but his policy and that of his paper was at the time directed more toward political democracy than toward communism. Furthermore, the sophisticated reasoning, what Heine once called "the terrible logic," of the Communists was definitely beyond the comprehension of the ordinary worker. Even in Cologne the Communists were almost exclusively middle-class intellectuals.

The average artisan, whether a master craftsman or a journeyman, tended to look not forward but backward. His greatest dread was that of losing respectability and sinking to the status of the true proletarian. His difficulties, as he saw them, derived from the machine and from the system of economic liberalism, that is, from free competition. Little interested in politics, the workers made concerted efforts to organize, nationally as well as locally, in a general labor union as well as in separate trade unions. Their great aim was to revive the guild system

---

[47] Paul Albrecht: *Die volkswirtschaftlichen und sozialen Fragen in der Frankfurter Nationalversammlung* (Halle, 1914), 29 ff.; Walter Schneider: *Wirtschafts- und Sozialpolitik im Frankfurther Parlament* (Frankfurt, 1923), 62 ff.; Hamerow: *Restoration, Revolution, Reaction,* chap. ix.

with all its protective features, and beyond that to enlist the aid of the state to guarantee work, to protect industry through tariffs, and to regulate if not actually check the spread of the factory system and of railway and steamship transportation.[48]

During the summer of 1848 various efforts were made to organize the artisans. An important congress, representative chiefly of the master craftsmen of southern Germany, met at Frankfurt from July 15 to August 18 and undertook to play an economic role co-ordinate with the political role of the Frankfurt Parliament, indeed, to draft a new labor code to supplement the new political constitution. The congress, which refused admittance to ordinary journeymen, called for return to the guild system and for free, compulsory elementary education, a progressive income tax, a protective tariff and state provision of employment when necessary.

From the very beginning the German labor movement was weakened by the rift between the masters and their employees, most of whom lived in the home of the master and were therefore subject to his authority.[49] On their exclusion from the masters' congress, the journeymen organized their own congress at Frankfurt. They were less enamored of the guild system than their employers and aimed at organization of the workers more or less in opposition to the guilds. Much of their attention was given to practical matters such as a minimum wage and a shorter workday, and to the demand for extensive state aid, foreshadowing the modern welfare state.

Even more important from the organizational standpoint was the Berlin Labor Congress (August 23–September 2), representing about ninety-five workers' clubs, mostly in North Germany. Its president was Stefan Born, the chief advocate of organization and self-help. It was an essentially moderate group which formulated the usual program with-

---

[48] Hans Meusch: *Die Handwerker-Bewegung, 1848–1849* (Alfeld, 1949); Theodore S. Hamerow: "The German Artisan Movement, 1848–1849" (*Journal of Central European Affairs*, XXI, 1961, 135–152); Obermann: *Die deutschen Arbeiter*, 180 ff.; Werner Conze: *Die Arbeiterbewegung in der nationalen Bewegung* (Stuttgart, 1966), 32 ff.; Noyes: *Organization and Revolution*, 122 ff. A useful collection of articles from the *New Rhenish Gazette* has been published under the title: *Karl Marx und Friedrich Engels: Die Revolution von 1848* (Berlin, 1953).

[49] In Frankfurt there were 2,696 shops with 3,965 employees, of whom 3,214 lived with the master. See Paul Kampffmeyer: *Geschichte der modernen Gesellschaftsklassen in Deutschland* (3 ed., Berlin, 1921), 234.

out attacking· the capitalist system or private property. Rejecting the guild system even more positively than the journeymen's congress, the Berlin group petitioned the Frankfurt Parliament to recognize and consider the needs of the workers, but at bottom its objective was effective organization to secure its demands. It set up a Labor Brotherhood (*Verbrüderung*) with twenty-six district committees to send delegates to an annual assembly which, in turn, should elect a central committee to transact business on a permanent basis. This organization, which managed to survive the revolution of 1848, went much further than anything attempted by the French workers and marked an important advance in the German labor movement.[50]

The Economic Committee of the Frankfurt Parliament was by no means unsympathetic to the cause of the workers and made an honest effort to balance the demands of the workers' congresses as well as of the numberless petitions that flowed in from local groups and individuals. The main task was to find a middle way between the guild system, called for by the master craftsmen, and economic freedom, which was a chief tenet of liberalism. However, a new industrial ordinance to regulate the conditions of labor was ultimately arrived at and submitted to the full Parliament. The members were all well aware of the social problem and many had read in the extensive literature that had poured out over the preceding years. They recognized that they had a mission to find "the solid ground of improved material and social conditions," and they engaged in long and earnest debates on various aspects of the labor problem. But they were liberals and could not get away from Malthusian thought. Pauperism, they argued, is due largely to the shortcomings of the workers, and in any case is bound to be transitional. Interference by the state would only make matters worse and, as for a return to the guild system, that would be a negation of all that liberalism stood for. The program of the workers, according to one liberal paper, reflected contempt for the demands of science and a shameless passion for monopoly. In the end the projected labor

[50] Ernst Schraepler: *Quellen zur Geschichte der sozialen Frage in Deutschland, I, 1800–1870* (Göttingen, 1955), 104 ff.; Max Quarck: *Die erste deutsche Arbeiterbewegung: Geschichte der Arbeiterverbrüderung, 1848–1849* (Leipzig, 1924); Wilhelm Friedensburg: *Stefan Born und die Organisationsbestrebungen der Berliner Arbeiterschaft* (Leipzig, 1923), 92 ff.; Rudolf Stadelmann: *Soziale und politische Geschichte der Revolution von 1848* (Munich, 1948), 166 ff.; Meusch: *Die Handwerker-Bewegung*, 43 ff.; Noyes: *Organization and Revolution*, 212 ff.

ordinance was quietly shelved. The workers had made a significant start, but they still had a long way to go.[51]

5. THE END OF ILLUSION

The Malmö armistice (August 28) marked the end of the Frankfurt Parliament's golden age. It had started out with illusions of grandeur, arrogating to itself the exclusive right to lay down the terms for the unification of Germany, setting up a federal government, and attempting to assume command of the armed forces. The refusal of the two great powers, Prussia and Austria, to abandon control over their armies was the first serious setback in domestic affairs, highlighting as it did the fact that the Parliament had no means for enforcing its decisions. In the foreign field the Malmö armistice, concluded without consultation of the Parliament, demonstrated, first, that any German state could and would, if its interests demanded it, act without reference to the elected assembly; second, that the question of German unity was not one for the Germans alone to decide. Prussia had acted under pressure from Britain and Russia, powers which left no doubt that they were entitled to be heard and proposed to insist on it. There were those, the historian Dahlmann for example, who counseled resistance at any cost and induced the Parliament at first to reject the armistice (September 5). One deputy talked of replying to the foreign powers with a *levée en masse* of a million and a half men. Count Schmerling, who was about to take over the premiership from Prince Leiningen, observed that war might not be a bad thing, as it would quickly unite all Germans in the national cause. Lord Cowley, the British representative, was horrified by the bellicose talk he heard in political circles. He thought the Parliament "a parcel of children who want whipping and caressing alternately."[52]

One can explain the attitude of the Parliament by the lack of experience of most of its members, but it was above all else a reflection of the ardent passion for national self-assertion which moved not only liberals and radicals but also workers and even Communists such as Marx.

[51] Wilhelm Mommsen: *Grösse und Versagen des deutschen Bürgertums,* 162 ff.; Eugen Barthelmess: "Sozialpolitisches im Revolutionsjahr" (in Wilhelm Keil, ed.: *Deutschland, 1848–1948,* 114–123); Noyes: *Organization and Revolution,* 221 ff.

[52] Günther Gillesen: *Lord Palmerston und die Einigung Deutschlands* (Hamburg, 1961), 40 ff.; Donald Southgate: "The Most English Minister" (New York, 1966), 226.

Ever since the crisis of 1840 they had been painfully aware of the helplessness of the Confederation. They were determined not only on the establishment of constitutional government but also on the attainment of a position commensurate with their numbers, their size, and their cultural achievements. Their economic development called for the extension of the *Zollverein* to the entire German area and the creation of a strong state that could hold its own in international affairs. In 1848 every German state, even the little county of Knyphausen, had its own commercial flag and its own (mostly honorary) consuls abroad. The foreign representatives of powers such as Prussia and Austria, or the great commercial city of Hamburg, were of course treated with respect, but those of the lesser states were often ignored.

The war with Denmark in 1848 emphasized to all the utter helplessness of the Germans at sea. Despite their long coastline and huge merchant marine, they had no fleet, not even a decent coastal defense force. The Danes blockaded the German harbors and captured German ships with impunity. Popular indignation was understandable. Countless pamphlets poured from the presses and everywhere navy societies were founded to agitate for a German fleet. After a navy congress at Hamburg (May 31), the Frankfurt Parliament on June 14 voted almost unanimously that a navy should be built for coast defense and commerce protection. But the Germans lacked the necessary naval shipyards, the experienced officers and the trained men. They converted some merchantmen and bought some warships in England and the United States. Meanwhile the Prussian government decided to build six frigates and six steam corvettes on its own account. But to construct a navy would take time. Prior to the autumn of 1848, very little had been accomplished.[53]

The naval program, whatever its merits, served among other things to arouse the suspicions of the British, who already ascribed German policy in the Schleswig question to the desire to get control of the duchies with the excellent potential naval base at Kiel. But what estranged the foreign powers more than anything else was the apparent claim that all territory inhabited by Germans should be included in the new national empire. This appeared from the affair of the duchies and from the effort to include nonfederal lands in the east, such as East and

---

[53] Archibald Hurd and Henry Castle: *German Sea-Power* (London, 1913), 72 ff.; Karl Haenchen: *Die deutsche Flotte von 1848* (Bremen, 1925), 12 ff.

West Prussia and the larger part of Posen, to say nothing of the voices that clamored for a Greater Germany in which parts of Switzerland, Belgium, the Netherlands and possibly Denmark might be included.[54]

What was particularly disconcerting to outsiders was the readiness of the Germans to incorporate in their national state many non-German territories, the populations of which had nationalist aspirations of their own. This meant the Czechs of Bohemia and Moravia, the Slovenes of Carniola and Carinthia, the Italians of the South Tyrol, the Danes of northern Schleswig and the Poles of Prussia's eastern provinces. The Germans were indignant over the refusal of the Czechs to participate in the elections to the Frankfurt Parliament and many were well pleased when Windischgrätz dealt Czech nationalism a blow by the reduction of Prague. They also subscribed to Prussia's suppression of the Polish movement in Posen, and refused to consider the petition of the South Tyrolese for permission to join the nascent Italian national state.

Meanwhile little progress was made toward the reorganization of the Germanic Confederation. The general sentiment at Frankfurt was in favor of unification under Prussian leadership, but Frederick William made no move to implement his promise that Prussia should be merged or fused with Germany, or to assume the leadership which he romantically believed belonged to the Hapsburgs. Actually the Austrian Empire, which in the spring had seemed done for, had by the summer shown greater vitality than most liberals had dreamed of. Radetzky's victory at Custoza revealed the Austrians as champions of German rights and claims and made the new liberal Austria seem more attractive than the old. One might say that the election of the Archduke John as vicar-general was a tribute to the Hapsburgs and a landmark in the revival of Austrian prestige.[55]

The vital question of precedence and leadership therefore remained open, while the tide was turning against the Parliament, as noted

---

[54] Richard Haufe: *Die Anschauungen über Gebiet, Staatsform und Oberhaupt des deutschen Nationalstaates in den Flugschriften, 1848–1849* (Leipzig, 1915), 8 ff., 25 ff.; Josef Pfitzner: "Die grenz- und auslandsdeutsche Bewegung des Jahres 1848" (*Historische Zeitschrift*, CLX, 1939, 308–322); Peter Rassow: *Deutschland und Europa im Jahre 1848* (Krefeld, 1954), *passim*.

[55] Adolf Rapp: *Grossdeutsch-Kleindeutsch* (Munich, 1922), xxiii; Hans G. Telle: *Das oesterreichische Problem im Frankfurter Parlament* (Marburg, 1933), 20, 33 ff.; Heinrich von Srbik: *Deutsche Einheit* (Munich, 1935), I, 332 ff.

above. With respect to the Malmö armistice, counsels of moderation finally prevailed. On September 17 the Parliament with heavy heart reversed its earlier decision and approved the armistice by a vote of 258 to 237. Among the opponents were the radicals, who were unwilling to surrender to the will of the hated German governments or the pressure of the foreigners. Marx, who denounced the signers of the armistice as a collection of impotent dreamers and a college of fools, mobilized the Democratic Society and the Workers' Society in Cologne for a huge demonstration (September 13), as a result of which a Committee of Public Safety, with Marx, Engels and other Communists as members, was set up. The Cologne radicals were evidently ready to start a civil war, but this was forestalled by the Prussian government, which proclaimed martial law, suspended the publication of the *New Rhenish Gazette,* and forced many of the Communist leaders to flee the city.[56]

The insurrection that broke out in Frankfurt itself on September 17 faced no such opposition, for the Parliament had no armed forces at its disposal. Radicals and workers threw up barricades and fought bitterly, ostensibly in protest against the approval of the humiliating Malmö armistice, but in reality probably in protest against the failure of the Parliament to make progress in the direction of democracy and relief for the poorer classes. The town garrison being altogether unequal to such an outbreak, the provisional government had to call in federal troops (Austrian, Prussian, Hessian) from the nearby federal garrison at Mainz. The insurrection was suppressed by the evening of September 18 and a week later an attempted republican rising in Baden was also defeated. But the upsurge of discontent and radicalism made a deep impression on the liberal members of Parliament, who had never envisaged barricade fighting at the very doors of the popularly elected assembly. Unable to protect itself, the Parliament would in the days to come have to depend on the collaboration of the governments for any progress toward reform and unification.

---

[56] Hermann Meyer: "Karl Marx und die deutsche Revolution von 1848" (*Historische Zeitschrift,* CLXXII, 1951, 517–537); Kotschetkowa: "Die Tätigkeit von Marx und Engels in der Kölner demokratischen Gesellschaft"; Becker: *Karl Marx und Friedrich Engels in Köln,* 117 ff.

Chapter Four

CLOSING THE CIRCLE

I. THE REPUBLIC WITHOUT REPUBLICANS

In France General Cavaignac, who had been given dictatorial powers to suppress the insurrection of the June Days, insisted on resigning his extraordinary powers, but was named by the National Assembly to be chief of the executive power. As such he replaced the executive commission set up in May and, as president of the Council of Ministers, named the members of his cabinet. Cavaignac was an incorruptible republican, a man of moderate views who served as the faithful servant of the Party of Order, which in turn commanded a majority in the chamber. He dissolved the dissident elements of the National Guard and brought radical clubs and newspapers to heel. Though the radicals branded him the "butcher" of the June Days, he suited the Assembly very well and worked effectively with it.[1]

During the summer and autumn of 1848 the Assembly devoted itself to the task for which it had been chosen, namely, the drafting of a new constitution. This was urgently necessary, for the charter of 1830 was a thing of the past, the monarchy had been swept away, the Orleanist Parliament had been dissolved, the cabinet of Louis Philippe had given way to a provisional government, then to an executive commission and most recently to a chief of the executive power. These were all makeshift arrangements, operating at a time when stability and permanency seemed so necessary.

The Constitutional Committee of the Assembly numbered eighteen members, among them some of the leading political figures of the time. Tocqueville, an outstanding theorist of that or any period, was among them, but held his colleagues in low esteem as lacking depth and deliberation: "I never witnessed a more wretched display in any committee on which I ever sat," he noted in his Recollections. His disparagement, however, may have been due in part to the unwilling-

<hr />

[1] General Ibos: *Le général Cavaignac* (Paris, 1930), 190 ff.; Paul Bastid: *Doctrines et institutions politiques de la Seconde République* (Paris, 1945), II, 5 ff.

ness of his colleagues to adopt his favorite recipe for a decentralized administrative system and a two-chamber Parliament. The committee-men knew little and perhaps cared less about the experience of the United States or Britain. They thought in terms of French history and French requirements.

The republican form, under the circumstances, had to be taken for granted. As for universal suffrage, radical though it might appear, it had proved itself in the elections of April, when the population at large had demonstrated its sanity in opposition to political and social extremism. Other provisions of a first draft were examined critically by delegates chosen by other committees of the Asssembly, after which another month was devoted to revision. From September 4 to October 23 the full Assembly debated the draft, article by article, and eventually on November 4 adopted the new constitution by a vast majority.

Nothing was done to change the highly centralized administrative system which Tocqueville blamed for so many of France's woes, but which Frenchmen of all stripes seemed to find both efficient and congenial. The constitution recognized the familiar civil rights, but boggled at recognition of the "right to work," which had been recognized by the provisional government and had underlain the establish-ment of the national workshops. Five full sessions were devoted to this topic. Most members were certainly in favor of rejecting it, but were fearful of further disturbances in Paris and other cities. Thiers, who had been elected to the Assembly in a by-election in June, argued that recognition of the right to work would run counter to the principles of economic liberalism and that, furthermore, it would be tantamount to paying workers a wage for doing nothing. By way of compromise the Assembly voted to recognize only the workers' right to relief: the state would provide for foundlings, for the infirm and for the aged. As for work, it would not recognize the laborers' right but would undertake to provide work as far as possible by favoring public projects suitable for unskilled labor.[2]

The principal debates, however, had to do with the nature of the legislature and the method of electing the executive. There was little sentiment for a two-chamber Parliament, on the theory that in Britain the upper chamber was designed for the aristocracy while in the United States the Senate was necessary because of the federal system.

---

[2] Bastid: *Doctrines et institutions politiques*, II, 82 ff.; Jean Dautry: *1848 et la Seconde République* (Paris, 1957), 214.

France, with a centralized administration, required only a single Assembly with concentrated power, competent to deal with any revolutionary emergency. Hence the constitution provided for a single chamber of 750 members, elected triennially by universal suffrage and by cantonal lists. The Assembly was to appoint a council of state, but this was to have the sole function of preparing legislation.

As for the executive, there was general agreement that its powers, too, should be concentrated: there should be a president with substantially the powers of the American president.[3] The key question, however, was whether the president should be elected by the Assembly, acting as the mandatory of the nation, or by direct vote of the people. Jules Grévy, a radical who was eventually to become president of the Third French Republic, warned that the populace, left to itself, might even elect a pretender to the throne. The Assembly would have sounder political judgment than the people at large. But Lamartine, in one of his most eloquent oratorical efforts, argued that election of the president by the Assembly would surely lead to corruption, which would not be possible in a popular vote: "One poisons a glass of water, but not a whole river." Dangers there were, of course, but if things should turn out badly, he was prepared to accept what fate had in store: "Even though the people should choose him whom perhaps my badly enlightened foresight dreads to see, no matter, the die is cast." The Assembly thereupon voted (October 9) that the president should be elected by universal suffrage for a four-year term, but be ineligible for re-election. In the event of none of the candidates receiving two million or more votes, the election was to revert to the Assembly. This is probably what most of the deputies expected to happen.[4]

The debate on the presidency was carried on very much with Prince Louis Napoleon, the Bonapartist claimant, in mind. The prince had hurried to Paris after the February Revolution and had evidently hoped to be included in the provisional government. But Lamartine had convinced him that his presence was not desired and he had returned to London to await developments. Some of his friends, however, had remained in France and had initiated a propaganda campaign on his behalf, with the result that he was elected to the

[3] The influence of the American constitution made itself felt only in this connection. See Eugene N. Curtis: *The French Assembly of 1848 and American Constitutional Doctrines* (New York, 1918), 186 ff.

[4] Bastid: *Doctrines et institutions politiques*, II, 107 ff.; André-Jean Tudesq: *L'élection présidentielle de Louis-Napoléon Bonaparte* (Paris, 1965), 51 ff.

chamber in a by-election in June. His supporters urged him to return, but in vain. Instead he declined his mandate (June 16) and decided to bide his time.

Members of the Assembly were distinctly troubled by the emergence of the Bonaparte pretender on the political scene and by the crowds that eagerly awaited his appearance at the Chamber. Lamartine proposed enforcement of the law which excluded the Bonaparte family from France, and others talked of nullifying the prince's election, which became unnecessary when he voluntarily resigned his seat. But there was, of course, no knowing what the future would bring. Louis Napoleon's friend and promoter, Victor Fialin de Persigny, soon badgered him into standing for election in the by-election of September 17, on which occasion he was again elected in Paris (Seine *département*) and in four other *départements*. In Paris he polled over 110,000 votes, as against 78,000 for his nearest competitor. This was enough to decide him. On September 24 he arrived in Paris, and two days later took his seat in the Assembly.[5]

Members of the Assembly were not so naïve as to think that a pretender with the charismatic name of Bonaparte would be content with the simple role of deputy. They realized that he might enter the race for the presidency and even attempt to restore the empire. But the prince did not seem a very formidable threat, for he was small, short-legged, and expressionless of countenance. When, on two occasions, he spoke briefly to avow his devotion to the Republic, his embarrassed stammer and his Swiss-German accent moved many of his colleagues to either scorn or ridicule. Experienced politicians put him down as a harmless halfwit (Thiers) or an insignificant numskull (Tocqueville).

The future was soon to tell, for Louis Napoleon announced his candidacy for the presidential elections fixed for December 10, thus entering into competition with Cavaignac, Lamartine, Ledru-Rollin and Raspail. Had the choice been up to the Assembly, it would almost certainly have elected Cavaignac, who, with support of the bureaucracy

[5] The basic account is still André Lebey: *Louis-Napoléon et la révolution de 1848* (2 vols., Paris, 1907–1908). Among more recent studies, F. A. Simpson: *The Rise of Louis Napoleon* (London, 1909), chap. xi, is excellent, and the following are important: Bernard de Vaulx: *L'échéance de 1852, ou la liquidation de 1848* (Paris, 1948); Maurice de La Fuye and Emile A. Babeau: *Louis-Napoléon avant l'Empire* (Amsterdam, 1951), chaps. xiv–xvi; Adrien Dansette: *Louis-Napoléon à la conquête du pouvoir* (Paris, 1961), chap. x; Heinrich Euler: *Napoleon III in seiner Zeit* (Würzburg, 1961), 446 ff. On the Napoleonic propaganda, see also Paul Chrétien: *Le duc de Persigny* (Toulouse, 1943), 27 ff.

as well as the army, seems in any event to have been so certain of success that, austere republican that he was, he refused to exercise administrative pressure and instead conducted an unaggressive campaign. He certainly had little to fear from his opponents on the left, for the democratic forces were weakened by the repression following the June Days and sadly divided as between republican democrats and social democrats. Ledru-Rollin represented the former and Raspail the latter. Neither had the remotest chance of obtaining even one million votes. Lamartine, on the other hand, thought he had reason for optimism, considering all he had done in the spring to hold the forces of radicalism in check. As for Louis Napoleon, he soon undeceived those who saw in him only a harmless imbecile. He conducted his campaign with great astuteness. His door was always open to those who had something to say and he showed himself ever ready to listen patiently to suggestions. With prominent politicians he posed as a man above class or party, intent on stabilizing the situation and conciliating conflicting factions. When necessary he would even go so far as to make definite commitments.

By the beginning of December the prince had enlisted the more or less sincere support of leading Orleanists (Guizot, Thiers, Barrot, Molé), of prominent Catholics (Berryer, Montalembert, Veuillot), of literary notables (Victor Hugo, Alexandre Dumas) and of influential editors (Girardin). What he lacked was financial support, for his personal fortune and the contributions of his devoted mistress, Miss Howard, were not sufficient. He managed to float a few modest loans with Paris bankers, but he was chronically short of funds and his backers mostly contributed their services without immediate reward. They launched newspapers, posted pamphlets and broadsides, formed election committees and dispatched agents to the provinces. They made effective use of the Napoleonic legend, which had long since established the great emperor as the champion of progress, the defender of religion and society, and the hero who had exalted France above all nations. The nephew, it was now argued, represented the very same principles. He could be depended upon to put an end to revolutionary agitation, to maintain order, restore property and revive French glory.[6]

The elections of December 10 were to show that Louis Napoleon

[6] Jean Lucas-Dubreton: *Le culte de Napoléon, 1815–1848* (Paris, 1960), chap. xviii; André-Jean Tudesq: "La légende napoléonienne en France en 1848" (*Revue historique*, CCXLIII, 1957, 64–85).

enjoyed the widest conceivable support not only throughout the rural areas of France but in the cities as well. Even in Paris the radical candidates, Ledru-Rollin and Raspail, received only 12.5 per cent of the votes. The capital and four other major cities gave the prince an absolute majority.[7] The results no doubt reflected the workers' hatred of Cavaignac and their distrust of Ledru-Rollin for his abandonment of the socialist program, but they certainly expressed also the appeal of Louis Napoleon, who had had nothing whatever to do with the struggles that culminated in the June Days and who, besides, had a well-known interest in the problems of the machine age and the plight of the urban workers. During his exile in England he had visited the industrial centers and made copious notes of his observations.[8] While in captivity in the fortress of Ham he had received the visits of Louis Blanc and had tried his own hand at social theorizing. In his pamphlet *The Extinction of Pauperism* (1844) he had argued that the days of social castes were over. In the future it would be possible to govern only with the support of the masses. The answer to unemployment and the constant fluctuation in the demand for labor was for the state to finance agricultural colonies to which unemployed urban workers could return, to work at a guaranteed soldier's wage until again required for work in the factories. The idea was by no means new. In fact, it was a favorite nostrum of the period. But it was new that a prince should demonstrate such awareness of the social problem and such interest in the welfare of the worker.[9]

Among the peasants, at the same time, the Napoleonic legend apparently had its most devoted adherents. The fact that the empire had meant heavy taxation, conscription and almost continuous war seemed no longer of much account. Bonapartists, said Victor Hugo, were like children: they liked what was flashy. The countryside, furthermore, had no use for revolution. It resented the 45-centime surtax, which was regarded as a case of rank discrimination in favor of worthless city loafers. Even after the June Days the peasants could not rid themselves of the fear of "communism." George Sand, herself accused of being a Communist, remarked that in the provinces one was

[7] Tudesq: *L'élection présidentielle*, 210–211.

[8] Ivor Guest: *Napoleon III in England* (London, 1952), 35.

[9] Ernest Labrousse: *Le mouvement ouvrier et les idées sociales en France de 1815 à la fin du XIXe siècle* (Paris, 1948), 135; Albert Guerard: *Napoleon III* (Cambridge, 1943), 55.

regarded as a Communist if one was a republican, and if one was a socialist republican one was suspected of drinking human blood, of killing babies, of beating one's wife, of being a bankrupt, a drunk and a robber, and one ran the real risk of being assassinated by some peasant who believed you mad because his bourgeois and his priest had told him so.[10]

It was fairly clear from the outset that the peasantry would vote for Louis Napoleon, many no doubt in the hope that he would put an end to the republic. It was thought that he would soon bring back prosperity. According to rumor he was planning to reduce the surtax from 45 centimes to 25 and to draw on his own "immense" fortune to relieve the rural poor. It took only the prince's election manifesto of early December to clinch the election. Though he had discussed it with Thiers, the manifesto was the prince's own work. A masterful political document, it promised in general all things to all men and once again pictured Louis Napoleon as the man above class or party, as the great conciliator.[11]

The victory of Louis Napoleon was, then, hardly the surprise of which many writers speak. The startling thing was not his election but the magnitude of his success, for of the 7,426,252 votes cast, he received 5,534,520, while Cavaignac had only 1,442,302, Ledru-Rollin 371,431, Raspail 36,920 and Lamartine a paltry 17,910. In most *départements* the prince obtained upward of 80 per cent of the votes, especially in the north and center. If the election did not exactly reveal what France wanted, it at least showed what the country did not want, namely, the existing republic. The influential groups, deputies, prefects, notables, editors, had all been swamped by the tidal wave of popular sentiment. Universal suffrage had brought the repudiation of the February Revolution and its fruits. In the words of Karl Marx, it was "the day of the peasant insurrection," marking "their entry into the revolutionary movement." But they entered it not to further it; rather, to ruin it.[12]

[10] Quoted in Pierre Labracherie: "Le paysan de 1848" (in *Esprit de 1848*, Paris, n.d., 215–246).

[11] Albert Soboul: "La question paysanne en 1848" (*La pensée*, No. 20, 1948, 48–56). On the manifesto see Vaulx: *L'échéance de 1852*, 107 ff.

[12] Karl Marx: *The Class Struggles in France*, 71. See also the discriminating evaluation of the election results in Tudesq: *L'élection présidentielle*, 211 ff.

2. ITALY: THE RADICAL PHASE

Many Frenchmen, when they voted for Louis Napoleon, expected him to restore France to its historic position as arbiter of Europe and it was, in fact, only a few months before the new president had involved his country in the traditional struggle for influence in the Italian peninsula. There the trend of events in the autumn of 1848 ran counter to that of most countries, for while elsewhere the forces of conservatism or reaction were in the ascendant, in Italy the liberal elements were being superseded by radical, democratic forces. To a large extent this was a reflection of the shock of the defeat at Custoza. For a time there was still hope that the mediation of Britain and France would bring Piedmont possession of Lombardy, but this mediation soon proved as ineffectual as the military operations. Palmerston preached to the Austrian government the virtues of abnegation and kept warning it of the imminent danger of French intervention, but in vain. In Vienna it was realized that the French were actually opposed to the aggrandizement of Piedmont and that the Cavaignac government, though it might put up a brave front, was intent on avoiding embroilment in foreign adventure. The Anglo-French partnership rested at bottom on distrust rather than confidence, for while the British objective was a strong North Italian state that would be an effective buffer between Austria and France, the French were concerned to keep North Italy divided and thus open to French influence. Neither government was moved by interest in Italian national aspirations. Their thought was of the balance of power and their objectives therefore diametrically opposed.

The Salasco armistice was a strictly military truce, which was periodically renewed while the effort at mediation continued. For months the Vienna government managed to temporize until, by November, the revolution in the Austrian capital had been finally mastered and Prince Felix zu Schwarzenberg had taken over as chief of the cabinet. Schwarzenberg at once struck a more positive note. He charged the British with desiring the annexation of Lombardy to Piedmont merely so as to obstruct French influence. No doubt this was an accurate expression of French opinion, too, for Cavaignac now began to warn the Piedmontese government not to expect French aid if it attempted to renew the war against Austria. Palmerston continued

for a time to exert pressure on Vienna until Schwarzenberg, in an
amazing dispatch to Austrian representatives abroad, called him to
order:

Lord Palmerston regards himself too much as the arbiter of Europe. We
for our part are not disposed to accord him the role of Providence. We
never impose our advice on him in Irish matters: let him spare himself
the trouble of advising us on the subject of Lombardy. . . . We are tired
of his eternal insinuations, his protective and pedagogical tone, both offensive and unwelcome. We are resolved to tolerate it no longer. Lord
Palmerston said one day to Koller (the Austrian chargé d'affaires in London), that if we wanted war, we could have it. I say, if he wants war, he
shall have it.[13]

As the outlook for mediation grew dimmer, the Piedmontese government found itself in a quandary. Some political leaders favored an
appeal for French intervention, but of this the king would hear
nothing and, besides, Cavaignac soon blasted all hopes that French
troops might serve as "mercenaries." Meanwhile the Turin government
was faced by a deteriorating economic situation, widespread unemployment and threat of social upheaval. Genoa, a center of radicalism like
other seaports, seemed on the verge of revolution, while in Turin itself
the democratic forces were becoming more assertive. Radical leaders,
organizations and newspapers blamed the king and his aristocratic
entourage for the defeat of the army. They clamored for constitutional
reform and a renewal of the patriotic war, arguing that once the sword
were drawn, the French Republic would be bound to aid. Count
Cavour, who was rising to prominence, counseled patience, insisted on
the need for more preparation and warned that France could no more
be counted on to support the Piedmontese than to aid the Poles. The
Italians, he thought, should wait at least until the Austrians had
become more deeply involved in the war against Hungary. On the
other hand, Gioberti was heart and soul with the war party, which was
steadily growing in influence. On October 17 a motion for war by the

---

[13] A. J. P. Taylor: *The Italian Problem in European Diplomacy, 1847–1849* (Manchester, 1934), 177 ff.; Vittorio Barbieri: "I tentativi di mediazione anglo-francesi
durante la guerra di 1848" (*Rassegna storica del Risorgimento*, XXVI/2, 1939,
683–726); Ruggero Moscati: *La diplomazia europea e il problema italiano nel 1848*
(Florence, 1947), and "L'Europa e il problema italiano nel 1848–1849" (in F. Catalano,
R. Moscati and F. Valsecchi: *L'Italia nel Risorgimento*, Verona, 1964, Part III, chap. iii);
Donald Southgate: *"The Most English Minister"* (New York, 1966), 230 ff.

democratic leader Angelo Brofferio was defeated by a vote of only 77 to 58.[14]

In December, when the chances of successful mediation had become hopeless, Charles Albert felt obliged to yield to popular pressure. He appointed a democratic cabinet with Gioberti at its head. The new administration promptly dissolved Parliament and in January, 1849, held elections which for the first time produced a democratic majority. Pressure for renewal of the war continued to mount, but Gioberti, now that he was in power, began to recognize many obstacles to a policy of unrestrained patriotism. The army, for instance, was still inadequately prepared and the new French president held out no hope of support. Furthermore, the pope, who had been obliged by the radicals to leave Rome, was appealing to the Catholic powers for intervention in his behalf and Gioberti, the champion of an Italian federation under papal leadership, now devoted his efforts to forging a coalition of Italian states for joint action in behalf of the pope which would make foreign intervention superfluous. Presently Gioberti, who showed no aptitude for constitutional procedures, fell out with his colleagues and resigned (February 21). He was succeeded by Urbano Rattazzi, who had long agitated for renewal of the war. On March 12 the Piedmontese government denounced the Salasco armistice and reopened hostilities.

A few words may be said about the projected Italian league or confederation which had become so popular after publication of the Gioberti book in 1843 and then cropped up continually in one form or another during the revolutionary years 1848-1849. After the defeat at Custoza, Gioberti had persuaded Charles Albert to send the eminent philosopher Antonio Rosmini to Rome, where the latter, in collaboration with a papal and a Tuscan representative, had worked out a plan for a confederation under papal leadership resting on an assembly sitting at Rome and having control over foreign policy, the armed forces and the trade policies of the entire peninsula (see Illustration 56). The plan is interesting chiefly as a reflection of Gioberti's thought

[14] G. F. H. and J. Berkeley: *Italy in the Making* (Cambridge, 1940), III, 384 ff.; Giorgio Candeloro: *Storia dell'Italia moderna* (Milan, 1960), III, 363 ff.; A. J. Whyte: *The Political Life and Letters of Cavour, 1848-1861* (London, 1930), 14 ff.; Adolfo Omodeo: *Vincenzo Gioberti e la sua evoluzione politica* (Turin, 1941), 78 ff.; Rosario Romeo: *Dal Piemonte sabaudo all'Italia liberale* (Turin, 1963), 108 ff. For the evolution of democratic doctrine in Italy, see Franco della Peruta: *I democratici e la rivoluzione italiana* (Milan, 1958).

and that of the patriotic nationalists. The Piedmontese government, now as ever, was opposed to any scheme that involved sacrifice of sovereignty. Its counterproposal (October) envisaged merely an alliance of independent states for the protection of their territorial integrity and for common military action in defense. In this plan the other governments rightly saw nothing but an effort to enlist support for Piedmontese designs and pretensions to hegemony. The effect of the Piedmontese proposal was to arouse distrust and fan hostility to the Turin government.[15]

Closely related to the problem of Italian confederation were developments in Tuscany and the Papal States. Social conditions in Tuscany, where most of the peasants were illiterate sharecroppers, were so desperate that an insurrection seemed imminent. In the towns, too, there was much unemployment and misery. In August there was an uprising in Livorno, a busy seaport, which forced officials and troops to flee the city. As it was, however, the lower classes were so illiterate, unorganized and leaderless as to be unable to assume power. Their demands were rudimentary: a larger share of the land and reduced obligations to the landlords; in the cities higher wages and public works to provide employment, along with restrictions on the introduction of machinery. There was occasionally a demand for recognition of the right to work and for the organization of labor, but these were only faint echoes of French socialist doctrine, the sole effect of which was to frighten the propertied classes and turn many of them toward reaction.[16]

The uprising in Livorno was finally suppressed by Francesco Guerrazzi, the well-known novelist, who rallied the *bourgeoisie* and organized a Civic Guard to restore and maintain order. Because of the limited franchise the moderate liberals were able to retain a majority in the Tuscan Parliament, but they were so beset by fears of all kinds that they left the government to Guerrazzi and to another celebrated writer,

[15] Antonio Monti: *L'idea federalistica nel Risorgimento italiano* (Bari, 1921); Berkeley and Berkeley: *Italy in the Making*, III, 384 ff.; Candeloro: *Storia dell'Italia moderna*, III, 293 ff.

[16] Gino Luzzatto: "Aspects sociaux de la révolution de 1848 en Italie" (*Revue socialiste*, n.s., Nos. 17–18, 1948, 80–86); Guido Quazza: *La lotta sociale nel Risorgimento* (Turin, 1951), 206 ff.; Franco Catalano: "Socialismo e communismo in Italia del 1846 al 1849" (*Rassegna storica del Risorgimento*, XXXVIII, 1951, 306–316); Salvatore F. Romano: "Le classi sociali in Italia, 1815–1918" (in *Nuove questioni di storia del Risorgimento*, Milan, 1961, 511–572).

Giuseppe Montanelli, who had just returned from volunteer service in the north. Guerrazzi, once in power, tended like Gioberti in Piedmont to adopt a moderate course. He turned his face against republicanism and denounced "the disgraceful greed of men without name, without country, without God, who have designs on the lands and houses of others."[17]

Montanelli for his part busied himself with schemes for an Italian confederation on a popular basis, such as Mazzini had long since advocated. Without union, he was convinced, the foreigner could never be expelled, and this, according to the program he submitted to the governments on November 7, was the real purpose of the confederation. What he proposed was the election of a constituent assembly by universal suffrage, this assembly then to decide what degree of integration was necessary. The Piedmontese government replied promptly that a popular assembly could hardly direct a war and then reverted to its own plan for military collaboration. The Montanelli proposal proved abortive, but remains interesting as a reflection of democratic aspirations. It was, in fact, to have a real influence on the course of events in Rome during the succeeding months.[18]

The situation as it emerged in the Papal States was both complicated and crucial. There, as elsewhere, the economic crisis provided the background for political developments. The government, struggling with a chronic deficit, could not hope to make ends meet without antagonizing influential strata of society. The cabinet of Count Terenzio Mamiani (May to August, 1848) enrolled some 3,000 Roman workers in what amounted to national workshops, only to discover that it had only about a third of the money required. The unrest was such that radical clubs sprang up everywhere and demonstrations became the order of the day. The most popular and powerful club was the Circolo Populare, led by Angelo Brunetti (*Ciceruacchio*), a brawny baker who was constantly proclaiming the right to work and demanding the abolition of want, chiefly through merciless taxation of the rich. The situation in Bologna was no better. An attempt by the Austrians

---

17 Quoted by Romano: "Le classi sociali in Italia." See also W. K. Hancock: *Ricasoli and the Risorgimento in Tuscany* (London, 1926), 130 ff.

18 R. Cessi: "Il problema della Costituente nel 1848" (*Rassegna storica del Risorgimento*, XLI, 1954, 304–311); A. M. Ghisalberti: *Giuseppe Montanelli e la Costituente* (Florence, 1947); and the heavily documented analysis of the various projects for federation in Renato Mori: "Il progretto di lega neo-guelfa di Pellegrino Rossi" (*Rivista di studi politici internazionali*, XXIV, 1957, 602–628).

in August to occupy the city led to such a ferocious popular outbreak that the troops had to retreat. For several weeks the city was at the mercy of unemployed workers and hoodlums who pillaged, murdered and tyrannized over the population without any specific program or objective. Eventually a government emissary backed by Swiss mercenaries succeeded in restoring order.[19]

The Mamiani cabinet, typical of the moderate liberal governments of 1848, was distrusted by the pope, not only because it was constantly pressing for participation in the war against Austria, but because it attempted to separate the administration of the Papal States from the administration of the Catholic Church. Mamiani had but little chance of success, for not even the Parliament, elected in May, afforded him much support. So great was the political immaturity of the country that of the restricted electorate only about a third had voted and of the successful candidates only about half had accepted their mandate. Though the well-to-do classes commanded a majority in the lower house, they showed themselves strangely apathetic, if not frightened. By way of contrast, the radical wing, led by the Mazzinian Pietro Sterbini and the renegade Carlo Bonaparte (prince of Canino), a nephew of the great French emperor, was aggressive and domineering. Crowds in the galleries and on the streets constantly cheered it on.[20]

The main issue was still that of war or peace. Pius and the cardinals, concerned about their ecumenical obligations, were unalterably opposed to participating in the war, the more so as they considered it primarily a campaign for the aggrandizement of Piedmont. But the majority in Parliament, the right as well as the left, was enthusiastically committed to war. The arrival of volunteers returning from the north, and of liberal and radical refugees from the Kingdom of Naples, added fuel to the fires of patriotism. The pope, in despair, finally appointed a cabinet under Cardinal Soglia, in which the sole member of note was Pellegrino Rossi, one of the truly significant personalities of the period. Rossi, an Italian by birth, had spent his mature years in France, where he enjoyed an enviable reputation as an economist of the liberal school.

[19] On the economic crisis in the Papal States, see Domenico Demarco: *Pio IX e la rivoluzione romana de 1848* (Modena, 1947), 92 ff., 105 ff., 122 ff.; also Quazza: *La lotta soziale*, 214 ff.

[20] Demarco: *Pio IX*, 77 ff. R. M. Johnston: *The Roman Theocracy and the Republic, 1846–1849* (New York, 1901), chap. x. See further, Guillaume Mollat: *La question romaine de Pie IX à Pie XI* (Paris, 1932), 225 ff.; Berkeley and Berkeley: *Italy in the Making*, III, 337 ff.; Candeloro: *Storia dell'Italia moderna*, III, 311 ff.

His friend Guizot sent him to Rome as French minister in 1846 and there he had quickly become one of the pope's chief advisers in matters of reform. Though disillusioned about constitutional government, Pius in the summer of 1848 seems to have still hoped that Rossi could make the system work and so save the country from chaos.

Rossi was convinced that war against Austria without foreign support would be sheer folly. For the pope to take part in it would mean working for the king of Piedmont when the Papal States required above all the restoration of order and reform of the administration. Like other liberals, Rossi held that good government was more important than popular government. He devoted himself, therefore, to realistic improvements: restoration of discipline in the army, modernization of the judicial system, increase of government income through taxation of church property, exploitation of the salt deposits, encouragement of trade through abolition of restrictions, and improvement of communications through railroads and telegraphs. Naturally he incurred the enmity of those who suffered from reforms. Unfortunately he made matters worse by the shortcomings of his own personality. A man of complete self-assurance and courage, he was cold and humorless in his dealings with others, contemptuous of opposition and disdainful of public opinion. His arrogance, sarcasm and offensive manners went a long way toward nullifying his great abilities.[21]

Rossi's cold and calculating attitude with regard to the war against the foreigner naturally made him anathema to all good patriots, whether moderate or radical. It was hardly surprising that a group of returned volunteers should plan to assassinate him, which they did on November 15 by stabbing him in the neck as he was ascending the staircase of the Parliament. This tragic event marked the end of the pope's effort to keep a middle course between the reactionary, clerical elements and the radical, nationalist forces. Of course, Pius had long since ceased to be the great hope of the patriots, since he had publicly refused to sacrifice the interests of the church to the cause of Italian unity. He was now in acute danger of being stripped of his worldly power as sovereign of the Papal States.

On the very day following Rossi's assassination, huge crowds

---

[21] Fundamental is Carlo A. Biggini: *Il pensiero politico di Pellegrino Rossi* (Rome, 1937), which deals almost exclusively with the years 1846–1848, but see also Laszlo Ledermann: *Pellegrino Rossi, l'homme et l'économiste* (Paris, 1929), and Tarquinio Armani: "Pellegrino Rossi, ministro federalista e costitutionalista" (*Nuova antologia*, CCCIV, July 1, 1939, 79–95).

gathered about the Quirinal Palace demanding the appointment of a democratic cabinet and a declaration of war against Austria. When the Civic Guard and even units of the armed forces began to fraternize with the populace, His Holiness recognized the hopelessness of his situation. As the mob began to invade the palace and threaten the Swiss palace guards with annihilation, Pius, under protest and in the presence of foreign diplomats, agreed to appoint a cabinet including the radical leaders Sterbini and Galletti. The new government was committed to declare war and call a popularly elected constituent assembly. Since Rome was now in the hands of the revolutionary elements, the pope on November 24 left the city in disguise. With the help of foreign diplomats he was able to reach Neapolitan territory and take refuge in the castle at Gaeta.[22]

Pius now appealed to the European governments to restore his temporal power. At the same time he embarked upon an acrid debate with the government in Rome. Arguing that it had been forced upon him, he now refused to recognize it and appointed a commission of three, under Cardinal Castracane, to take over the administration. The cabinet, while rejecting this attempt to supersede it, sent a deputation to Gaeta begging the pope to return to the capital. Pius, now completely under the influence of Cardinal Antonelli, declined even to receive this delegation, whereupon the cabinet took a further step in setting up a Council of State, an act which Pius again declared illegal and void. The situation was thus completely deadlocked.

Nonetheless, the Rome cabinet proceeded to convoke a constituent assembly for the Papal States, which was to be elected on January 21, 1849, by universal suffrage. Once more Pius tried to intervene. He denounced the projected election as "a monstrous act of unconcealed treason and open rebellion," and excommunicated those responsible for it. Nevertheless, the election took place and returned a democratic majority, chiefly because of the fact that the conservative and moderate elements abstained from voting. Even in Rome itself it is said that only 23,000 out of a possible 60,000 exercised the franchise.[23]

This stirring chapter of Roman history came to a close with the meeting of the constituent assembly on February 5. After a few days of

[22] Berkeley and Berkeley: *Italy in the Making*, III, 411 ff., quotes the accounts of several ambassadors who were eyewitnesses of the events of November 16 and the flight of the pope.

[23] E. E. Y. Hales: *Pio Nono* (London, 1954), 97; Charles Pouthas: *Le pontificat de Pie IX* (Paris, 1962), 47 ff.

debate it declared the temporal power of the popes at an end and proclaimed the Papal States to be thenceforth the Roman Republic (February 9). The vote on this crucial matter was 120 to 10 (with 12 abstentions), but this should not be taken to indicate an overwhelmingly strong republican movement. There was, for the time being, no acceptable alternative. The flight of the pope, like the defection of the princes, had transformed the democratic movement in central Italy into a republican movement and had so paved the way for the victory of Mazzinian principles.

3. ROME: THE ORDEAL OF A REPUBLIC

The European powers, even the Protestant ones, believed that the pope must be restored to his temporal power if he was to have the independence necessary for discharge of his spiritual functions. The problem was simply how the restoration could be accomplished. In France, "the eldest daughter of the Church," the question had from the beginning marked political overtones. Cavaignac, evidently in the hope of securing the support of the Catholic party in the elections of December 10, had (November 26) ordered 3,500 troops to be concentrated at Marseilles preparatory to embarkation for Civitavecchia, the seaport of Rome. At the same time he had dispatched Count François de Corcelle to Gaeta to offer the pope asylum in France. The arrival of His Holiness on French soil would no doubt have been a feather in Cavaignac's cap. Perhaps for that very reason Pius declined the offer, whereupon the French expedition to Civitavecchia was suspended.[24]

On December 4 the pope, despairing of bringing his rebellious subjects to submit, appealed to the powers for armed intervention to restore him to his states. The Spanish government proposed (December 21) a congress of the Catholic powers, but the Piedmontese government, ever fearful of foreign interference in Italian affairs, countered by insisting that the matter be left to the Italians. Gioberti made every effort to effect a reconciliation between the pope and the Roman authorities and was prepared to send troops south into Tuscany and the Papal States to "restore order." But the papal court, as ever suspicious of Piedmontese designs, declined the advances of Turin.

[24] Ross W. Collins: *Catholicism and the Second French Republic* (New York, 1923), 153 ff.; Guillaume Mollat: *La question romaine de Pie IX à Pie XI* (Paris, 1932), 243 ff.; Guido Quazza: *La questione romana nel 1848–1849* (Modena, 1947), 43 ff.

On February 18, 1849, Pius appealed officially to the Catholic powers (omitting Piedmont) and Gioberti was obliged to resign as Piedmontese prime minister, in favor of Rattazzi.[25]

The Austrian government was at this time still seriously hampered by the threat of renewal of the war by Piedmont and, what was perhaps even more grave, by the major operations against Hungary. France, then, was free to make its decision. Communications being still very poor, several weeks were lost in the mission of various agents and the dispatch of countless messages. During this span of time the Roman Republic had a chance to organize. Mazzini, who arrived on March 5, has generally been credited with having made the short-lived Roman Republic a unique example of a democracy devoted to "God and the People," high-minded and moral to an unprecedented degree. It should be noted, however, that prior to his arrival the government had already introduced many drastic reforms: the nationalization of church properties, the abolition of clerical control over the university, the suppression of the Inquisition, and the abolition of the censorship. It had also made concrete efforts to relieve the sufferings of the poor: church buildings were turned into cheap housing, church lands were being divided and assigned to peasant ownership, the salt and tobacco monopolies were being reformed. Considering the brevity of its existence, this was a not insignificant achievement.[26]

Mazzini approved of all these measures wholeheartedly, but his own contribution was rather on the intellectual and moral plane. On the day after his arrival he expounded to the Roman assembly his doctrine of a Third Rome, the symbol of a new and higher humanity.[27] In concrete terms, he aimed at the union of Tuscany with Rome and the convocation of an Italian constituent assembly to establish an Italian Republic and prepare for resumption of the crusade to drive out the foreigner. He had spent some weeks in Florence prior to coming to

[25] Luis Garcia Rives: *La Repubblica Romana de 1849* (Madrid, 1932); Quazza: *La lotta soziale,* chap. vi an.' 139 ff.; Candeloro: *Storia dell'Italia moderna,* III, 387 ff.

[26] Still worth reading is R. M. Johnston's *The Roman Theocracy and the Republic* (New York, 1901), 240 ff. The best recent study is Luigi Rodelli: *La Repubblica Romana del 1849* (Pisa, 1955), 161 ff. Important also are Domenico Demarco: *Una rivoluzione sociale: la Repubblica Romana del 1849* (Naples, 1944); Georges Bourgin: "L"oeuvre sociale de la République Romaine de 1849" (*Actes du Congrès du Centenaire de la Révolution de 1848,* Paris, 1948, 149–156); Fausto Fonzi: "La Repubblica" (in *La mostra storica della Repubblica Romana,* Rome, 1949, 31–34).

[27] See above, Chapter VIII.

Rome and had tried to persuade Guerrazzi to adopt his program. But the latter had evaded a definite commitment, partly no doubt from fear of provoking intervention by either Piedmont or Austria, but perhaps also from reluctance to merge Tuscany with the radical Roman Republic. Particularism was as strong a force in Italy as in Germany.[28]

The prospect of a united central Italy and a republican war against Austria decided the Piedmontese government to take the plunge which it had been contemplating for several months. It denounced the Salasco armistice (March 12) and prepared for hostilities. The French minister at Turin, who, like his British colleague, had done his utmost to dissuade the Piedmontese from resumption of the war, regarded the decision as "heroic folly." The Piedmontese army was still not completely ready and could not put into the field a force larger than that of a year before. The king had been induced to name as chief of staff and *de facto* commander the Polish general, Joseph Chrzanowski, who, though a competent soldier, had arrived in Italy only six months earlier and had only an imperfect command of the language. Chrzanowski, pessimistic by nature, was hardly edified to note that neither the king, nor the politicians, nor the generals had much hope of success. They were embarking on the war for reasons of prestige and to anticipate action by the republicans of central Italy. By taking the initiative they trusted that other states would come to their support.[29]

Chrzanowski favored a cautious strategy, avoiding a major engagement for the time being. But the king and his advisers, thinking the Austrians far weaker than they were, insisted that a vigorous offensive would oblige Radetzky to fall back and make possible the Piedmontese reoccupation of Milan. Radetzky, for his part, had long anticipated denunciation of the armistice and had done everything possible to encourage the mistaken notions of his opponents. "Give me the opportunity," he wrote to Schwarzenberg on March 7, "and you shall soon see me lay the whole of Italy up to the frontier of the noble king of Naples at the feet of His Majesty the Emperor."[30] In an order of the

[28] Gwilyn O. Griffith: *Mazzini* (New York, 1932), 205 ff.; Fausto Fonzi: "Mazzini" (in *La mostra storica*, 55–59); Giorgio Falco: *Giuseppe Mazzini e la Costituente* (Florence, 1946); Ivanoe Bonomi: *Mazzini, triumviro della Repubblica Romana* (3 ed., Milan, 1946), chap. iii; Candeloro: *Storia dell'Italia moderna*, III, 382 ff., 429 ff.

[29] César Vidal: "La Deuxième République et le royaume de Sardaigne en 1848" (*Rassegna storica del Risorgimento*, XXXVII, 1950, 505–530); Piero Pieri: *Storia militare del Risorgimento* (Turin, 1962), chap. ix.

[30] A. J. P. Taylor: *The Italian Problem in European Diplomacy* (Manchester, 1934), 213 ff.

day following the resumption of hostilities, he cheered his troops on to the advance on Turin. They responded with enthusiastic demonstrations and ovations.[31]

The Piedmontese advance across the Ticino was given short shrift. Radetzky had deployed his forces from Milan to Pavia. On March 20 the Austrian forces, like the Piedmontese, crossed the boundary river, but Radetzky's army turned northward to take the enemy on the right flank. The Piedmontese hastily recrossed the river and fell back on Novara, to which Radetzky, expecting to meet the enemy at Mortara, had dispatched only one army corps, under General D'Aspre. The latter, discovering on March 23 that he had the entire Piedmontese army before him, called for support, which was promptly dispatched to him. For several hours D'Aspre was badly outnumbered, but Chrzanowski failed to take advantage of his opportunity. By four in the afternoon the whole Austrian army was on the scene and by early evening the Battle of Novara was over. The Piedmontese were completely defeated. Charles Albert, still nominally in command, abdicated his throne on the field of battle, and his successor, Victor Emmanuel II, promptly sent an emissary to Radetzky with the request for an armistice.

Radetzky was well impressed with the new ruler when he met him in conference on March 26. Victor Emmanuel was known to have disapproved of the war and now declared that he was determined to re-establish royal authority by curbing the pretensions of his democratic Parliament. Radetzky therefore decided to give him a chance. He eschewed an advance on Turin, in part certainly to avoid provoking French intervention. Furthermore, he asked for no cession of Piedmontese territory, but only for occupation of the frontier fortress of Alessandria pending the payment of a formidable indemnity. After some months of quibbling over details, the terms of the armistice were enshrined in the peace treaty of Milan (August 6).[32]

[31] Oskar Freiherr von Wolf-Schneider: *Der Feldherr Radetzky* (Vienna, 1934), 86 ff.; Viktor Bibl: *Radetzky, Soldat und Feldherr* (Vienna, 1955), 304 ff.; Oskar Regele: *Feldmarschall Radetzky* (Vienna, 1957), 287 ff.

[32] The patriotic legend that Radetzky offered Victor Emmanuel easy terms on condition that he agree to "modify" the Piedmontese constitution and that the young king nobly rejected the offer was exploded by Howard M. Smyth: "The Armistice of Novara: a Legend of a Liberal King" (*Journal of Modern History*, VII, 1935, 141–152). Smyth's conclusions have been accepted by authoritative Italian historians such as Angelo Filipuzzi: *La pace di Milano* (Rome, 1955), ii ff.; Candeloro: *Storia dell'Italia moderna*, III, 405 ff.

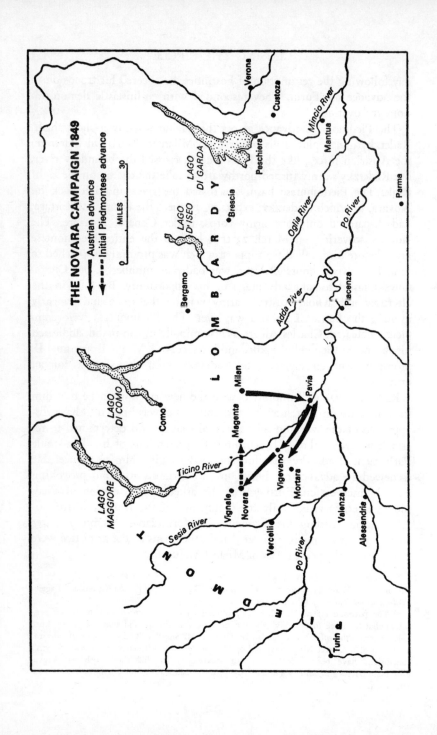

Novara was not, in military terms, a major engagement. It lasted only a few hours and the casualties were extremely modest. But it was decisive in the sense that it brought to an abrupt end Piedmontese aspirations to expel the Austrians from Italy and annex Lombardy and Venetia to form a North Italian kingdom. It left the Austrians free to occupy all central Italy and restore the fugitive princes. Schwarzenberg bemoaned the fact that Radetzky had not gone on to Turin and there imposed on the Piedmontese an indemnity so heavy that the kingdom could barely survive. But the genius of the aged field marshal was political as well as military. He argued that a Carthaginian peace would have generated ever greater animosity, that a huge indemnity would in any case prove uncollectible, that it would only discredit the Piedmontese monarchy and that it might well entail conflict with France. If Piedmont could be kept quiet by easy terms, the Austrians could not only carry through their intervention in central Italy but could redeploy their forces to the Hungarian front.[33]

For France, too, Novara was decisive, in the sense that the government must now intervene in Italy or abandon the affairs of the peninsula to the Austrians. Louis Napoleon, who valued the support of the church in his campaign to restore order in France, was under heavy pressure from the influential minister of public instruction, Count Frédéric de Falloux, and other Catholic notables who clamored for military action on behalf of the pope. The president yielded to the extent of being ready to send an army across the Alps to save the Piedmontese from the wages of their "heroic folly," but was dissuaded by Thiers, who urged negotiations instead. In any case, the leniency of Radetzky's terms obviated the need for French action to save the Piedmontese from occupation.[34]

There remained the threat of Austrian action in central Italy and especially in the Papal States. It was well known in Paris that Naples and Spain as well as Austria were about to intervene against the Roman Republic, which was regarded throughout Europe, even by some liberals, as a den of thieves and ruffians, imposed on the inhabitants by a group of dangerous radicals. The French thought it impera-

[33] Bibl: *Radetzky*, 313; Filipuzzi: *La pace di Milano*, 11 ff.

[34] F. A. Simpson: *Louis Napoleon and the Recovery of France* (3 ed., London, 1951), 61 ff.; César Vidal: "La Deuxième République et le Royaume de Sardaigne en 1849" (*Rassegna storica del Risorgimento*, XXXVII, 1950, 505–530).

tive to forestall Austrian domination of central Italy and ensure that the pope, when restored to his capital, would not revert to the old regime, but would maintain and develop the lay institutions introduced in the spring of 1848. It was believed in Paris that the Romans would greatly prefer French to Austrian intervention. The radicals in Parliament, to be sure, protested against coercion of a sister republic and raised the awkward question what was to be done in the event of resistance. But theirs were voices crying in the wilderness.[35]

On April 16 the French assembly, by a huge majority, voted credits for an expedition to Rome and on April 24 a force of 10,000 men landed at Civitavecchia, thirty-five miles from the city. Since there was no resistance, the commander, General Nicolas Oudinot, set out for Rome "full of vain anticipation of a glorious reception and a gratuitous banquet," to quote the report of a British agent.[36] He had at least some justification for his confidence, for the Roman army, while it had secured some munitions abroad, was still far from ready for combat. Conditions in the city were bad and morale low.[37] Only the extremists had faith in the survival of the republic, reported a German consul. Most people, he continued, wished they were a thousand miles away and even some of the leaders were talking of the need for compromise. But Mazzini, who on March 29 had become a member of the directing triumvirate, opposed all accommodation and rallied the non-Roman Italians (exiles and volunteers, who flocked to Rome in great numbers) to organize resistance. He probably realized that the city could not long hold out, but he had an insuperable aversion to French pretensions and in any case felt that the Romans must act as "men working for eternity." The Third Rome, if it had to go under, should meet its doom in a blaze of heroism.[38]

[35] Collins: Catholicism and the Second French Republic, 217 ff.; Emile Bourgeois and Emile Clermont: Rome et Napoléon III (Paris, 1907), 13; Ruggero Moscati: La diplomazia europea e il problema italiano nel 1848 (Florence, 1947), 80 ff.; Franco Valsecchi: "Luigi Bonaparte e gli intenti della sua politica d'intervento a Roma nel 1849" (Rassegna storica del Risorgimento, XXXVII, 1950, 500–504). George M. Trevelyan: Garibaldi's Defence of the Roman Republic (new ed., London, 1908), 101, 109, comments on British hostility to the Roman Republic.

[36] Collins: Catholicism and the Second French Republic, 228 ff.

[37] For details, see the excellent analysis in Luigi Mondini: "L'aspetto militare della difesa di Roma nel 1849" (in Giuseppe Mazzini e la Repubblica Romana, Rome, 1949, 37–62).

[38] The reports of the Württemberg consul, Kolb, are of great interest. They were published by Moscati: La diplomazia europea, 138 ff. For Mazzini's position, see also Alberto M. Ghisalberti: Roma da Mazzini a Pio IX (Milan, 1958), chap. ii.

Mazzini's position was reinforced by the arrival, on April 27, of 1,200 Garibaldian legionnaires and 600 Lombard volunteers under Colonel Luciano Manara. Garibaldi had been in Rome since February, but had left his followers at Rieti. Like the Lombards, they were hard-bitten fighters. On Oudinot's approaching the San Pancrazio Gate on April 30, he was suddenly attacked on the flank by the Garibaldians and forced to retreat. Garibaldi was all for pursuing him, but Mazzini vetoed such action on the theory that it would be a mistake to

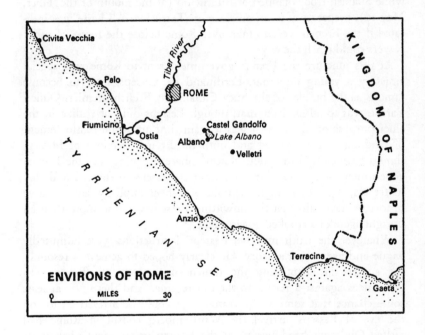

antagonize the French government before seeking a peaceful solution.[39]

The effect of Oudinot's unexpected reverse was to harden French policy. The president wrote at once to the commander: "Our soldiers

[39] The classic account of the military operations is Trevelyan's book, already cited, but this should now be supplemented with Vittorio E. Giuntella: "La difesa della Repubblica" (in *La mostra storica della Repubblica Romana,* 73–77); Pieri: *Storia militare del Risorgimento,* chap. xii; and recent biographies of Mazzini such as Arturo Codignola: *Mazzini* (Turin, 1946), chap. vi, and Garibaldi, such as Denis Mack Smith: *Garibaldi* (New York, 1956), and Christopher Hibbert: *Garibaldi and His Enemies* (Boston, 1966).

have been received as enemies; our military honor is involved. I shall not suffer it to be stained. You will not lack reinforcements." Additional men and munitions were rushed to Oudinot. There was indeed no time to lose, for Austrians, Neapolitans and Spaniards were all poised for action. Early in May the Austrians invaded Tuscany and occupied Pisa and Lucca (May 6), then Livorno (May 11) and, after fierce resistance, Bologna (May 16) and Florence (May 25). Concurrently Neapolitan forces advanced to Albano and Velletri (May 8), while Spanish troops landed at Fiumicino (at the mouth of the Tiber, May 17), preparatory to an advance on Terracina. All haste was indicated if the French were to take over Rome before the forces of other powers could reach the city.

At this juncture the French government sent to Rome as a special emissary a young diplomat, Ferdinand de Lesseps, later to become famous as the builder of the Suez Canal. The French premier, Odilon Barrot, was to admit later that, though Lesseps did not realize it, the chief purpose of his mission was to gain time until the reinforcement of Oudinot was completed and until the French elections of May 19 should have cleared the political atmosphere. Arguing that the French government neither expected nor desired Lesseps to succeed and that its treatment of the Roman Republic was sheer duplicity, authoritative historians have said that the unwitting Lesseps was "no more than an upright agent of a crooked government."[40]

Whatever the truth may be, Lesseps' instructions were admittedly vague and even contradictory. He clearly hoped to achieve a resounding success in negotiating the return of the pope to Rome with guarantees against a return to the old regime. And there was at least some chance that some such arrangement could be arrived at, for on the eve of Lesseps' arrival the Württemberg consul in Rome had visited Oudinot's headquarters at the Roman government's behest, to inquire what the terms of the French might be.[41] However, there is no doubt that Lesseps was overeager and precipitate. He exceeded his in-

[40] The standard and by no means friendly account is that of Bourgeois and Clermont, noted above, and the preface by Gabriel Monod. See further Trevelyan: *Garibaldi's Defence of the Roman Empire*, 145 ff.; Griffith: *Mazzini*, 224; and, most recently, G. Edgar-Bonnet: *Ferdinand de Lesseps, le diplomate, le créateur de Suez* (Paris, 1951), 80 ff.

[41] Moscati: *La diplomazia europea*, 154; Mollat: *La question romaine*, 260 ff.; Simpson: *Louis Napoleon*, 70 ff.

structions and outraged the French military men by arranging a suspension of hostilities so as to give Garibaldi time to drive back the Neapolitans from Albano (May 18) and threaten the invasion of the kingdom. Then Lesseps proposed to the Roman government that it request French protection and admit French troops to aid in defense of the city against possible attack by Austria. The city was to be left free, however, to decide its own form of government. Mazzini rejected this offer, evidently in the fantastic hope that the French election would prove a victory for the radicals and that presently the French would come to the help of a sister republic. Only in response to an ultimatum did the Roman government agree (May 31) that the French might occupy cantonments outside the city walls, in return for a promise of aid in repelling an eventual attacker. Oudinot flatly refused to sign this agreement and the French government, on learning of it, not only refused to sign it but recalled Lesseps, who, so rumor had it, had gone plumb mad.

Oudinot was now ordered to attack the city. He had by now some 30,000 men and ample artillery, including thirty siege guns. The defenders, sadly deficient in equipment, could muster hardly half the number of Oudinot's troops. Their army was a miscellaneous force, consisting of former papal troops, Roman Civic Guards, volunteers, students, conscripts, and, of course, many patriots from the north.[42] They were commanded by a competent professional soldier, General Pietro Roselli, for whom, understandably, Garibaldi was a veritable thorn in the flesh. But the latter certainly gave moral courage and dash to the defense. Incapable of commanding large units and often reckless in handling even small ones, he did have a quick sense for tactical situations and the nerve to make decisions. Thus, when Oudinot on June 3 unexpectedly attacked and occupied the villas commanding the approaches to the San Pancrazio Gate, Garibaldi speedily organized resistance and staged one counterattack after another to defeat the French assault.

For the better part of a month the French bombarded the city while constructing approach trenches preparatory to an attack on the walls. The outlook for the defenders became ever more desperate and there

---

[42] Alberto M. Ghisalberti: "Popolo e politica nell' 49 romano" (in *Giuseppe Mazzini e la Repubblica Romana,* 79–102) disputes the charge that the Romans themselves were apathetic and made but a minor contribution.

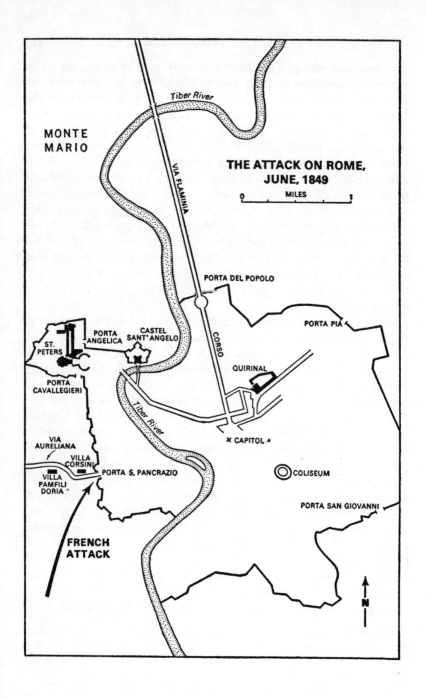

MONTE
MARIO

Tiber River

**THE ATTACK ON ROME,
JUNE, 1849**

0   MILES   1

VIA FLAMINIA

PORTA DEL POPOLO

PORTA PIA

PORTA
ANGELICA

CASTEL
SANT' ANGELO

ST.
PETERS

CORSO

QUIRINAL

PORTA
CAVALLEGIERI

Tiber River

× CAPITOL

VIA
AURELIANA

VILLA
CORSINI

PORTA S. PANCRAZIO

VILLA
PAMFILI
DORIA

COLISEUM

PORTA SAN GIOVANNI

**FRENCH
ATTACK**

N

was much popular pressure for surrender. Garibaldi recommended that the army abandon the city and conduct a war of harassment in the open country. But Mazzini, of whom it has been well said that he was less interested in getting the best peace terms than in putting up the best possible battle, was for fighting to the last ditch and then going down in a never-to-be-forgotten blaze of glory. When the assembly voted against such romantic heroism (June 30), Mazzini and his colleagues resigned. Garibaldi, with several thousand men, then left the city (July 2) and tried to make his way north to join in the defense of Venice. Harassed by Austrian forces, many of his party were captured and executed. Others simply disappeared and Garibaldi himself barely succeeded, after a dramatic flight, in reaching the Tuscan coast and escaping by sea. Mazzini remained undisturbed in Rome for some days before he, too, took refuge on a ship at Civitavecchia.

The French troops occupied the city on July 3, after which the Roman assembly was dissolved, the clubs closed down, the population disarmed and the press subjected to censorship. Presently a commission of three cardinals arrived from Gaeta to prepare for the restoration. Oudinot, an innocent in politics, turned over the administration to them, with the result that before long the institutions of the past were re-established. The French were shocked by the prospect of a return to the benighted rule of the priesthood. They made desperate attempts to salvage the liberal institutions, but in vain, for the pope had the support of Austria and other Catholic powers, and even of Russia and Prussia. When French pressure became too irksome, Cardinal Antonelli, the soul of reaction, would threaten the removal of the papal Curia to Austrian-occupied territory. Meanwhile the pope deferred his return from Gaeta until the restoration was substantially completed (April 12, 1850). Thus the French, by their intervention, prepared the ground for the reaction which, in the premises, it had been their objective to forestall.[43]

"In the few hundred meters between the bastions of the Porta San Pancrazio and the Villa Corsini," says an Italian historian, "the Revolution of 1848 was really brought to its close."[44] The Austrians

---

[43] Bourgeois and Clermont: *Rome et Napoléon III*, 192 ff.; Mollat: *La question romaine*, 269 ff.; Roger Aubert: *Le pontificat de Pie IX* (Paris, 1952), 36 ff.; Hales: *Pio Nono*, 149 ff.; and the interesting article by Charles H. Pouthas: "Un observateur de Tocqueville pendant les premiers mois de l'occupation française" (*Rassegna storica del Risorgimento*, XXXVII, 1950, 417–430).

[44] Giuntella: "La difesa della Repubblica."

had all but completed the work of restoration by the time of Rome's capitulation. On July 28 the Grand Duke Leopold had resumed his Tuscan throne. Long before that the Sicilian revolution had met its doom. The British and French had exerted themselves to arrive at a compromise settlement which would have given the island complete autonomy, with a connection with Naples only through a common ruler. Ferdinand, however, had balked at the notion of an independent Sicilian army and eventually ordered his troops to attack (March 29, 1849). Catania fell to the Neapolitans on April 6, after which operations were extended to the west coast. Palermo was obliged to capitulate after the arrival of the Neapolitan fleet (April 27). The populace then rose in revolt, but this could be little more than a gesture of despair. After some severe barricade fighting, the insurrection was suppressed (mid-May) and the island, which a year before had attained *de facto* independence, was once again under Bourbon domination.[45]

There remained only the Venetian Republic, for the other Adriatic seaport, Ancona, had fallen to the Austrians on June 19 after a month of siege and blockade. The Republic of St. Mark, cut off from the mainland and blockaded by the Austrian fleet, had played only a peripheral role in the developments of the period following Custoza. Daniele Manin, the very soul of caution and moderation, had been given dictatorical powers, under which he repudiated the act of fusion with Piedmont, on the plea that the omission of Venice from the provisions of the Salasco armistice had annulled all previous agreements. He appealed to the British and French for support, but received from them little more than the good advice to make the best terms he could with the Austrians. It was obvious to all that Venice's doom would be sealed as soon as the Austrians had disposed of the Piedmontese and the radicals of central Italy.

The day of reckoning approached on the morrow of the Battle of Novara. Yet the Venetian assembly, when called upon by the Austrians to submit, voted to resist. On May 4 the Austrians began to bombard the Venetian fortifications. By July the city, now tightly blockaded, was running out of food and suffering severely from epidemics of cholera and typhus. Finally, on August 22, almost two months after the fall of

[45] For an excellent, succinct account, see Federico Curato: *La rivoluzione siciliana del 1848-1849* (Milan, 1940), 207 ff. For the military operations, see Pieri: *Storia militare del Risorgimento,* chap. xiii.

Rome and ten days after the capitulation of the Hungarians at Világos, the city was obliged to surrender. Manin and other leaders were permitted to leave.[46]

The radical phase of the Italian revolution proved just as abortive as the moderate, liberal phase which preceded it. Born of the disillusionment and discouragement following the Custoza disaster, the radical movement was an affair of the lower classes, tradesmen, artisans, journeymen, of the cities, the very people who in March had mounted the barricades but had then left the conduct of the revolution and the war of independence to the upper, educated classes. But the lower classes were no better educated, no better organized in the summer and autumn than they had been in the spring. The radical leaders who now emerged, the men such as Guerrazzi, Montanelli and Galletti, were democrats and republicans, but chiefly in theory. They were themselves disturbed by the prospect of mob rule, and in any case had no thought of serious social revolution. Not even Mazzini, for all his concern for the common man, would have anything to do with socialism or attacks on private property. These men, once they were in power, were almost as intent as their predecessors on the restoration and maintenance of order.

This being so, the debate provoked by Marxist politicians and historians seems rather bootless. They argue that the radicals had only themselves to blame for their failure, because they should have faced up to the need to liquidate the feudal regime and should have roused the peasantry to share in the struggle. To this one can only reply that the radical like the moderate leaders positively dreaded a social upheaval and had not the slightest intention of encouraging the ignorant peasantry to revolt; that, furthermore, many of them, like Mazzini, knew, very little about the peasantry and its problems and sufferings, for they were city-bred intellectuals; and lastly, that the peasantry was so backward and unorganized that it could hardly have been an effective partner.[47]

[46] For a vivid account, see George M. Trevelyan: *Manin and the Venetian Republic of 1848* (New York, 1923); and for a more sober treatment, Pieri: *Storia militare del Risorgimento,* chap. xi.

[47] This debate was given impetus by the Communist leader A. Gramsci: *Il Risorgimento* (3 ed., Turin, 1950) and continued by Palmiro Togliatti: "Le classi popolari nel Risorgimento" (*Studi storici,* III, 1964). On the "bourgeois" side, see Antonio Monti: "Guerra regia e guerra di popolo nel Risorgimento" (in Ettore Rota, ed.: *Questioni di*

In the last analysis it was not so much the shortcomings of the revolutionary regimes as the brutal fact of military power that proved decisive. Radetzky had both the military and political insight to bide his time and take every advantage of the complicated Italian situation. He pressed the Italians as fast and as far as he dared without provoking the intervention of the French and, whether wittingly or not, left it to the French Republic to liquidate the Roman Republic and pave the way for the restoration of clerical rule in the Papal States.

4. FRANCE: THE CONSTITUTIONAL DEADLOCK

Louis Napoleon as president of the French Republic was the choice of the nation, not of the Assembly elected in the previous April. The Assembly had good reason to question the sincerity of the new president's devotion to the Republic, but could do nothing about it, for the recently enacted constitution, that "newfangled bundle of bad laws," made it as impossible for the Assembly to remove the president as for the president to dissolve or even prorogue the Assembly. Not only that: it was all but impossible, too, to revise the constitution. For the first two of the three years of its term the Assembly was forbidden even to entertain motions for revision, and after the two years a motion required for its adoption a two-thirds vote in three consecutive sessions, each a month apart. It would have been literally unthinkable to trammel political action more completely.[48]

At first Louis Napoleon did not appear as a formidable opponent. He allowed Thiers to all but name the members of the new cabinet under the Orleanist Odilon Barrot, and the cabinet in turn worked closely with the conservative elements in the Assembly without much reference to the views or desires of the chief executive.[49] The details of French political life must be omitted in a summary account like the present. The first important landmark of the period was the election of May 13, 1849, held after the Assembly, which had completed its task of

---

storia del Risorgimento, Milan, 1951, 183–216); and Rosario Romeo: Risorgimento e capitalismo (Bari, 1959). For recent critical reviews, see John W. Cammett: "Two Recent Polemics on the Character of the Italian Risorgimento" (Science and Society, XXVII, 1963, 433–457); Franco Valsecchi: "Le classi popolari e il Risorgimento" (Cultura e scuola, No. 15, 1965, 82–93).

[48] F. A. Simpson: Louis Napoleon and the Recovery of France (3 ed., London, 1951) is still one of the best treatments of this period.

[49] Paul Bastid: Doctrines et institutions politiques de la Seconde République (Paris, 1945), II, 162.

providing a constitution, had reluctantly agreed to dissolve. The monarchical groups—Legitimists, Orleanists, Bonapartists—managed to pull together in a "coalition of fear" directed against radicalism and socialism. On the other hand, the radical or democratic elements had also come together in a "new Mountain," with a program of mildly socialist reforms. The moderate republicans, on the other hand, failed to take advantage of their position. Léon Faucher, the minister of the interior, took his liberalism so seriously that he refused to bring administrative pressure to bear on behalf of his associates.[50] The result was that the monarchists won almost 500 seats out of 750 in the new Assembly, and the leftists some 200. The moderate republicans, who had dominated the previous Assembly, came off with only 80 seats in the new one. The shift toward conservatism was generally expected, but the radical victory was both surprising and alarming. It rested, of course, on the urban populations, where the radicals were fairly well organized. Paris gave them 106,100 votes as against 106,300 for the Party of Order and only 42,300 for the moderate republicans. Ledru-Rollin, who in the presidential election had polled only 370,000 votes, was now elected in no less than five *départements,* with a total vote of 2,000,000. Taking the country at large, the monarchists polled 3,310,000 votes, the "new Mountain" 1,955,000, and the moderate republicans 834,000.[51]

The radicals were so elated by their gains that they presently overreached themselves. In the Assembly the question of French intervention on behalf of the pope was being hotly debated when on June 11 Ledru-Rollin moved the impeachment of the president and the members of the cabinet for violation of Article V of the constitution, which forbade the use of French armed forces against the liberty of any other people. He and his party, declared Ledru-Rollin, would defend the constitution "if necessary by arms." On defeat of his motion, he and the deputies of the Mountain left the assembly and on June 13 attempted to stage an insurrection. They seized the Conservatoire des Arts et Métiers, in the crowded workers' section of Paris, and called on the people to throw up barricades.

The rising proved, however, to be a fiasco. Karl Marx was to ridicule

[50] Theodore Zeldin: "Government Policy in the French General Election of 1849" (*English Historical Review,* LXXIV, 1959, 240–248).

[51] Simpson: *Louis Napoleon,* 37 ff.; Bastid: *Doctrines et institutions politiques,* II, 204 ff. On the recovery of radicalism, see Georges Duveau: *La vie ouvrière en France sous le Second Empire* (Paris, 1946), 57 ff.; and the Communist analysis of N. Zastenker: "La 'Montagne' en 1849" (*Questions d'histoire,* No. 2, 1954, 101–138).

the exaggerated hopes of the Mountain and to compare its noisy claims to the Biblical trumpets of Jericho: "Whenever they stand before the ramparts of despotism, they seek to imitate the miracle."[52] In his opinion recollections of the June Days and distrust of the radical leadership explained the failure of the Paris populace to rise in support of the men they had just elected to the chamber. A further factor no doubt was the severe cholera epidemic which was claiming 600–700 victims daily. People had other things than revolution to think about. Besides, they had been disarmed and were under martial law, that is, state of siege, which was at once proclaimed by the government. General Changarnier easily dispersed the demonstrators, while Ledru-Rollin and his colleagues escaped from the Conservatoire by a back door or, as some would have it, through a skylight. The point has been well made that whereas in June, 1848, the insurrection had plenty of men but no leaders, in June, 1849, it had more than enough leaders but no men.[53]

There was a more serious uprising in Lyons, which cost some 200 lives but was also quickly suppressed. The upshot of these revolts was to provide the government with ample excuses for repression. Some thirty radical deputies were deprived of their seats, martial law was continued in both Paris and Lyons, units of the National Guard from the workers' sections were disbanded, clubs were suppressed and newspapers, though not abolished, were put under strict surveillance.

Louis Napoleon, meanwhile, set out on a tour of the provinces, including some that were known to be unfriendly. His reception was generally satisfactory, sufficiently so to warrant his dismissal of the Barrot cabinet and his appointment of one which, though undistinguished, could be counted on for loyalty. This assertion of control over the executive came as a disagreeable surprise to the majority in the Assembly, but the president carefully abstained from further challenges. It was not that he lacked an organized following, for he had nothing but contempt for party rule and aimed to stand above parties and to set up an efficient administration by nonpolitical experts who could overcome class antagonisms by building a modern, well-

[52] Karl Marx: The Eighteenth Brumaire of Louis Bonaparte (1852).

[53] Raoul de Félice: "La journée du 13 juin, 1849 à Paris" (La Révolution de 1848, VI, 1909–1910, 135–157, 242–252, 314–325); Alvin R. Calman: Ledru-Rollin and the Second French Republic (New York, 1922), chaps. xxiii and xxiv; Duveau: La vie ouvrière en France, 57 ff.

integrated, productive society.[54] He probably shared the concern of most people over the continued unrest and spread of radicalism and may well have been content to have the Assembly assume the onus of reactionary measures which he regarded as necessary and to which at the very least he assented. For another period of many months he continued to co-operate with the parliamentary majority.

The campaign against radicalism produced, in the spring of 1850, two important acts of Parliament: a new education law and a revised electoral law. In the field of education the Guizot Law of 1833 had marked an important advance, but the situation still left much to be desired. Fully 40 per cent of the French communes had by 1848 failed to open a primary school. Many of those that had opened schools used a barn or granary for the purpose. More than half of the primary-school teachers earned less than 300 francs a year and were obliged to supplement their salary by serving as bell ringer in the church or even as gravedigger.[55] The situation, in brief, was such that liberal, radical and socialist writers all clamored for a system of free, obligatory primary education, in socially integrated schools where the children could be given instruction in both natural and social sciences, to meet the requirements of the modern world.[56]

Following the February Revolution, the provisional government had therefore commissioned Hippolyte Carnot, the minister of instruction and a follower of Saint-Simon, to draft an appropriate bill. When completed, it provided for compulsory education to the age of fourteen, with instruction in civics, history, hygiene, music and other cultural subjects. Private organizations (even the Jesuits) were to have the right to conduct their own schools, but in the public schools religious instruction was to be imparted outside the school building. The salaries of teachers were to be raised to the 600–1,200-franc level. All told, the Carnot project was enlightened and forward-looking. But it was promptly stamped "socialistic" by his opponents and after the June Days Carnot was dismissed.

[54] Duveau: *La vie ouvrière en France,* 46, and various biographies that stress the modernity of Napoleon's views and objectives, such as Albert Guerard: *Napoleon III* (Cambridge, 1943); T. A. B. Corley: *Democratic Despot: a Life of Napoleon III* (London, 1961).
[55] George Bourgin: "La question scolaire en 1848 et la loi Falloux" (*Accademia dei Lincei: Atti dei Convegni,* X, 1949, 329–347).
[56] Georges Cogniot: *La question scolaire en 1848 et la loi Falloux* (Paris, 1948).

In the Barrot cabinet, appointed after the presidential election, Count Frédéric Falloux became minister of public instruction. He was an outstanding Legitimist, had been one of the chief advocates of suppression of the national workshops, and was to be an ardent proponent of intervention on behalf of the pope. As a devout Catholic, he was convinced that the most effective way to combat radicalism was to strengthen clerical influence in education, in line with the campaign for "liberty of instruction" long since being waged by Count Charles de Montalembert and other Catholic leaders, who wanted the right to establish church schools at the secondary as well as the primary level, and aimed to end all state regulation or supervision. Montalembert and his friends, who at first had welcomed the February Revolution, now joined the so-called Party of Order. So did many former anticlericals, such as Thiers, who, thoroughly frightened by the threat of social revolution, declared: "Today I regard religion and its ministers as the auxilliaries, the saviors, perhaps, of the social order."[57]

Falloux shelved the Carnot draft and appointed an extraparliamentary commission to re-examine the school problem. Thiers, who served as chairman, came out frankly against free, compulsory education and made no secret of his belief that radical teachers were at the root of much of France's troubles. "To read, to write, to count, that is what needs to be taught; all the rest is superfluous," he declared. Had he had his way, the entire primary-school system would have been turned over to the clergy. This was more than even Montalembert or Falloux desired. The new bill therefore provided for some measure of state control. It was laid before the Assembly in June, 1849, debated at length in various committees and finally adopted on March 15, 1850.

The "Falloux Law" has been called one of the major events in French political history in the nineteenth century, and has also been described, by a Marxist writer, as a law of fear and hate.[58] Its effect was to enhance greatly the influence of the church, for it authorized private organizations to maintain both primary and secondary schools. At the primary level the communes were authorized to entrust the school to the priest, and even to dispense with a public school if the

[57] Quoted by Ross W. Collins: *Catholicism and the Second French Republic* (New York, 1923), 271–272. See also Jean Leflon: *L'Eglise de France et la révolution de 1848* (Paris, 1948); R. Aubert: *Le pontificat de Pie IX* (Paris, 1952), 42 ff.

[58] René Rémond: *La droite en France* (2 ed., Paris, 1963); Cogniot: *La question scolaire,* chap. v.

church already provided one. Schooling was not made free or compulsory; religious instruction was made obligatory; state supervision was hardly more than administrative, for the entire educational system was to be under a Superior Council of Public Instruction, with lower departmental councils. On these councils the clergy (Protestant and Jewish as well as Catholic) was to be represented. The Assembly, in its struggle against radicalism, had now enlisted the support of the church. "Fear of the Jacobins outweighed fear of the Jesuits," says Pierre de La Gorce. The extreme wing of the Catholic party, it is true, denounced the law as a betrayal of the church's interests, inasmuch as it did not abolish state "interference," but even the extremists came to see what important gains the church had made.[59]

A few days before passage of the Falloux Law an election took place to fill the seats of the thirty radical deputies excluded in June, 1849. To the disagreeable surprise of political circles, twenty-one radicals were returned. Yet more ominous was the result of a Paris by-election on April 28, when the writer Eugène Sue carried the day against a prosperous merchant who had fought against the workers in the June Days. Sue, who had made millions from his writings, notably his *Mysteries of Paris,* was a confirmed socialist whose victory was hailed with jubilation by radicals of every stripe. Fear of possible revolution led the Assembly to appoint a commission, with well-known members such as Thiers, Molé and Montalembert, to draft additional provisions for the electoral law, which were enacted into law on May 31 by a vote of 433 to 241.

The new law was designed to reduce the electorate by excluding the workers and other undesirables, whom Thiers described publicly as "the vile multitude." Henceforth three-year residence in the canton, to be demonstrated by tax receipts or employers' affidavit, was required for the franchise. In effect this provision raised the voting age from twenty-one to twenty-four, since men were not enrolled on the tax lists until the age of twenty-one and could only vote if they had been on these lists for three years. The reduction in the electorate was drastic: about 30 per cent (from nine and a half million to six). The degree of disfranchisement varied from one region to another. In the *département* of the Rhone it was 40 per cent, in the Nord 51 per cent, in the

[59] Collins: *Catholicism and the Second French Republic,* 298 ff.; John K. Huckaby: "Roman Catholic Reaction to the Falloux Law" (*French Historical Studies,* IV, 1965, 320–321).

Seine 63 per cent. In Paris, where the indigent were numbered at 120,000, fully 144,000 out of the previous 220,000 were deprived of the vote.[60]

Another aspect of the new electoral law had an important bearing on the election of the president. The two million votes required for popular election had thus far constituted about one-fifth of the total vote. Under the new law it would amount to about one-third. In other words, the chances of election by popular vote were markedly diminished, and those of election by the Assembly correspondingly enhanced.[61] If Louis Napoleon nevertheless signed the new law, it may well have been that he too was concerned by the rising tide of radicalism, or that he was not yet ready to defy the conservative elements in the assembly. It has been suggested that perhaps he was glad to have the Assembly compromise itself and to leave the reckoning to the future. In any case, it is impossible to believe that he ever positively approved of so drastic a curtailment of universal suffrage, to which he owed so much.

The royalist majority in the Assembly had no more burning desire than to arrange for the restoration of the monarchy. In the summer of 1850 leaders of both the Legitimist (Bourbon) and Orleanist factions conferred with the Bourbon claimant ("Henry V") in Germany, and with the Orleanist family in England. Louis Philippe having died (August 26), it was ardently hoped that his son would agree to "fusion," that is, to a deal by which the Bourbon Henry, who was childless, should ascend the throne, to be succeeded on his death by the Orleanist claimant. In short, there would within a foreseeable time be a return to the July Monarchy. But the project was doomed by the recalcitrancy of the Bourbons. They hated their Orleanist relatives and saw no point in preparing the way for their restoration. Furthermore, Henry was so firmly convinced of his divine right to the throne that he flatly refused to recognize the right of the people to determine the form of government, as they had done in 1830.[62]

During the years 1849–1851 the economic situation continued to be bad, in the countryside as in the cities. The workers appear to have

[60] Bastid: *Doctrines et institutions politiques*, II, 256 ff.; Duveau: *La vie ouvrière en France*, 59 ff.

[61] Heinrich Euler: *Napoleon III in seiner Zeit* (Würzberg, 1961), 669.

[62] Simpson: *Louis Napoleon*, 98; Rémond: *La droit en France*, 101; Bernard de Vaulx: *L'échéance de 1852* (Paris, 1948), 168 ff.

accepted the new electoral law without much protest and refused to react to the constant prodding of radical leaders in exile to organize resistance. At most they talked about the regular elections due to take place in May, 1852, when they would take their revenge. It seems clear that there was a steady increase of radicalism, especially in the provinces, where the petite *bourgeoisie* of the rural towns and even the peasants were more democratic, republican and even socialist than they had ever been before.[63]

While the members of the Assembly were working to restore the monarchy, Louis Napoleon was scheming to retain his office beyond May, 1852, the date of the next presidential as well as parliamentary election, in which under the constitution he would not be eligible for re-election. He therefore toured the country once again, appealing for popular support for a revision of the constitution in his favor. Departmental councils were encouraged to petition the Assembly in this sense, and the president took every opportunity to replace prefects, judges and other officials who were unfriendly, while he cultivated the commanders of the local *gendarmerie,* who, in the last resort, controlled the situation in their area. By military reviews and other attentions he flattered the army and secured enough support to enable him, in January, 1851, to insist on the replacement of General Changarnier, who was commander of the Paris garrison and National Guard and at the same time a deputy. The general, regarding Louis Napoleon as an obstacle to an Orleanist restoration, had done what he could to discredit him. He was heard to call him a melancholic parrot and to express his readiness to lock him up in Vincennes whenever the Assembly might so order. Naturally, his dismissal provoked a storm in the Assembly, which ended by censure of the cabinet. The president thereupon replaced the cabinet with one of much the same stripe.[64]

[63] Ernst Labrousse: "La propagande napoléonienne avant le coup d'état" (*Accademia dei Lincei: Atti degli convegni,* X, 1949, 313–324); Duveau: *La vie ouvrière en France,* 60; and the interesting analysis of three southern *départements* by Leo A. Loubère: "The Emergence of the Extreme Left in Lower Languedoc, 1848–1851" (*American Historical Review,* LXXIII, 1968, 1019–1051). Of great interest is also the official report of December 1, 1851, which reviews the situation in many parts of France and discusses the ramifications of the radical movement. This was published by Juda Tchernoff: *Associations et sociétés secrètes sous la Deuxième République* (Paris, 1905), chap. ix. Other unpublished reports are cited in Euler: *Napoleon III,* 660 ff.

[64] Bastid: *Doctrines et institutions politiques,* II, 278 ff.; Vaulx: *L'échéance de 1852,* 175 ff.; Howard C. Payne: "Preparation of a Coup d'Etat" (in *Studies in Modern European History in Honor of Franklin Charles Palm,* New York, 1956, 175–202).

By the summer of 1851 matters were approaching a crisis. By that time more than fifty departmental councils, no doubt inspired by the prefects, had petitioned for revision of the constitution so as to allow Louis Napoleon to stand for re-election in May, 1852. The favorite argument was that only thus could a government overturn of which the radicals would take advantage be avoided. The Assembly in fact voted a bill for revision on July 14, but the vote fell far short of the two-thirds required by the constitution. It had now become clear, however, that there was next to no hope that the deadlock resulting from the rigidity of the constitution could be broken by parliamentary action. There was more and more talk of the need for a *coup d'état,* that is, a subversion of the constitutional order by force. Business circles in particular were becoming convinced that stability and confidence depended on the president's taking matters in hand and putting an end to what Palmerston was presently to call "the day-before-yesterday tomfoolery which the scatter-brained heads of Marrast and Tocqueville invented for the torment and perplexity of the French nation." "There is a pronounced feeling in England," wrote *The Times* on November 19, "that financial conditions would be much better if the French political squabble were settled by a successful coup d'état." This was the sentiment everywhere in Europe. The revolutions had been suppressed and only in France did the republic hang on, with radicalism threatening a revival of disorder, with unpredictable ramifications.[65]

5. THE COUP D'ÉTAT OF LOUIS NAPOLEON

The assembly was not deterred by the smoldering crisis from taking its annual vacation from August to November, which gave the president ample time for completing his plans. A number of reliable prefects were appointed and some hard-bitten soldiers brought home from Algeria. General Leroy Saint-Arnaud, famous for his toughness, was made minister of war. Another highly important recruit was the president's half-brother, Count (later Duke) Auguste de Morny, an able, cool-headed and utterly ruthless man of the world, who had made a fortune in industry and banking and had for some years been a deputy under the July Monarchy.[66]

[65] Palmerston's comment quoted by Simpson: *Louis Napoleon,* 167; *The Times* quoted in Franklin C. Palm: *England and Napoleon III* (Durham, 1948), 66.

[66] Morny was the illegitimate son of Queen Hortense and Count Charles de Flahault, who in turn was an illegitimate son of Talleyrand. In the absence of a really adequate

Morny insisted that the coup must wait until the assembly was once more in session, so as to forestall efforts by the members to organize resistance in their constituencies. Planning was made difficult by lack of funds, for the Assembly had kept the president on somewhat less than short rations. Some money was scrounged from bankers and friends, but the major contribution came from Miss Howard, the president's mistress, who mortgaged her London house, pawned her jewels and sold her horses. Her cash contribution is said to have amounted to some 200,000 francs.[67]

When the chamber reassembled early in November, the president at once requested the abrogation of the electoral law and the restoration of universal suffrage, on the plea that the law as it stood was being exploited by radicals for subversive purposes. No doubt Louis Napoleon fully expected the conservatives to reject his proposal, which they did by a vote of 355–348, thus enhancing his own popularity. The majority tried to counter by submitting a bill that would enable the questeurs of the Assembly to requisition troops for its protection and to appoint the commanding officer of such troops. In effect, the assembly proposed to arrange for its own protection in the form of a little private army under the command of Changarnier. In response Saint-Arnaud offered to provide all the protection that might be desired, but insisted that only he, as minister of war, could appoint the commander. After much acrimonious debate the bill was defeated on November 17, the elements of the left all uniting against it.

By this time rumors and dire forebodings were everywhere afloat. There was talk of the return of Ledru-Rollin from his exile in England, and of plans for a grand insurrection in May, 1852. The Orleanists, too, were said to be girding for action. They allegedly were planning to nominate the Prince de Joinville for the presidency and may even have had some thought of provoking insurgency in the provinces. The evidence on these matters is scanty and inconclusive. In

biography, see Marcel Boulenger: *Le duc de Morny* (Paris, 1925). Popular biographies are those of Maristan Chapman: *Imperial Brother: the Life of the Duke de Morny* (New York, 1931), and A. Augustin-Thierry: *Son Elégance, le duc le Morny* (Paris, 1951).

[67] Simone André-Maurois: *Miss Howard, la femme qui fit un empéreur* (Paris, 1956), 80–81, 96. On the financial problem in general, see Adrien Dansette: *Louis-Napoléon à la conquête du pouvoir* (Paris, 1961), 291 ff.

any event the plans of others had no bearing on those of Louis Napoleon and his entourage.[68]

The date chosen for the coup was December 2, the anniversary of the great Napoleon's victory at Austerlitz. The detailed plans were executed with exemplary promptitude and efficiency, due largely to the management and direction of Morny. Early in the morning Paris was placarded with three announcements, printed under heavy guard during the night. The first declared the Assembly dissolved, universal suffrage restored, a popular referendum to be held later in the month, and the establishment of martial law in the Paris area. The second charged the Assembly with having become the center for conspiracies against the president, the choice of the people: "When men who have already lost two monarchies wish to tie my hands so that they may destroy the Republic also, it becomes my duty to save the Republic and the country by appealing to the solemn judgment of the people, the sole sovereign I recognize in France." The people were to vote on a new constitution, admittedly based on Napoleon's constitution of the Year VIII (1799), which established a representative but authoritarian regime. The third announcement called upon the army, "the elite of the nation," to make its voice heard.

Early on the same morning the police arrested at their homes sixteen deputies, of whom six were generals, seven radical leaders and three Orleanists. The police took into custody sixty-two other undesirables, most of them men of the left. As news of these happenings spread, a number of deputies hurried to the Chamber, only to find it closed and under military guard. A few managed to get in by back doors, but were quickly ejected by the troops. They then gathered at the homes of various chiefs to denounce the president's action and plan resistance. Most of these groups were soon dispersed by the police, but at 11 A.M. about 250 deputies, mostly royalists, assembled at the town hall of the tenth *arrondissement*. The meeting declared itself a regular session of the Assembly, deposed Louis Napoleon and assumed supreme power. After some hours of debate the military appeared and marched the protesters off to the barracks. By way of resistance the deputies refused

[68] Most of the evidence comes from the correspondence of Count de Flahault, Morny's father, who was privy to Napoleon's plans. See Earl of Kerry and Philip Guedalla, eds.: *The Secret of the Coup d'Etat* (New York, 1924), 36 ff., 159; and the discussion of the problem in Simpson: *Louis Napoleon*, 125 ff., and appendix B; Dansette: Louis-Napoléon, 340–341; Euler: *Napoleon III*, 763 ff.

the liberation pressed upon them by the government, but their resistance met with little sympathy or response. Louis Napoleon and his generals, when they rode through the city on horseback, found perhaps not popular enthusiasm but at least calm acceptance of what had been done.

The Paris workers, many of them still unemployed, had no reason to regret the Assembly which had deprived them of the vote. They were probably more pleased by its discomfiture than by Louis Napoleon's success. In any case they were unarmed and confronted with military forces of some 50,000 men. Under the circumstances an insurrection would indeed have been pure folly.[69] The nearest thing to it was the effort of a few radical leaders, among them the poet Victor Hugo, to initiate a barricade war. Hugo, originally a member of the Party of Order, had deserted the majority in protest against the repressive measures following the abortive uprising of June, 1849, and had become a confirmed radical and republican. He and his friends exhausted themselves in street-corner agitation, but the workers, so Proudhon reported, instead of heeding the call to arms, continued their game of billiards. The revolutionaries rallied only about a thousand supporters, who, in the night of December 3–4, threw up barricades in the congested sections of the city, between the boulevards and the Right Bank of the river.[70]

General Magnan, commander of the Paris garrison, followed the now well-established strategy of allowing the insurrection to mature before attacking the disaffected area from all sides. The barricades were soon taken and the defenders captured or killed. However, a tragic episode occurred in the course of the operation. Large numbers of the curious had collected on sidewalks and balconies to watch the show. The soldiers, excited by taunts hurled at them and fearful of the crowds that hedged them in, suddenly opened fire. In the ensuing panic artillery was turned on the elegant shops while the troops stormed the buildings and cut down everyone they could reach, without discrimination. Many persons, men and women, who had not the slightest intention of resisting fell victims to this fury. Some have

[69] Duveau: *La vie ouvrière en France,* 70 ff. Karl Marx: *The Eighteenth Brumaire of Louis Bonaparte,* 93 ff., rightly stressed the importance of the economic stagnation.

[70] Hugo's own account is in his *Histoire d'un crime.* For his role, see Matthew Josephson: *Victor Hugo* (New York, 1942), chaps. xii and xiii.

charged Louis Napoleon and Morny with having wanted the massacre in order to cow the populace into submission, but this is perhaps going too far. All one can say is that Morny throughout urged firmness. All told, over 500 people, civil and military, were killed or wounded in the aftermath of the *coup d'état,* the big black mark on the record of Louis Napoleon.[71]

The resistance in the provinces was more formidable than in Paris, especially in the poorer *départements* of the center and south (notably Drôme, Ardèche, Gard, Hérault, Aude, Var and Basses-Alpes), where the local lawyer or teacher led the protests of villagers and peasants. There was relatively little violence or plunder, but the resistance was sufficiently widespread and determined to frighten the propertied classes and conjure up the "red specter." Officials, too, were so firmly convinced of the existence of a huge conspiracy that they took this resistance to be the prelude to the grand insurrection planned for May, 1852. Consequently stories were rife of a dreadful *Jacquerie,* of murder, pillage and rape. Even so well-informed a person as the Count de Flahault could write in private letters that only a tenth of the atrocities were being reported in the press. There were, he asserted, whole schools of young girls violated and women killed after horrid tortures. In short, the insurgents were cannibals corrupted by civilization.[72]

The disturbances, such as they were, gave the authors of the *coup d'état* ample excuse for systematic repression. Martial law (state of siege) was proclaimed in thirty-two *départements* and some 27,000 persons were arrested. They were tried by special commissions which had been instructed by Morny to treat as bandits and criminals all members (even past members) of secret societies and opponents of the regime. Verdicts were arrived at on the basis of evidence provided by local officials, many of whom had already prepared lists of undesirables. In the short space of a month (February, 1852) the commissions

[71] Simpson: *Louis Napoleon,* 172 ff.; Dansette: *Louis-Napoléon,* 355 ff.; Henri Guillemin: *Le coup d'état du 2 décembre* (Paris, 1951), 390 ff.; Howard C. Payne: *The Police State of Louis Napoleon Bonaparte, 1851–1860* (Seattle, 1966), chap. ii.

[72] Kerry and Guedalla: *Secret of the Coup d'Etat,* 190, 193, 200; Duveau: *La vie ouvrière en France,* 77 ff.; Dansette: *Louis-Napoléon,* 358 ff.; Guillemin: *Le coup d'état de 2 décembre,* chap. vii; Albert Soboul: "La question paysanne en 1848" (*La pensée,* Nos. 18–20, 1948); and the important studies of Marcel Dessal: "Le complot de Lyon et la résistance au coup d'état dans les départements du Sud-Est" (*1848: Revue des révolutions contemporaines,* No. 189, 1951, 83–96); Loubère: "Emergence of the Extreme Left."

disposed of the thousands of cases before them. Over 11,000 prisoners were released and another 8,000 interned under police surveillance; 9,581 were deported to labor camps in Algeria and 239 to the prison colony in Guiana.[73]

Since Louis Napoleon, on taking office, had promised "to remain faithful to the democratic republic," and "to regard as enemies of the nation all those who may attempt by illegal means to change the form of the established government," it is clear that by the *coup d'état* he violated his oath. However, the moral aspects of his action concerned only those good democrats who bemoaned the shipwreck of their dreams. Heinrich Heine, who idolized the great Napoleon and had nothing to say in favor of the "blockheads" of the Assembly, felt his heart bleed:

The noble ideals of political morality, legality, civic virtue, liberty and equality, the rosy morning dreams of the eighteenth century, for which our fathers went so heroically to their deaths, and which we dreamed after them in the same spirit of martyrdom—there they now lie at our feet, shattered, dashed to pieces, like fragments of chinaware.[74]

But these outbursts were exceptional. Most people, in France and abroad, approved of what Louis Napoleon had done. The Legitimists are said to have secretly rejoiced at the assault on radicalism and socialism, and especially at the suppression of the dreaded *Jacquerie*. The Orleanists, while outraged, were soon reconciled and joined the victorious faction. Like business circles in general, they welcomed the end of uncertainty and the return of confidence. The business recovery was truly phenomenal. In two weeks the quotation of government bonds rose from 91.60 to 100.90.

In London joy was as unconfined as in Paris: "The great French difficulty which has so long loomed like a dim and gigantic terror through the mist, has met with its solution," wrote *The Economist* (December 13). "The French," added the *Illustrated London News*

---

[73] Pierre Dominique: *Louis Napoléon et le coup d'état du 2 décembre* (Paris, 1951) prints in the appendix the verdicts in the *département* of Basses-Alpes. See also Dansette: *Louis-Napoléon*, 370 ff.; Payne: *Police State of Louis Napoleon, op. cit.*, 40 ff., 64 ff.

[74] Heine, letter of February, 1852, quoted in William Rose: *Heinrich Heine, Two Studies of His Thought and Feeling* (Oxford, 1956), 81. The same plaint is in the letters of the Countess d'Agoult to the German poet Georg Herwegh: "There is no longer any law or right: Rome is in the hands of the pretorians, who are gorging themselves on blood and gold" (Marcel Herwegh: *Au printemps des dieux*, Paris, 1929, 157).

(December 27), "begin to love their business much better than they love theories of government." The workers, too, were reported gratified by the economic recovery: "Six weeks ago society was living from hand to mouth," reported Walter Bagehot: "now she feels sure of her next meal. And this, in a dozen words, is the real case—the political excuse for Prince Louis Napoleon."[75]

Foreign governments were relieved that now, at long last, the revolution had been everywhere suppressed. Lord Palmerston was so hasty in his expression of approval that the outraged queen insisted on his resignation, though many of his cabinet colleagues shared his sentiments. The Austrian ambassador in Paris could see in the president only "the chosen instrument of Providence to deal the mortal blow to parliamentarism on the Continent." Even Nicholas of Russia shared in the general satisfaction. At just about all levels of society moral issues were ignored and the gratification of practical interests was supreme.[76]

Under the circumstances, the outcome of the plebiscite of December should cause no surprise. In reply to the question whether or not they desired the maintenance of the president's authority and whether they delegated him to draft a new constitution, 7,439,216 voted in the affirmative and only 640,737 in the negative. Eighty-two per cent of the electorate voted and of these 91.65 per cent expressed approval. These figures seemed for long so implausible that the government was suspected of having doctored them, but recent study of the records has dispelled all such doubts. Incidentally, latter-day dictators have demonstrated that such landslide votes are by no means unobtainable.[77] Nonetheless, the figures of Louis Napoleon's plebiscite do tend to conceal the degree of opposition to his *coup d'état*. The disturbances in several *départements* are instructive in this regard, and so are the abstentions. After all, it may be taken for granted that the almost 20 per cent of the voters who, despite official pressure, refused to cast a ballot were almost all of them opponents of the regime. In some *dé-*

---

[75] Norman St. John-Stevas: *Walter Bagehot* (Bloomington, 1959), 418 ff.; Palm: *England and Napoleon III,* 68 ff.; Guillemin: *Le coup d'état de 2 décembre,* chap. ix.

[76] Herbert C. Bell: *Lord Palmerston* (New York, 1936), chap. xxi; Richard Salomon, "Die Anerkennung Napoleons III" (*Zeitschrift für osteuropäische Geschichte,* II, 1911–1912, 321–366).

[77] Gisela Geywitz: *Das Plebiszit von 1851 in Frankreich* (Tübingen, 1965) provides a definitive analysis.

partements the abstentions ran to more than 50 per cent. In the large cities both the percentages of abstentions and of negative votes were remarkably high: in Lyons, 27 per cent and 35.3 per cent respectively; in Bordeaux, 31 per cent and 33.6 per cent; in Strasbourg, 41 per cent and 36 per cent. Paris, as might be expected, was definitely hostile. There the abstentions were 25.5 per cent and the negative votes 26.2 per cent even in the well-to-do sections, while in the workers' sections the negative votes were as high as 42.9 per cent. Considering the administrative pressure brought to bear by prefects and subprefects and the systematic propaganda picturing Louis Napoleon as the savior of the country from the atrocities of the radicals, the opposition to his coup was by no means negligible. But the fact remains that his action met with overwhelming approval. By and large the rural areas were more favorable than the urban, the poorer rural areas more favorable than the prosperous, the latter more favorable than the provincial towns, and the larger cities least favorable. The conclusion is inescapable that the country, which had become a republic by default, was never really reconciled to the Second Republic and therefore welcomed the rule of a man whose name signified something to all men and who promised the restoration of order, the return of confidence and the recovery of business.

Chapter Five

CENTRAL EUROPE: THE MARCH OF REACTION

I. BALKAN INTERLUDE: THE WALLACHIAN REVOLUTION

THE June Days in France and Radetzky's victory at Custoza marked the turn of the revolutionary tide in Europe. The governments were recovering from their paralyzing fright and were ready to use their armed forces against the insurgents when necessary. Czar Nicholas, too, had completed the deployment of his armies on his western front and reiterated his readiness to come to the aid of his fellow princes if they so desired. No doubt they preferred to settle their problems in their own way and with their own means, but it was comforting to know that the Russian armies stood ready to intervene in case of emergency.

The first instance of Russian armed intervention was in the Danubian Principalities, where, the reader may recall, the czar exercised a certain protectorate by treaty. There was much opposition, even on the part of the upper classes, to Russian domination; and when news arrived of the revolutions in Western and Central Europe, a number of patriotic boyars in April provoked huge demonstrations against the prince of Moldavia. The latter, however, refused to be intimidated. Sure of Russian support, he had the ringleaders arrested and deported. Only a few managed to escape to Transylvania.[1]

Much more serious and important was the revolution which broke out in Wallachia in June. This was largely the work of the young boyars who had been educated in Paris and had there imbibed the ideas of nationalism, democracy and socialism.[2] Despite the repeated warnings of the Russian consul, the government did nothing to supervise or control the activities of these ardent young men on their return home.

---

[1] R. W. Seton-Watson: *A History of the Roumanians* (Oxford, 1934), chap. ix; John C. Campbell: "1848 in the Roumanian Principalities" (*Journal of Central European Affairs*, VIII, 1948, 181–190); Michael Roller: "Les Roumains en 1848" (in François Fejtö, ed.: *Le printemps des peuples*. Paris, 1948, II, 239–266).

[2] See above, Chapter VIII.

In a secret meeting at Islaz on the Danube they drew up a program calling for abolition of the Organic Statute, recognition of the equality of rights, election of a Parliament representing all classes, universal education, emancipation of Gypsies and Jews (both numerous in the Principalities), and emancipation of the peasantry, redistribution of the land, and indemnification of the landowners by the state. When the prince rejected these demands, a revolution broke out in Bucharest. The prince was obliged to appoint a revolutionary cabinet before fleeing the country (June 23).

The revolutionary forces now quickly broke ranks. The majority, led by Eliade-Radulescu, was intent on liberating the country from foreign domination and effecting a union of the Rumanian lands. But a radical minority of intellectuals, of whom Nicholas Balcescu was the leader, was determined on fundamental social changes, especially abolition of forced labor by the peasants and distribution of the land among them. The moderates were able for some time to defer elections to a constituent assembly and to exclude the radicals from important offices. But the unrest in the country was such that the provisional government was obliged to set up a commission (composed equally of landlords and peasants) to study the agrarian problem. At the meetings of this commission (August 22–31), the peasants were unexpectedly aggressive: they objected to being bound to the soil and forced to labor on the estates. They demanded land, even if the state had to compensate the landlords. Such shocking talk had never before been heard and to the propertied classes was utterly intolerable. On August 31 the government closed out the work of the commission.[3]

The Wallachian Revolution was doomed from the start because the ideas of the leaders, particularly of the radicals, were imported from the West and far too advanced for Rumanian society at that time. Only a few of the boyar families had any part in it. Most of them were

[3] The radical side is presented in the anonymously published account of Balcescu: *La question économique de. Principautés Danubiennes* (Paris, 1850), and in the defense of Balcescu by A. G. Golesco: *De l'abolition du servage dans les Principautés Danubiennes* (Paris, 1856). On the more conservative side, Ion Eliade-Radulescu: *Mémoires sur l'histoire de la régéneration roumaine* (Paris, 1851). Among modern treatments, see Marcel Emérit: *Les paysans roumains depuis le traité d'Andrinople* (Paris, 1937), 297 ff.; Helmut Haufe: *Die Wandlung der Volksordnung im rumänischen Altreich* (Stuttgart, 1939); Andre Oțețea: "La révolution de 1848 et les paysans roumains" (*Revue d'histoire comparée*, VII, 1948, 19–34); Vasile Maciu: "De la conception sociale et politique de Nicolae Balcescu" (*Nouvelles études d'histoire*, 1955, 373–390).

outraged by the program of the radicals, which went far beyond anything the upper classes had in view. When the agrarian problem was raised they became completely soured on the revolution and probably regarded the intervention of the powers as a godsend.

The insurgent leaders had tried hard to conciliate their Turkish overlords and enlist the support of the French and British. Lamartine was and always had been sympathetic to Rumanian aspirations, but by June he had already been eclipsed by more realistic politicians. His successor at the Foreign Office, Bastide, was frightened by the whole business, which he thought premature and likely to provoke Russian intervention. Palmerston, too, rejected Rumanian advances, holding that if the Principalities, in the name of nationality, were to be allowed to break away from the Ottoman Empire, the Bulgarians and other Balkan peoples would soon register similar claims and thereby undermine the empire which it was British interest to uphold.[4]

Lord Stratford de Redcliffe, the British ambassador at Constantinople, considered the Bucharest revolution nothing but the work of "a number of young boyars educated abroad, gypsies and students who demanded universal suffrage and the election of every Wallachian to the office of hospodar (prince)." He urged the Turks to intervene and restore order, but the Turks, already under pressure from Czar Nicholas to join in military occupation of the Principalities, were reluctant to collaborate with their traditional enemy. The result was that at the end of July the Russians alone invaded Moldavia, thus almost forcing the Turks to send troops across the Danube into Wallachia (early September). Some weeks later the Turks occupied Bucharest, where they were soon joined by the Russians (October 11). The revolutionary leaders were driven into flight and the revolution was at an end. In May, 1849, the Russians and Turks signed a new convention at Balta Liman. This provided that in the future the two powers should jointly choose the princes, whose term of office should be seven years. The former elected assemblies were to be replaced by appointed councils (*divans*) composed of members of the great nobility and high clergy. Russia and

---

[4] Paul Henry: *La France devant le monde* (Paris, 1945), 165 ff.; Harold Temperley: *England and the Near East: the Crimea* (London, 1936), 258 ff.; Radu R. Florescu: "Stratford Canning, Palmerston and the Wallachian Revolution of 1848" (*Journal of Modern History*, XXXV, 1963, 227–244); Dan Berindei: "La politique extérieure de la Valachie pendant la révolution bourgeois-démocratique" (*Nouvelles études d'histoire*, 1965, 285–297).

Turkey were to name commissioners to "advise" the princes, and were to maintain forces of occupation until a new statute had been worked out. Actually they evacuated only in 1851.[5]

2. THE REDUCTION OF VIENNA

In the Hapsburg dominions the fate of the revolution hinged largely upon the war in Hungary, which broke out in September, 1848 and then precipitated the October Revolution in Vienna. In order to avoid undue fragmentation of the narrative, attention will be directed first to the affairs of the capital. There the radical elements—students, artisans, workers—were firmly in control, for in the absence of the Court at Innsbruck the official government and the city council were helpless, at least where local matters were concerned. The Committee of Safety, really a revolutionary assembly, was directed by Dr. Fischhof and other academic leaders who looked to the Student Committee (the *Aula*) as a link to the general public and especially the workers.

The Committee of Safety, like the Paris provisional government, was confronted by a severe economic crisis and its concomitant unemployment. It appointed a Committee of Labor under an eloquent and enthusiastic student named Willner, who promptly proclaimed the "right to work" and set up "workshops" much like the French national workshops, where large numbers of the indigent were employed on grading and other jobs at relatively attractive pay. Presently 20,000 workers were enrolled and the financial burden was becoming formidable. The propertied classes grumbled about the experiments of this new Louis Blanc and became increasingly impatient with the revolutionary regime. They induced the emperor and Court to return (August 12) and applauded the appointment of Ernst von Schwarzer as minister of public works. He in turn reduced the wage rate in the workshops and thereby precipitated the serious disorders of August 21–23. Students and suburban National Guards backed the protests of the workers, while the National Guards of the Inner City defended the government. Fighting broke out and there were a number of dead. While not comparable in magnitude to the Paris June Days, this clash of conservative and radical forces and the defeat of the workers was a similar class conflict. The Committee of Safety was obliged to disband and the government took over command of the National Guard. But the student committee and the Democratic Society remained in existence, while the workers boiled with resentment and desire for revenge.[6]

Meanwhile elections for the Austrian Parliament had been held in mid-June and the National Assembly (*Reichstag*) had opened its sessions in Vienna on July 22. The voting had been by universal but indirect suffrage, but there had been many irregularities and many abstentions. In terms of social class the deputies were for the most part members of the lower middle class and peasants, of whom many were illiterate. In terms of nationality it should be noted that no elections were held in Hungary or in the Italian provinces. In the Parliament the Germans were in a minority, as they were in the general population. Of some 400 deputies there were 160 Germans and 190 Slavs. Proceedings of the Parliament were much hampered by the language problem. Fully 25 per cent of the membership were ignorant of German, the only possible language for debate, so that the meaning of the discussion had to be explained to them by interpreters.[7]

Like other revolutionary assemblies, the Austrian devoted itself first to the drafting of a constitution and especially to the formulation of a bill of civil rights. Difficulties between Germans and Czechs soon developed, for while the Germans took the unity of the Hapsburg Monarchy (exclusive of the Kingdom of Hungary) as almost axiomatic, the Czechs now formed a conservative wing determined to work for the federalization of the empire, through which alone they could hope to attain self-government and, as a strong unit, exercise an important if not dominant influence.[8]

The Parliament did, however, act harmoniously in resolving one major problem, that of the peasantry. Emancipation within a year had

---

[6] Ernst W. Zenker: *Die Wiener Revolution 1848 in ihren socialen Voraussetzungen und Beziehungen* (Vienna, 1897), 200 ff.; Heinrich von Srbik: "Die Wiener Revolution des Jahres 1848 in sozialgeschichtlicher Beleuchtung" (*Schmollers Jahrbuch*, XLIII (3), 1919, 19–58); Rudolf Kiszling: *Die Revolution im Kaisertum Oesterreich* (Vienna, 1948), I, 206 ff.; R. John Rath: *The Viennese Revolution of 1848* (Austin, 1957), 219 ff., 289 ff.

[7] Peter Burian: *Die Nationalitäten in 'Cisleithanien' und das Wahlrecht der Märzrevolution* (Graz, 1962), 36 ff.

[8] Josef Redlich: *Das oesterreichische Staats- und Reichsproblem* (Leipzig, 1920), I, 119, 140; Kiszling: *Die Revolution in Kaisertum Oesterreich*, I, 201 ff.

already been decreed for Bohemia, Moravia and Silesia, as well as immediately for Galicia, but there was much pressure for prompt and more drastic action. On July 26 Hans Kudlich, the son of a Silesian peasant who at the age of twenty-five had already distinguished himself as a student leader, proposed the abolition of all feudal dues and obligations. Adoption of the bill in one form or another was a foregone conclusion because the landlords everywhere, haunted by the fear of peasant insurrection, realized that they must abandon their traditional privileges. But since Kudlich demanded emancipation as a human right, rather than as an economic measure, there was much debate as to whether the holders of these rights should be indemnified and, if so, to what extent and by whom. After forty sessions, during which over a hundred amendments were proposed, it was agreed that there should be no compensation for loss of patrimonial jurisdiction but that, under a law passed on September 7 by a modest majority (174–134), there should be indemnification for loss of rights attached to the land, the amount to be determined by a special commission. The act, whatever its shortcomings, was of major importance and of direct interest to far more people than the political issue then under debate. The Parliament and the government, by satisfying the demands of the peasantry, drained off one of the most dangerous sources of revolutionary unrest. Thenceforth the peasantry as a class showed but little interest in efforts at reform.[9]

Despite the setback suffered in August, the radical press and the clubs became more and more aggressive in September. Many well-to-do people began to leave the city, while the National Guards of the better quarters became discouraged. Class lines were now clearly drawn: on the one hand the Constitutional Club, founded to oppose radicalism, and on the other the Democratic Club, which labored to co-ordinate all radical activities.

Such was the situation when the Croatian forces began to approach Vienna. In mid-September Jellachich had advanced on Budapest until the Hungarians on September 29 made a stand at the towns of Pakozd and Velencze, some forty miles southwest of the capital.

[9] Zenker: *Die Wiener Revolution 1848*, 185 ff.; Jerome Blum: *Noble Landowners and Agriculture in Austria, 1815–1848* (Baltimore, 1948), 232 ff.; Josef Buchinger: *Der Bauer in der Kultur- und Wirtschaftsgeschichte Oesterreichs* (Vienna, 1952), 168 ff.; and on Kudlich, the scholarly biography of Friedrich Prinz: *Hans Kudlich* (Munich, 1962), especially chap. viii.

Though the fighting was indecisive, Jellachich halted his advance and turned northwestward towards Vienna. He had evidently reckoned on the defection of many Hungarian regiments and was now fearful of meeting yet greater forces if he persisted in his effort to take the Magyar capital. It seems that his new plan was to put himself in position to co-operate with the imperial armies advancing from the west.[10]

In Hungary the Croat invasion produced important political changes. Batthyány and most members of the cabinet began to doubt the ability of the Hungarians to maintain their independence and tried repeatedly to arrive at some accommodation with the Court. The high aristocracy or magnates were even more dubious and were disgruntled with the Batthyány government, which they blamed for the impasse in which the country found itself. They counseled the king to break with the ministry and persuaded him to appoint Count Franz Lamberg, who had large estates in Hungary, to be commander-in-chief of all forces in Hungary. These conservative elements had gone along with the revolution in March because, in view of popular pressure, there seemed to be no alternative. Now, eager to break the power of radicalism, they were above all intent on avoiding a conflict with Vienna, the more so as Hungary was already beset with revolt on all its borders.[11]

The liberal gentry, on the other hand, were outraged by what they regarded as the treachery of the Court. They rallied to Kossuth, who already enjoyed the support of all popular elements. He now became the dominant figure of the Committee of National Defense set up by Parliament on September 25. The Lamberg appointment was promptly denounced as illegal and army officers were ordered to refuse him obedience. So great was the excitement and hostility in Budapest that when Lamberg was seen crossing the Danube bridge he was set upon by a mob and brutally murdered (September 28). Unwilling to defend this attack on the royal authority, Batthyány resigned. Kossuth, on the

---

10 Ferdinand Hauptmann: "Banus Jellačič und Feldmarshal Fürst Windischgrätz" (Südostforschungen, XV, 1956, 373–402); Gunther E. Rothenberg: "Jelačič, the Croatian Military Border and the Intervention against Hungary" (Austrian History Yearbook, I, 1965, 45–67).

11 Heinrich Friedjung: Oesterreich von 1848 bis 1860 (2 ed., Stuttgart, 1908), I, 77; Julius Miskolczy: Ungarn in der Habsburger Monarchie (Vienna, 1959), 112 ff.; Erzsebet Andiés: "Kossuth en lutte contre les ennemis des réformes et de la révolution" (Studia historica, XII, 1954, 1–169).

other hand, set out on a tour of the provinces to secure recruits for the army. The peasants, who regarded him as the author of their emancipation, gave him an enthusiastic reception. Soon thousands of young peasants were flocking to the colors.[12]

Kossuth, far from the capital, did not learn of the fighting at Pakozd until several days later. It strengthened his conviction that the country, if properly inspired, could defend its independence successfully and he therefore urged pursuit and destruction of Jellachich's army. But the commander of the Hungarian forces, Field Marshal Franz Moga, had grave doubts about the legality of the war and little confidence in the fighting qualities of his militia (*Honved*) regiments. In his opinion the first requirement was to ensure the defense of Budapest. Count Denes Pazmandy, presiding officer of the lower chamber of Parliament and temporarily chairman of the Committee of National Defense, shared Moga's opinion.

On Kossuth's return to the capital (October 7) he learned that a royal decree of October 3 had ordered the Hungarian Parliament dissolved, had declared its decisions null and void, and had named Jellachich high commissioner and commander-in-chief of all troops in Hungary. All troops were absolved from their oath of allegiance to the Hungarian constitution. Thus at last the Vienna court had abandoned all pretense and thrown down the gauntlet to the revolutionary regime. Kossuth at once denounced the decree in the most scathing terms and declared that the country would in three weeks provide 300,000 men to defend its honor and independence. Parliament thereupon declared the royal decree illegal and charged Jellachich and all his supporters with treason.

Kossuth, who now became chairman of the Committee of National Defense, pressed for vigorous action by the army. When news arrived of a great insurrection in Vienna on October 6, he urged that Hungary make common cause with the Viennese, even to the extent of invading Austrian territory. Moga was ordered to pursue Jellachich and destroy his forces before they could be reinforced. But Moga still hesitated,

---

[12] François Eckart: "La révolution de 1848 en Hongrie et la cour de Vienne" (*Actes du Congrès Historique du Centenaire de la Révolution de 1848*, Paris, 1948, 229–242); Gyözö Ember: "Louis Kossuth à la tête du Comité de la Défense Nationale" (*Studia historica*, VI, 1953); György Spira: "L'alliance de Lajos Kossuth avec la gauche radicale et les masses populaires de la révolution hongroise de 1848–1849" (*Acta historica*, II, 1953, 49–150).

hoping against hope that an accommodation might still be arrived at. Two precious weeks were lost, since Kossuth was reluctant to provoke dissension in the ranks of government.[13]

Before pursuing this theme further, attention must be given to the developments in Vienna, on which so much depended. In the Austrian Parliament many of the German deputies, who were radicals, supported the Hungarian cause enthusiastically, while the Czechs and other Slavs, who were mostly conservatives, stood firmly by the Court. A crisis ensued when, on September 30, it became known that the minister of war, Count Theodor von Latour, had been supplying Jellachich with money and munitions. The decree making Jellachich commander of all the troops in Hungary followed almost at once. Thereupon the radical press began to vilify Latour and demand that he and other ministers be hanged. To all intents and purposes the populace was invited to give Latour the treatment already meted out to Lamberg by the Budapest mob.[14]

The crisis broke on October 6, when a German regiment was being dispatched to reinforce Jellachich. The populace offered resistance, tore up the railroad tracks and blocked the bridge over the Danube. Fighting broke out in the city, so serious that Count Auersperg, the commander of the garrison troops, felt obliged to evacuate his forces to the suburbs. The crowds then besieged the Ministry of War, where the cabinet was in session. Most of the members of the government managed to escape, but Latour was hunted through the building and murdered, after which his body was stripped naked, mutilated and strung up on a lamppost. The final act of this ferocious outbreak was an assault on the arsenal, which was forced to surrender 30,000 rifles to the crowd.[15]

The radicals and the mob were now in undisputed command of the capital. On October 7 the Court fled to Olmütz (in Moravia) and a general exodus of the upper classes followed. Even the Parliament,

---

[13] For much interesting detail, based on the documents, see the article by Ember: "Louis Kossuth" and Friedrich Walter: "Die Ursachen des Scheiterns der madjarischen Waffenhilfe für die Wiener Oktober-Revolutionäre, 1848" (*Südostforschungen*, XXII, 1963, 377–400).

[14] Hermann Meyer: *1848: Studien zur Geschichte der deutschen Revolution* (Darmstadt, 1949), 43 ff., has revealed the contacts and relations between Hungarian agents and Vienna radicals.

[15] Kiszling: *Die Revolution in Kaisertum Oesterreich*, I, 237 ff.; Rath: *Viennese Revolution of 1848*, chap. xiv.

from which thirty-two Czech deputies had departed, was so shocked by the brutality of the mob that it hesitated to take any initiative. The real power now rested with the Central Committee of the Democratic Societies, which in turn dominated the National Guard. The Guard, from which all but the radical elements had defected, now numbered only 18,000 and was commanded by the radical journalist Wenzel Messenhauser, who, though a former army officer, was better fitted to conduct a propaganda campaign than to wage war. Messenhauser was assisted by General Joseph Bem, hero of the Polish war against Russia in 1831. They felt that, if necessary, they could muster some 50,000 men, with seventy pieces of artillery.

The Viennese radicals were in constant touch with Hungarian headquarters and repeatedly called for assistance. But in the Hungarian camp all was confusion and indecision. Kossuth and his adviser, General Francis Pulszky, favored energetic action, arguing that if the Vienna revolution were snuffed out, all Austrian forces would be turned against Hungary. But Moga, uncomfortable in the role of opponent of the king, hesitated to cross the frontier (the Leitha River) unless formally invited to do so by the Austrian Parliament, which in turn evaded incrimination. Moga must also have had doubts about his own forces. He had only 5,000 regular troops, plus 1,400 cavalry. In addition there were some 15,000 fairly well-armed but untrained troops and 5,000 National Guards armed only with scythes or pitchforks. There was grave reason to fear that many of the men, who had enlisted only for defense of the fatherland, would desert if ordered to cross the frontier.[16]

Jellachich crossed the Leitha on October 10 and joined forces with Auersperg and the Vienna garrison. Had he had his way, he would have attacked the city at once, before the Hungarians could arrive. But he was ordered to await the arrival of Windischgrätz, who had been appointed a field marshal and given command of all troops, including Jellachich's. The attacking forces totaled about 70,000 men, with 200 guns. By October 20 the army advancing from the north began to reach the city, which by October 23 was fairly well encircled. Hostilities soon became general. On October 28 Jellachich delivered an assault on the city and an armistice was agreed to, which, however, was almost at once broken under popular pressure.

[16] For details see the articles by Ember and Walter, cited above.

The Viennese were heartened by news that the Hungarians, who had already once sent some men across the frontier river, only to recall them, had now at last cast the die and were on the march toward the city. But on October 30 Jellachich defeated them at Schwechat and forced them to fall back. Kossuth blamed the Viennese for this reverse, remarking that they watched the battle from the cathedral tower without sending forces to the rescue. But Kossuth had throughout overestimated the military strength of the Viennese. He had calculated on assistance by a force of 25,000 or more men, which was utterly out of the question. In any case, the cause of the revolutionaries was now hopeless. On October 31 the city was attacked in the vicinity of the imperial palace. There was vigorous resistance, but the trained and well-equipped troops were soon able to overrun and occupy the entire Inner City. The losses on the government side were about 1,200 men, while the defenders had some 3,000 casualties. Martial law was at once proclaimed, the National Guard and the Academic Legion dissolved, the political clubs suppressed and the newspapers put under rigid censorship. The active insurgents were mostly taken prisoner. Of some 2,400 about half were released after some months, while 400 were given long prison terms and twenty-five were executed. Many of the radical leaders managed to escape and others were protected by their status as deputies. But Messenhauser faced the firing squad and so did Robert Blum, the well-known Saxon radical and member of the Frankfurt Parliament. Blum had come to Vienna not as the official representative of the Parliament but merely as the representative of his radical colleagues, who wished to encourage the Viennese insurgents. He had taken an active part in the operations and was therefore subject to court-martial. His conviction and execution, while technically justifiable, were openly defiant of liberal as well as radical opinion throughout Germany. It was, in a sense, notice given that the Vienna government was not to be trifled with and that, when it came to a showdown, it would ignore the pretensions of the popularly elected Parliament.

3. THE SUBMISSION OF BERLIN

The course of events in the Prussian capital followed closely the developments in Vienna, and the Prussian government's moves were clearly influenced by those of the Hapsburg Court. The Prussian Parliament had been elected early in May and turned out to be much more radical than the Frankfurt Parliament, elected at the same time. Not only the larger cities but also the agricultural regions of Silesia and East Prussia returned confirmed democrats. None of the 1,500 great landholders of Silesia was elected, for example. The majority of the members were lower judges, local officials, schoolteachers and clergy of both faiths. Though there were no organized parties, there was a group of about forty on the right; a center of moderate liberals, much influenced by the economist Karl Rodbertus; and a democratic, republican left led by Franz Waldeck, a prominent judge of known integrity. Since the left wing of the center tended to vote with the left, the more advanced elements could usually command a majority.[17]

The Parliament had been called by the king to "collaborate" with the government in drafting a constitution, and was therefore suprised to find a constitution modeled on the Belgian waiting for its approval. It promptly voted down the government draft as inadequate, and appointed its own Constitutional Committee, under Waldeck, making clear its intention to assume full constituent powers. The king allowed matters to run their course, much to the exasperation of the court Camarilla, which was becoming ever more insistent on the assertion of royal authority. The populace, meanwhile, was becoming more and more assertive. There were endless demonstrations and petitions, while the newspapers bombarded the citizenry with programs worked out by the radical clubs. Of the latter the most influential was the Democratic Club, with a membership of some 1,200 journalists, students and artisans. The workers had in addition the Workers' Club, organized and led by Stefan Born, which aimed at self-help in the attainment of labor's demands. To alleviate the widespread unemployment the government in Berlin as in Vienna assigned some 3,000 workers to road and grading jobs, and at the same time instituted an inquiry into the conditions of the agrarian laborers.[18]

The task of maintaining order under these circumstances devolved

[17] Gerhard Schilfert: *Sieg und Niederlage des demokratischen Wahlrechts in der deutschen Revolution, 1848–1849* (Berlin, 1952); Ernst R. Huber: *Deutsche Verfassungsgeschichte* (Stuttgart, 1960), II, 584 ff. On the attitude of the rural areas, see Gunter Franz: "Die agrarische Bewegung im Jahre 1848" (*Hessisches Jahrbuch für Landesgeschichte*, IX, 1959, 150–178); Hans Hübner: "Die ostpreussichen Landarbeiter im Kampf gegen junkerliche Ausbeutung und Willkür, 1848–1849" (*Zeitschrift für Geschichtswissenschaft*, XI, 1963, 552–569).

[18] Ernst Kaeber: *Berlin, 1848* (Berlin, 1948), 101 ff., 137 ff.; Hermann Meyer: *1848: Studien zur Geschichte der deutschen Revolution* (Darmstadt, 1949), 67 ff.

upon the Civic Guard (*Bürgerwehr*), which consisted of some 22,000 men organized in battalions and companies. Associated with it were several "flying corps," one composed of students, another of young workers, another of artists, all of them highly activist. However, neither the Civic Guard nor the flying corps had a clear mandate or charter defining their duties. The Civic Guard, like its Vienna counterpart, tended to be fluid, the well-to-do elements shirking their obligations except on crucial occasions. On June 14 there was a serious clash between the Guard and the populace when the latter attempted to storm the arsenal and seize weapons. Another grave episode occurred on October 12 when the Guard fired on unruly canal workers, with some loss of life. By that time the Guard, long since ridiculed by the regular troops, was scorned even by the radicals.[19]

By the autumn the conservative elements were regaining confidence and beginning to organize for resistance to radicalism. Prince William returned from exile to take the seat in Parliament to which he had been elected. Presently Fatherland Societies and Prussian Societies sprang up and a new and influential newspaper, the *Gazette of the Cross* (*Kreuzzeitung*), began to assert the rights and virtues of the old order. On August 18–19 a group of landlords met in a so-called Junker Parliament to protest against proposed laws to end tax exemptions of the nobility and labor obligations of the peasants. They founded an Association for the Protection of Property which soon courted the support of the workers by agitating against the Civic Guard and the cabinet, while at the same time denouncing the system of free competition and advocating a return to the guild system.[20]

The aggressiveness of the Junkers, among whom were many army officers, provoked the ire of the liberals and radicals, who detested the army as an instrument of repression and aimed at replacing it by a popular militia. On August 9 a resolution was introduced in Parliament directing army officers to refrain from reactionary agitation or else resign. So flagrant was this attack on the royal prerogative that Frederick William at long last decided to take action. He worked out a plan for dissolving Parliament and introducing a government-made

[19] O. Rimpler: *Die Berliner Bürgerwehr im Jahre 1848* (Brandenburg, 1883). Rimpler was the last commander of the Guard.

[20] Kaeber: *Berlin, 1848*, 182 ff.; Theodore S. Hamerow: *Restoration, Revolution, Reaction* (Princeton, 1958), 177 ff.; Sigmund Neumann: *Die Stufen des preussischen Konservatismus* (Berlin, 1930).

constitution. But before plans were complete a crisis developed which led to the resignation of the Auerswald-Hansemann cabinet and its replacement by a cabinet of bureaucrats under General Ernst von Pfuel. The latter was an enlightened soldier of the earlier reform period, who was interested in the success of the constitutional experiment. To the utter disgust of the Court and the army, he accepted the resolution of the Parliament, which, in turn, became more and more arrogant in its dealings with the government.[21]

The situation came to a head in October, in Berlin as in Vienna. The Prussian Parliament, coming at last to discussion of the constitution, voted on October 13 to make the Civic Guard permanent, and to abolish the hunting rights of the nobility. Far more defiant was the vote (217–134) to strike the words "by the Grace of God" from the king's title, to forbid the use of all titles of nobility and eventually to abolish the nobility itself. This was too much for Pfuel, who resigned. Co-operation between the government and the elected Parliament had clearly become impossible, the more so as the radicals were becoming intransigent. On October 26–29, just as the Vienna insurrection was coming to a head, a great Democratic Congress, with delegations from 140 cities, was held in Berlin. While much given to theoretical debate, the congress called upon the Prussian Parliament to aid the Viennese revolutionaries. On October 31 there were great demonstrations in front of the theater which was the seat of the Parliament. But in the end the Parliament rejected a motion for military intervention at Vienna and belatedly referred the whole question to the Frankfurt Parliament for decision.[22]

News of Windischgrätz' victory at Vienna emboldened the king to take the offensive against his own revolutionaries. On November 1 he appointed General Friedrich Wilhelm von Brandenburg, a natural son of Frederick William III, to be minister-president. The Parliament promptly protested, demanding a cabinet which could enjoy its support. This time the protest was ignored and Brandenburg was instructed to liquidate the entire revolutionary movement. On November 9 he announced the adjournment of the Parliament to November 27

[21] Gordon A. Craig: *The Politics of the Prussian Army* (Oxford, 1955), 115; Huber: *Deutsche Verfassungsgeschichte*, II, 736 ff.

[22] Karl Obermann: *Die deutschen Arbeiter in der Revolution von 1848* (Berlin, 1953), 234 ff.; Huber: *Deutsche Verfassungsgeschichte*, II, 706 ff.

and its transfer to the provincial town of Brandenburg. But this attempt to imitate Windischgrätz' procedure met with more resistance than had been expected. The Parliament voted by a huge majority (252–30) to declare the decree illegal and refuse compliance. The Civic Guard ignored orders to keep the Parliament from meeting and the Workers' Club offered to support the assembly against the reactionary government. But there was no popular upheaval. The populace was evidently weary of turmoil and disorder and above all appears to have been deeply discouraged by the news from Vienna.[23]

General Wrangel, who occupied the capital with 13,000 troops on November 10, met with no significant opposition from the Civic Guard or the populace. There was no bloodshed as in Vienna. Troops closed the Parliament building, whereupon a substantial number of deputies attempted, during the following days, to meet in other places. As a parting shot they called upon the country to refuse taxes. But these moves proved ineffectual. The Parliament remained closed and only the diehard radicals, such as Karl Marx, attempted to carry through the denial of taxes.[24]

In Berlin as in Vienna martial law was proclaimed, the Civic Guard dissolved, the clubs closed and the newspapers subjected to censorship. On November 26 about 260 of the original 400 members of the Parliament, mostly the conservative and moderate elements, assembled dutifully at Brandenburg. Had the court Camarilla had its way, the Parliament would have been abolished entirely and the objectionable members arrested. The king, while unwilling to go back on his promise of March, wanted to couch the future constitution in traditional terms. But the cabinet, unwilling to provoke further crises, proposed that Parliament be dissolved while the government at the same time promulgated a reasonably liberal constitution based on the Parliament's earlier draft. There was to be a two-chamber Parliament, of which the lower chamber was to be elected by universal suffrage. Parliament was to have the right to initiate legislation and the cabinet was to be responsible to it. The king reluctantly agreed, but only after adding a provision giving him an absolute veto on legislation and the

---

[23] Rimpler: *Die Berliner Bürgerwehr*, 86 ff.; Obermann: *Die deutschen Arbeiter*, 243 ff.; Hamerow: *Restoration, Revolution, Reaction*, 185 ff.

[24] Hermann Meyer: "Karl Marx und die deutsche Revolution von 1848" (*Historische Zeitschrift*, CLXXII, 1951, 517–537).

power to rule by decree in an emergency. On December 5 the Parliament was dissolved and the new constitution proclaimed.[25]

The evidence suggests that Count Brandenburg and the Court intended the constitution to be provisional, designed to pacify the country and tide matters over until revisions in a conservative direction became feasible. But the elections to the new Parliament on January 22 again produced a lower chamber strongly oriented toward the left: as against 184 conservatives and moderates, there were 160 radicals. In response to this situation the government submitted and Parliament approved a new labor code which to some extent undid the work of 1845 and restored some of the controls of the guild system, for which the workers had been clamoring. At the same time a bid was made for support of the peasantry by out-and-out abolition of patrimonial jurisdiction.[26]

The strength of the radicals made it difficult if not impossible for the government to carry through its plan for conservative revision of the constitution. So when the Parliament, on April 27, 1849, called upon the government to approve the liberal constitution worked out for all Germany by the Frankfurt Parliament, the decision was taken to dissolve it and then promulgate a new electoral law that would produce a more satisfactory chamber. The new law introduced the three-class system of voting, which remained in effect until 1918. While every adult and "independent" male retained the franchise, the electorate was divided into three classes according to taxpaying ability. The first class, paying in the aggregate one-third of the direct taxes, comprised only 5 per cent of the population but elected one-third of the deputies. Its voting power was four times as great as that of the second class and about twenty-five times as great as that of the third class. In Berlin, for instance, the first class in 1849 numbered 2,000, the second 7,000 and the third 70,000 persons. Obviously, the effect of the law was to exclude from the franchise the miners, factory workers and domestics who could be classified as not independent. Political control

[25] Friedrich Meinecke: *Weltbürgertum und Nationalstaat* (1962 ed.), 349 ff.; Friedrich Frahm: "Entstehung und Entwicklungsgeschichte der preussischen Verfassung" (*Forschungen zur brandenburgischen und preussischen Geschichte*, XLI, 1928, 248–301); Huber: *Deutsche Verfassungsgeschichte*, II, 763 ff.

[26] Rudolf Stadelmann: *Soziale und politische Geschichte der Revolution von 1848* (Munich, 1948), 171; Hamerow: *Restoration, Revolution, Reaction*, 188 ff.; P. H. Noyes: *Organization and Revolution* (Princeton, 1966), 318.

was in the hands of the propertied classes, the large landholders and the upper middle class. These people had never favored universal suffrage and asked nothing better than a franchise based on property, as in France, Belgium and Britain. In the elections of June, 1849, the results were entirely satisfactory tó the government. The lower classes were accorded so little power that many of them ignored the election. In the industrial Rhineland and Westphalia abstentions were as high as 80 or even 90 per cent. Even in rural Brandenburg they reached 60 per cent.[27]

The new Parliament worked harmoniously with the government in revising the constitution, which was promulgated on January 31, 1850. The upper chamber now became a house of peers, the cabinet became responsible to the king alone, and in general the royal authority was fully restored. The revolution was over. What is surprising is that in Prussia it should have had so radical a complexion. It is readily understandable that in the industrialized areas, where unemployment was prevalent, the democratic forces should have enlisted support among the workers. Evidently the situation of the rural workers under feudal conditions was just as bad and produced just as much radicalism. The situation in Prussia, which was ostensibly favorable was actually parlous. But the forces of radicalism were too unorganized and the leadership too inexperienced to establish effective control. Furthermore, the government still had the loyalty of the armed forces and so was able, when the time seemed ripe, to defeat the revolution. Nonetheless, much had been gained. The old system of government through the patrimonial estates had been replaced by a form of parliamentary government; absolutism had given way to constitutionalism. The common people, it is true, had suffered defeat and were not to play a much larger role under the new system than under the old. But the upper middle class, which had led the opposition in the years before 1848, had established its position on the political stage. Popular insurrection, for all the fear and danger it involved, had forced the governments to accept a large installment of liberal demands. To master insurgency the governments had been obliged to purchase the support of the moderates by adopting reforms which, though partial, breached the walls of the old order and opened the way to modernization.

[27] Schilfert: *Sieg und Niederlage,* 267 ff.; Jacques Droz: *Les révolutions allemandes de 1848* (Paris, 1957), 476 ff.; Huber: *Deutsche Verfassungsgeschichte,* III, 49 ff.

4. SCHWARZENBERG AND THE HUNGARIAN WAR

The suppression of the revolution in Vienna enabled the court Camarilla to prepare openly for the counterrevolution. On the recommendation of Windischgrätz a new cabinet was appointed under Prince Felix zu Schwarzenberg, who, however, insisted that first of all the dynastic change, so long planned by the Archduchess Sophia and her entourage, should be carried through. On December 2, then, the Emperor Ferdinand abdicated in favor of his nephew Francis Joseph, who had just turned eighteen and was therefore legally of age.[28] For the next three years, however, the government was in the firm and energetic hands of Schwarzenberg, who is generally regarded as the prototype of the realistic statesmen who were to dominate both domestic and international politics during the ensuing period. The new chancellor was a man of high intelligence but quite unhampered by moral considerations. Though a member of one of the greatest landholding families, he was by no means the rock-ribbed feudalist that Windischgrätz was. Determined to put an end to revolution, he nevertheless recognized the need for some progressive change. His own class, the high aristocracy, was too hidebound for the modern world. It was necessary and desirable, he thought, to bring at least the upper middle class into political life. He had associated with him in the cabinet Count Franz Stadion, the liberal-minded governor of Galicia; Alexander Bach, an outstanding lawyer and former leader of the liberal *bourgeoisie;* and Karl Ludwig Bruck, a Rhinelander by birth who had made himself a great merchant and shipowner. These men, whatever their differing views on details, were united in the effort to counteract revolutionary agitation by overhauling and modernizing the old system of feudal privilege. Schwarzenberg, in presenting his cabinet to the Austrian Parliament, which had been transferred to Kremsier, near Olmütz, announced the intention of the government to work with the representatives of the people in establishing a constitutional state: "We honestly and unreservedly desire the constitutional monarchy."[29]

The sequel was to demonstrate that Schwarzenberg was insincere in this affirmation, made no doubt to rally popular support until the

---

[28] Josef Redlich: *Emperor Francis Joseph of Austria* (New York, 1929), 27 ff.

[29] Rudolf Kiszling: *Die Revolution im Kaisertum Oesterreich* (Vienna, 1948), I, 303 ff.; Adolf Schwarzenberg: *Prince Felix zu Schwarzenberg* (New York, 1946), 27 ff.; Rudolf Kiszling: *Fürst Felix zu Schwarzenberg* (Graz, 1952), 45 ff.

revolutionary unrest had been ended. Nonetheless, the work of the next few years must not be ignored. For example, the government made no effort to return to the feudal system, nor to undo the emancipation of the peasantry. Much was done to put the administration, the tax system and the tariff on a uniform basis. The administration of justice was taken from the bureaucracy and trial by jury was introduced. The civil service was thoroughly reformed and a substantial measure of local self-government instituted. All in all, the upheaval of 1848 brought not inconsiderable changes in the direction of modernization.

Schwarzenberg's immediate objectives were to restore the authority of the government throughout the empire, and to re-establish the position of Austria as a great power in German and European affairs. Most pressing was the need for liquidating the Hungarian problem, which meant the military defeat of the "rebel" kingdom and the destruction of the historic rights and claims of the Crown of St. Stephen. The Hungarian government refused to recognize the accession of Francis Joseph as king of Hungary on the plea that the dynastic change had been engineered without consultation with the Budapest Parliament. The Hungarians were further provoked and outraged by Schwarzenberg's contention that the new ruler was not bound by the concessions which had been extracted from his predecessor under duress. By the new year the break between the two governments was complete. Francis Joseph declared Kossuth and his supporters rebels and traitors and ordered Windischgrätz to proceed militarily against them.[30]

The commander of the forces was slow in getting operations under way, partly because he doubted the ability of the Austrians to subdue the Hungarians without Russian help and therefore hoped to induce the Hungarian aristocrats to assert themselves against Kossuth and the extreme nationalists, and then offer their submission to the emperor-king. These hopes were by no means groundless, for many of the Hungarian magnates felt that Kossuth had driven matters too far and that the revolutionary reform movement might well end in the destruction of the entire social structure. Had Windischgrätz been willing to

[30] C. M. Knatchbull-Hugessen: *The Political Evolution of the Hungarian Nation* (London, 1908), II, 108 ff.; Heinrich Marczali: *Ungarische Verfassungsgeschichte* (Tübingen, 1910), 151.

agree to terms short of unconditional surrender, a compromise might indeed have been arrived at.[31]

Initially the prospects of the Hungarians seemed dim indeed. General Arthur Görgei, a thirty-year-old engineer officer, who had been appointed to command of the army, had a hard time in recruiting, training and equipping a force of even 30,000 men. When Kossuth tried to induce him to attack the Austrians, he flatly refused, with the result that serious dissension quickly developed between the politician Kossuth and the soldier Görgei, who resented civilian interference with operations. Görgei, like many others, had doubts about Kossuth's extreme nationalism and was not ill-disposed toward negotiations which might lead to a return to the *status quo*.[32]

When finally Windischgrätz began his advance (December 15), Görgei refused battle and fell back so as to keep his forces intact. Since he did not believe defense of the capital militarily advisable, Kossuth and the government were obliged to move to Debreczen, to the east of the Tisza (Theiss) River. On January 5, 1849, Austrian troops occupied Budapest, to the immense rejoicing of those who, like Windischgrätz, considered the war all but concluded, especially after a victory over the Hungarian field forces at Kapolna on February 26.

This easy success probably decided Schwarzenberg to cut short the constitutional labors of the Austrian Parliament, which had reached completion. The Parliament had eschewed consideration of Austria's place in the projected German Empire, partly because the Czech deputies were so firmly opposed to the program of German unity and partly because that problem was within the province of the Frankfurt Parliament, in which Austria had representation. Hungary, too, had been omitted from its deliberations on the grounds that that kingdom had been granted virtual independence in March, 1848. The long and arduous debates had therefore focused on the knotty problem of organizing a state in which there were many nationalities living inter-

---

[31] Friedrich Walter: *Die Nationalitätenfrage im alten Ungarn* (Munich, 1959), 8k ff.; Erzsebet Andics: *Das Bündnis Habsburg-Romanow* (Budapest, 1963), 139 ff.

[32] Fritz Valjevec: "Ungarn und die Frage des oesterreichischen Gesamtstaates zu Beginn des Jahres 1849" (*Historische Zeitschrift*, CLXV, 1941, 81–98); Gyözö Ember: "Louis Kossuth à la tête du Comité de la Défense Nationale" (*Studia historica*, VI, 1953, 40 ff.); Erzsebet Andics: "Kossuth en lutte contre les ennemis des réformes et de la révolution" (*ibid.*, XII, 1954, 82 ff.); Julius Miskolczy: *Ungarn in der Habsburger-Monarchie* (Vienna, 1959), 114.

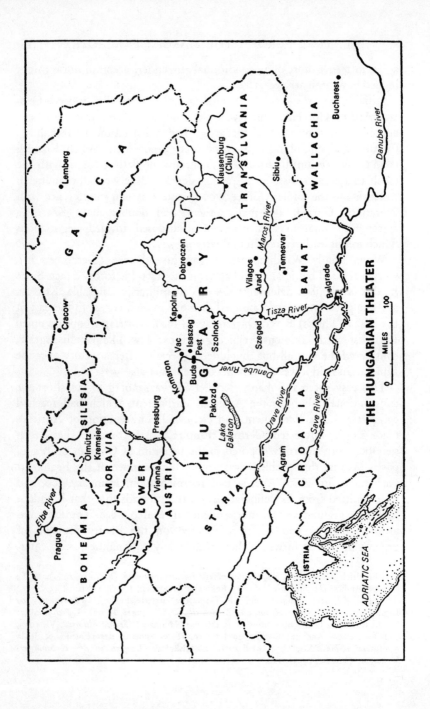

THE HUNGARIAN THEATER

spersed in many areas and having various historic rights and claims. The Czechs took the conservative view and opposed all efforts at centralization, which they believed certain to end in domination by the German element.

The Parliament's draft, the so-called Kremsier Constitution, was unanimously approved by the assembly on March 1, 1849. It is historically of great interest, for it proposed a compromise solution for the multinational empire. In the first place it provided for popular sovereignty and so marked the end of absolutism and the patrimonial state. The emperor was to appoint the ministers, but they were to be responsible also to the Parliament. The emperor's veto on legislation enacted by Parliament was to be only suspensive, and his power to dissolve Parliament was limited by the proviso that a new Parliament should meet within three months. Parliament was to consist of an upper house (*Länderkammer*) composed of delegations from the historic local diets or *Landtage*. The lower house (*Volkskammer*) was to be popularly elected by direct vote. The constitution declared all peoples of the monarchy to have equal rights in matters of language and administration. The provincial Diets were to have broad autonomy in cultural matters, and the districts (*Kreise*), into which the historic lands (*Länder*) were to be divided, were to be based on nationality and to have popularly elected councils. In sum, the Kremsier draft constitution envisaged a liberal representative system and at the same time a federal organization based on the historic lands with a large measure of local self-government and full scope for national self-expression. This was probably as close to a satisfactory solution of the nationalities problem as one could hope to come.[33]

Schwarzenberg, who had been watching the work of the Parliament with ill-concealed hostility, had long since made up his mind to dissolve it as soon as possible. If he had not done so prior to March 1, it was chiefly out of consideration for public opinion in Germany, where Austria's position would be further weakened by an attack upon the popularly elected Parliament. Now, when the assembly voted

---

[33] The basic study is Josef Redlich: *Das oesterreichische Staats- und Reichsproblem* (Leipzig, 1920), I, Part III. See also Paula Geist-Lanyi: *Das Nationalitätenproblem auf dem Reichstag zu Kremsier* (Munich, 1920); Fritz von Reinöhl: "Die Frage der deutschen Einheit und der Wien-Kremsier Reichstag" (in *Festschrift für Ritter von Srbik*, Munich, 1938, 276–286); Robert A. Kann: *The Multinational Empire* (New York, 1950), II, 21 ff.

approval of the draft constitution, further delay was impossible. On March 4 the Parliament was prorogued and the government promulgated its own constitution, largely the work of Count Stadion. In many respects this "provisional constitution" was hardly less liberal than that of the Parliament, though the franchise was restricted to taxpayers and the powers of the emperor were more extensive. The important difference was in the projected organization of the empire. The government constitution was to apply to all Hapsburg possessions, described as "the free, indivisible, indissoluble, constitutional hereditary monarchy." This meant the inclusion of Hungary, of which the constitution was to remain valid only in so far as it did not conflict with the imperial constitution. Hungary was reduced to the status of any other crown land, and was to be deprived of all its historically associated territories (*partes adnexae*). Thus Croatia, Slavonia, Voivodina and Transylvania were all given the status of individual crown lands, each with its own Diet.[34]

An eminent authority has described the government constitution of March 4 a "supreme piece of political jugglery," designed by its ostensible liberalism to mislead German public opinion and by its all-inclusiveness to challenge Hungarian nationalism.[35] This it certainly did, despite the fact that in April the tide of victory had begun to turn in favor of the Hungarians. Windischgrätz, by his procrastination, had given Görgei time to complete his preparations. In a brilliant campaign the Hungarian army evaded the Austrians and, marching north, joined forces with the new levies concentrated east of the Tisza River. On March 5 Görgei had won a first victory at Szolnok, to be followed by a second at Isaszeg (April 6). Meanwhile another Hungarian force, commanded by the Polish general Bem, who had escaped from Vienna, drove the Austrians out of Transylvania and threatened to invade Galicia. Under these favorable auspices Kossuth was able to override the compunctions of the more moderate elements. In response to Schwarzenberg's constitution he proclaimed the Hapsburg dynasty deposed and Hungary completely independent, with the inclusion of

---

[34] Redlich: *Das oesterreichische Staats und Reichsproblem*, I, Part IV, chap. i; Kann: *Multinational Empire*, II, 59 ff. The important documents are printed in the fundamental study of Hanns Schlitter: *Versäumte Gelegenheiten: die okroyierte Verfassung vom 4 März, 1849* (Vienna, 1920); see also Walter: *Die Nationalitätenfrage im alten Ungarn*, 88 ff.

[35] Redlich: *Emperor Francis Joseph*, 77.

Transylvania and other associated territories (April 14). The Committee of National Defense was dissolved and Kossuth became governor-president. Though not officially a republic, the new regime was in every respect *de facto* republican.

For a month or six weeks the miracle of Hungarian victory was several times repeated. Görgei advanced to Budapest, which he besieged and finally captured (May 21). By this time the Vienna government was panic-stricken, fearing a Hungarian advance on Vienna and a recrudescence of insurgency in the capital. Windischgrätz was replaced by General Welden, who, after inspecting the situation, gave up all hope. There was now no alternative to calling on Czar Nicholas for aid.

The czar felt bound by the agreements of Münchengrätz (1834) and by his promise to the Emperor Francis in 1835 to stand by his successors. Fearful lest the revolutionary upheaval in Central Europe spread to Russia, he had concentrated large armies on the frontiers so as to be ready to intervene when necessary. He watched developments in Germany with as much interest as the affairs of his own country and as for Austria was convinced that its maintenance as a great power was of supreme interest to Russia, not only as a bulwark against revolutionary ideas coming from the West, but also as a counterweight to a possible united Germany under Prussian leadership. "No one needs a strong and powerful Austria more than I do," he had written the Archduchess Sophia when she begged his support for her son in December, 1848. Nicholas kept urging the Hapsburg government to take a strong line against the revolutionaries and had applauded every success of Windischgrätz, Jellachich and Radetzky. Time and again he reiterated his readiness to help, but only on condition that he be appealed to by the emperor himself and that he be allowed to conduct the intervention on his own terms.[36]

On the Austrian side Schwarzenberg as well as Windischgrätz had envisaged the probable need for Russian aid against Hungary, but the chancellor was naturally reluctant to suffer the humiliation of an

---

[36] Fundamental are the studies of Revekka Averbuch: *Tsarkaiia interventsiia v borbe s vengerskoi revolutsiei* (Moscow, 1935); Eugene Horvath: "Russia and the Hungarian Revolution" (*Slavonic Review*, XII, 1934, 628–659); Dionys von Janossy: "Die russische Intervention in Ungarn im Jahre 1849" (*Jahrbuch des Wiener Ungarischen Historischen Instituts*, I, 1931, 314–335); A. S. Nifontow: *Russland im Jahre 1848* (Berlin, 1954); Andićs: *Das Bündnis Habsburg-Romanow*, 68 ff.

appeal. He tried to induce the Russians to intervene spontaneously and secretly encouraged the Austrian commander in Transylvania to call upon General Lüders and the Russian forces occupying the Danubian Principalities for support when Bem threatened to take over the entire area. When, on March 11, Bem defeated both the Austrians and the Russians near Sibiu, Schwarzenberg felt obliged to ask for 30,000 Russian troops to intervene in Transylvania.[37]

Finally, on April 20, when the Austrian commander ordered the evacuation of Budapest and there was reason to fear that the Hungarians might presently stage an advance on Vienna, Schwarzenberg formally requested Russian intervention in Galicia, despite the fact that the cabinet was still reluctant to take the plunge. Nicholas, dreading the possibility of an invasion of Galicia by Bem and an eventual Polish insurrection, ordered General Paskievich to act. The intervention was publicly announced on May 8 as urgently necessary to forestall the spread of revolution. The presence of Polish officers and refugees in the Hungarian army, possibly 5,000 in number, was greatly exaggerated by the Austrian authorities, who reported 20,000 Poles, organized in separate regiments and corps, so as to impress the Russians. In any case, the czar felt that he must crush the revolution or be incessantly menaced by it.[38]

On June 6 the main Russian army of 100,000 men poured over the Carpathians and into Galicia and Hungary, while another force of 30,000 invaded Transylvania from Wallachia. But the opening of the campaign was delayed not only by the indecision and circumspection of the commander-in-chief, Field-Marshal Paskievich, but by lack of provisions and supplies and by the outbreak of a severe cholera epidemic which, during July and August, took a heavy toll. However, more and more troops were dispatched to clinch the victory, until ultimately the Russians had sent about 360,000 men into the country. The Hungarians, who had enjoyed a superiority in numbers over the

---

[37] Hugo Kerchnawe: *Feldmarshall Fürst Windischgrätz und die russische Hilfe, 1848* (Innsbruck, 1930); Andiés: *Das Bündnis Habsburg-Romanow*, 106 ff., 116 ff., 126 ff., 136.

[38] His remarks to the French representative, cited by Constantin de Grunwald: *Tsar Nicholas I* (New York, 1955), 249 ff. See also Nifontow: *Russland im Jahre 1848*, chap. viii; Walter: *Die Nationalitätemfrage im alten Ungarn* 107 ff.; Andiés: *Die Bündnis Habsburg-Romanow*, 137, 144 ff.

Austrians, now saw the scales swing violently against them. There was, in fact, little or no hope of holding out for long.[39]

In this extremity Kossuth tried to arrive at a separate agreement with the czar, suggesting the possibility of electing a Russian grand duke to the Hungarian throne, but Nicholas would not parley with a revolutionary. Kossuth also approached the Frankfurt Parliament, stressing the common interest of Germans and Hungarians in forestalling the domination of Central Europe by the Slavs. But his appeal impressed only the German radicals, and came to nothing. Britain and France, on whom Kossuth for a time placed high hopes, proved equally disillusioning. Both powers were interested chiefly in preserving the Hapsburg Monarchy as a bulwark against Russia. Though radicals such as Cobden and Urquhart might sympathize, Palmerston refused to be moved, even by suggestions of a favorable trade treaty. On July 21 he summed up the British interest as he saw it, in a speech to Parliament:

The political independence and liberties of Europe are bound up . . . with the maintenance and integrity of Austria as a great European power; and therefore anything which tends by direct or even remote contingency to weaken and to cripple Austria, but still more to reduce her from the position of a first-rate Power to that of a secondary State, must be a great calamity to Europe, and one which every Englishman ought to deprecate and to try to prevent.[40]

With conservative circles in all countries, even Britain, on the Austrian and Russian side, the Hungarians had only the military genius of Görgei, the determination of Kossuth, and the valor of the troops to fall back upon. Fortunately for them Paskievich, who had been ordered by the czar to "strike like a thunderbolt," did nothing of

[39] One of the best studies of the campaign is the contemporary account of Max Schlesinger: *The War in Hungary* (London, 1850). Of modern treatments, see Kiszling: *Die Revolution im Kaisertum Oesterreich*, II, and John S. Curtiss: *The Russian Army under Nicholas I* (Durham, 1965), chap. xv.

[40] Quoted by Charles Sproxton: *Palmerston and the Hungarian Revolution* (Cambridge, 1919), 21. For other aspects of the international situation, see Wilhelm Alter: *Die auswärtige Politik der ungarischen Revolution* (Berlin, 1912), 25 ff.; Eugene Horvath: "Kossuth and Palmerston, 1848–1849" (*Slavonic Review*, IX, 1931, 612–631); N. J. Szenczi: "Great Britain and the War of Hungarian Independence" (*ibid.*, XVII, 1939, 556–570); Denes A. Janossy: "Great Britain and Kossuth" (*Archivum Europae Centro-Orientalis*, III, 1937, 53–190); Andićs: *Die Bündnis Habsburg-Romanow*, 165 ff.

the kind. Though the Hungarians were obliged to abandon Budapest and move the government to Szeged (July 2), Görgei succeeded in evading the Russian armies and retreating to the northeast, whence he then marched southward beyond the Tisza River toward Szeged. At the same time, however, the Austrian general, Count Julius von Haynau, advanced from the west, crossed the Tisza and defeated a Hungarian force under General Dembinski near Temesvar. Since the Russians had managed also to drive the Hungarians in Transylvania across the border into Turkey, the Hungarians were being gradually surrounded. Görgei, who had been at odds with Kossuth for some time, insisted on his resignation (August 11) and two days later surrendered with his 25,000 men at Világos, not to Haynau and the Austrians, but to the Russians. Kossuth and other leaders fled to Turkish territory, where their presence soon created an international crisis. The Austrians and Russians demanded their extradition, while the British and French supported the sultan in refusing it. Under threat of a British-French naval demonstration, Austria and Russia finally gave way.[41]

Görgei was given his freedom by the Russians, who found it easy to get along with the Hungarians, whose plucky resistance they admired. But Russian efforts to intercede in their behalf with the Vienna government proved utterly futile. The Austrians were furious with the Hungarians for having forced upon them the humiliation of appealing for foreign help. They had even considered asking the czar for a tract of territory in northern Asia to which they could exile the revolutionaries. Haynau, an able general but a heartless brute, was beside himself when the Hungarians surrendered to the Russians. He secured from the emperor a free hand to try and execute thirteen Hungarian generals, as well as the former premier, Count Batthyány.[42] Thousands of other Hungarians were sentenced to long prison terms. Pleas for moderation by the British and other governments were ignored or

[41] Eduard von Wertheimer: "Die Kossuth-Emigration in der Türkei" (*Ungarische Jahrbücher*, VIII, 1928, 377 ff.); Harold Temperley: *The Crimea* (London, 1936), 292 ff.; Vernon J. Puryear: *England, Russia and the Straits Question, 1844–1856* (Berkeley, 1931), 153 ff.

[42] For a discussion of responsibilities, see Walter: *Die Nationalitäten Frage im alten Ungarn*, 123 ff.; Andić: *Die Bündnis Habsburg-Romanow*, 158, 195.

rejected. In a letter to the British ambassador in Vienna, Palmerston felt impelled to describe the Austrians as "the greatest brutes that ever called themselves by the undeserved name of civilised men."[43]

For some years Hungary remained under martial law, divided into five military districts and ruled by German officials sent from Vienna. Croatia, Slavonia and other lands, which had espoused the imperial cause against the Hungarians, were treated no better. All nationalities, it was said, were given equal rights to Germanization. Soon it became clear that the March 4 constitution had been meant solely as window dressing. It was never put into effect. Once the Hungarian problem was solved, the government felt free to ignore it and eventually (December 31, 1851) it was replaced by an imperial decree or "patent" which restored absolute rule. There was to be an appointed council (*Reichsrat*) with consultative powers only, but the government was in reality left to a ministry appointed by the emperor and a bureaucracy recruited from the German population. German was made the official language. This was the so-called "Bach System," from the name of the man who had started as a liberal and had in 1849 succeeded Count Stadion as minister of the interior. Actually it was inspired by Baron von Kübeck, a close adviser of the emperor and an unrepentant conservative.[44]

The surrender of the Hungarians capped the victory of the counter-revolutionary forces in the Hapsburg Empire. Looking back on the great revolutionary upheaval, it is rather surprising that it ever developed as far as it did, for the truly revolutionary forces were weak and unorganized. The liberal elements, who never contemplated a resort to violence, were carried away by the students and workers of Vienna and were soon so frightened that they either retired from the scene or actively supported the government. The threat of peasant insurrection, which was real and formidable, was eliminated by the prompt abolition of remaining feudal obligations and dues.

There remained the problem of nationalities, which gave the court an opportunity to play off one group against another, the more so as

[43] Sproxton: *Palmerston and the Hungarian Revolution*, 109–111.

[44] Redlich: *Das oesterreichische Staats und Reichsproblem*, I, Part IV, chap. iii; Kann: *Multinational Empire*, II, 115 ff.; Schwarzenberg: *Prince Felix zu Schwarzenberg*, 98 ff.; Kiszling: *Fürst Felix zu Schwarzenberg*, 166 ff.

the Hungarians, under Kossuth's influence, overshot the mark in demanding a degree of independence that might have destroyed the monarchy as a great power and in any case antagonized the other nationalities. The majority of the Hungarian aristocracy and even many of the gentry disapproved of Kossuth's policies, but he was able to rally the support of the workers and peasants and eventually over-reached himself. Even so, the resistance of the Hungarians was truly impressive. It is most unlikely that the government would have been able to suppress the Hungarian revolution without the massive aid of the Russians.

The story of the Hapsburg insurrections is filled with subterfuges, deceits and brutalities of many kinds. Yet the fact remains that despite the repression some progress was made. The government leaders, Radetzky, Schwarzenberg, Stadion, Bach, whatever their transgressions, were not dyed-in-the-wool feudalists like Windischgrätz. True, they were determined to forestall popular sovereignty and representative government and to frustrate the reorganization of the empire along federal lines, but they would not go back to the patrimonial system of hoary privilege and feudal rights. The revolution, it must be said, had at least the effect of opening the way to modernization in Central Europe.

5. GERMANY: THE DILEMMA OF NATIONALISM

It was indeed a tragedy that the Parliament at Frankfurt should have arrived at debate on the composition and organization of the new national state at a time when the revolutionary movements in the two principal capitals were being suppressed and the governments again securing control of their affairs. The Parliament has sometimes been blamed for spending months on discussions in the Constitutional Committee and so allowing the golden moment when the governments were relatively helpless to pass. But a few months devoted to so difficult and complicated a problem would hardly seem excessive. In France the Constitutional Committee took almost as long to debate a far less thorny problem. The Frankfurt committee included many of Germany's most outstanding scholars. It is not true that they lost themselves in rhetoric and theory. The records of their proceedings reveal much hardheaded thinking in addition to an impressive knowledge of the British, French and American constitutional systems and their operation.[45]

There was basic agreement among the men of the Frankfurt Parliament that the new German state must be a federal state (*Bundesstaat*), that is, something more than a mere confederation of states (*Staatenbund*), such as the Germanic Confederation of 1815. The federal government would have extensive executive power, including control over foreign policy, the armed forces, justice, trade, and so on. The more conservative men of the right wished to preserve as much as possible of the authority of the individual states; they were "particularists." Those on the left, by contrast, wanted the powers of the princes and their governments pared to the bone and almost complete authority vested in the federal government. In between were the center groups whose members, far from being contemptuous of local traditions and interests, were enamored of the variety of German life. While desirous of preserving the individuality of the member states, they were nevertheless determined to have a federal system endowed with effective power. Differences of opinion in these matters were susceptible of compromise and what finally emerged was an intermediate solution.

Far more baffling was the question what territories should be included in the new German Empire. In the early months of the revolution it was generally believed that the Hapsburg Monarchy was doomed to disintegration and that, if it survived at all, it would be little more than a loose aggregation of national units. The Germans of Austria were, in these circumstances, eager to be included in the new Germany, and the non-Austrian Germans were just as keenly desirous of having them. In the summer of 1848 it still looked as though the emerging German state would comprise all major German populations, that is, would be a truly national state.

Yet after Radetzky's victory at Custoza it seemed increasingly likely that the Hapsburg government would regain its footing. By October the chances of the counterrevolution were even brighter. At Frankfurt some of the radicals began to argue that if the Hapsburg Empire was to be disrupted, it was high time to act. They pleaded for aid to the

[45] Anton Scholl: *Der Einfluss der nordamerikanischen Unionsverfassung auf die Verfassung des Deutschen Reiches vom 28 März, 1849* (Leipzig, 1913); Eckart G. Franz: *Das Amerikabild der deutschen Revolution von 1848–1849* (Heidelberg, 1958); Halvdan Koht: *The American Spirit in Europe* (Philadelphia, 1949), chap. iv, who stresses the profound influence of Tocqueville's *Democracy in America*.

Viennese insurgents and support for the Hungarians. But the majority would not hear of such a provocative policy. Most members were convinced that it would be a fatal mistake to antagonize the governments, with which co-operation was necessary if the German problem was to be solved without major ructions. So the Parliament remained inactive while the counterrevolution triumphed, while Windischgrätz defiantly executed Robert Blum, one of the most prominent leaders of the left.[46]

Just as the revolution in Vienna was about to go under, the Frankfurt assembly on October 27 voted (316–90) approval of paragraphs II and III of the constitutional draft, which specified that no part of the new German Empire should be connected with non-German territories save through purely personal union. This posed the "great query" which the Austrian government would have to answer: whether to allow its German provinces to join the new Germany and reorganize the Hapsburg Monarchy as a loose conglomeration of lands held together only through the dynastic tie, or whether to accept its exclusion from the projected German national state.

Austrian historians have complained that the historian Gustav Droysen, who drafted these fateful paragraphs, was a North German who lacked understanding or appreciation of Austria's position and mission; that he looked upon the monarchy simply as "an irrational complex of states." Perhaps so, but the fact remains that of the 115 Austrian deputies in the Frankfurt Parliament, 74 voted in favor of Droysen's draft. Like their colleagues, most of the Austrian deputies had set their hopes on the nascent German state and were prepared to bid the Hapsburg Monarchy farewell.[47] The great majority of the members had convinced themselves that the Hapsburg government would never accept the solution offered it and that therefore the inclusion of the German lands of Austria was impossible. With heavy hearts they had decided that it was better to abandon the Austrian Germans than to jeopardize the future of all Germany. It seems that the Austrian Germans (in contrast to the Austrian deputies in the Parliament) were in fact opposed to any plan that involved the breakup of

[46] Hans G. Telle: *Das oesterreichische Problem im Frankfurter Parlament im Sommer und Herbst, 1848* (Marburg, 1933), 78 ff.

[47] Heinrich von Srbik: *Deutsche Einheit* (3 ed., Munich, 1940), I, 366 ff.; Rudolf Kiszling: *Die Revolution im Kaisertum Oesterreich* (Vienna, 1948), I, 337 ff.

the historic Hapsburg Empire. They had a deep conviction of mission to rule the congeries of nationalities in the Danube Basin. Yet, unwilling to sacrifice the monarchy, they were indignant at the attempt to exclude them from German affairs.[48]

Following the subjugation of Vienna, the Austrian government made it increasingly clear that the empire would be maintained as a single state (*Gesamtstaat*) and that, as soon as it had put its own house in order, it would discuss its relations with the rest of Germany. In other words, while the Italian and Hungarian problems were still unsettled, the Vienna government did not propose to challenge the Frankfurt Parliament.

Schwarzenberg's negative stand led to the resignation (December 15) of the Frankfurt cabinet of Anton von Schmerling, a prominent Austrian liberal. Heinrich von Gagern headed the new cabinet, while Eduard von Simson succeeded him as presiding officer of the Parliament. Gagern, it will be recalled,[49] had from the outset held that the only feasible solution of the German problem lay in establishment of a federal state under Prussian leadership, with the exclusion of the German provinces of Austria. The German and the Austrian Empires could then be united through a constitutional alliance. It was an integral part of his plan, however, that the king of Prussia should exchange his royal crown for the imperial one, which was to carry real power and authority. Meanwhile, in order to avoid the domination of the new federal state by one powerful member, and to establish something like equality between the member states, Prussia was to be dissolved and each of its eight provinces was to become a separate member state of the empire, while many of the smallest German states were to be merged with the larger states. The end result would be the emergence of eight German states to match the eight former provinces of Prussia. Lest the reader suppose that such a fundamental recasting was fantastic, he should be reminded that Napoleon in 1803 had carried through just such a restructuring of the German world and that, since most of the German states had existed in their present form only since 1815, they could all be regarded as still in a formative stage. This was particularly true of Prussia, which many looked upon as a mere

[48] Adolf Rapp: *Grossdeutsch-Kleindeutsch* (Munich, 1922), xxiv; Jacques Droz: *L'Europe centrale: évolution historique de l'idée de 'Mitteleuropa'* (Paris, 1960), 79 ff.

[49] See above, Chapter XII.

"bundle of provinces." Bismarck was partially to remake the German world in 1866, while later, in 1919, many liberals were to advocate the dissolution of the Prussian state. It was something of a tragedy that this was accomplished not in 1848 but only after two world wars.[50]

That Frederick William of Prussia had a genuine interest in the larger problem of German unity is not in dispute. Indeed, in the days of his tribulation he had talked of his readiness to "merge" or "fuse" Prussia with Germany. But these were merely beautiful words, designed to still the popular clamor. Neither the king nor the court had any intention of breaking up the glorious monarchy of Frederick the Great. They were particularists, almost to a man. Even the liberal leaders of the industrialized Rhineland, where separatist feeling was stronger than elsewhere, were opposed to disruption of the monarchy. Gagern and other members of minor South German states might cook up alluring schemes, but neither one of the two great powers was willing to be carved up or merge its identity in a still-nebulous national state. The Frankfurt leaders had soon to deal with the further fact that the so-called "middle states," that is, those of intermediate size, were one and all opposed to the surrender of substantial authority to the projected federal government. All told, the Gagern program, however intelligent and carefully planned, from the outset ran serious danger of shipwreck.

The suppression of the Berlin revolution in November led many to fear that Prussia would adopt an out-and-out reactionary policy and so make itself impossible as the leader of liberal Germany. Gagern himself hurried to Berlin, which, incidentally, he had never before visited. He tried to persuade the king to replace the cabinet of Count Brandenburg by one enjoying the confidence of the Prussian Parliament and did what he could to forestall the promulgation by the government of a constitution that might conflict with that being worked out at Frankfurt. By holding before Frederick William the prospect of the imperial crown, he hoped to prevent a reorganization of the Prussian state that would nullify plans for its dissolution. His efforts, however, proved vain and his sole consolation was the realization that the Prussian

---

[50] For full treatment of this subject, see the classic study of Friedrich Meinecke: *Weltbürgertum und Nationalstaat* (7 ed., now in his *Werke*, Munich, 1962).

constitution of December 5 was more liberal than might have been expected.[51]

Despite the independent procedure of the Berlin government, the Frankfurt Parliament proceeded on what was now the only remaining course of action. On January 3, 1849, it adopted the Gagern plan for an "inner" federal state and an "outer" federation to include the Austrian Empire. Two days later it defeated a radical proposal for a federal republic under a popularly elected president and adopted a motion for a federal empire under a hereditary emperor. The Parliament had by this time split into a greater German (*grossdeutsch*) and a lesser German (*kleindeutsch*) faction. The former, commanding some 125 votes, favored inclusion of either the German provinces of Austria or the entire Hapsburg Monarchy in the new federal state, and looked with disdain on the lesser German faction, which commanded more votes (about 225), as compromisers who would exclude Austria and so betray the German national cause.[52]

The final decision was forced on the Frankfurt Parliament when Schwarzenberg on March 4 promulgated the constitution which treated the Hapsburg Monarchy as a single unit and then followed up (March 11) with the demand that the entire empire be included in the new German state. This state, he proposed, should be governed by a directory of seven, assisted by a chamber of states (*Staatenhaus*) appointed by the state governments, and in this Austria, on the basis of population, should have thirty-eight seats, as against thirty-two for all the other German states combined.

This was too much for the *Kleindeutschen*. Gagern and his associates now made a deal with the radicals: they agreed that provision for an upper house of Parliament should be dropped and that election for the lower house should be by universal, equal and direct suffrage. In return, the radicals undertook to vote the rest of the constitution and not to obstruct the election of the king of Prussia as emperor. The constitution was then voted on March 27 and the final step, the election

[51] Meinecke: *Weltbürgertum und Nationalstaat*, 340 ff.; Huber: *Deutsche Verfassungsgeschichte*, II, 756 ff.

[52] The two terms appeared first in December, 1848. See Heidrun von Möller: *Grossdeutsch und Kleindeutsch; die Entstehung der Worte in den Jahren 1848–1849* (Berlin, 1937).

of Frederick William as emperor, was taken on March 28, by a vote of 290 in favor and 248 abstaining.

On April 2 the presiding officer, Eduard von Simson, led a delegation of thirty prominent members of the Parliament to offer Frederick William the imperial crown. The king was gracious but enigmatic. He spoke of the desirability of strengthening the powers of the executive and referred to his obligations toward his fellow princes, without whose approval he could not consider acceptance. The majority of the delegation took the royal remarks as a veiled refusal and they were right. As the king's letters to his friends (published much later) were to reveal, he was most contemptuous of the Frankfurt Parliament and its pretensions to organize the future of Germany. He would have nothing to do, so he wrote, with a crown offered him by bakers and butchers, and reeking with the stench of the revolution. He would not allow the revolutionaries to fasten about his neck a dog collar by which to chain him forever to the principle of popular sovereignty and so make him the slave of the revolution. In short, he would accept the crown only if it were offered to him by his fellow princes. As for the German national state, he could envisage that only in medieval terms, with the Hapsburgs at the head and with government by divinely appointed princes, assisted by their feudal estates.

The temptation is strong to ridicule the king and his antiquated romanticism. It was a real misfortune that at this crucial moment the Prussian crown should have been worn by a man so little fitted to the requirements of the modern world. The men of Frankfurt were as saddened as they were helpless in the face of this situation, for their wisdom would not compensate for their lack of material power. They could neither force the Hapsburgs to accept their exclusion from the new Germany nor induce the Prussian king to change his nature.

At first there was a period of confusion, during which the definitive reply of the king was awaited. There was still some hope that, at the price of certain concessions, he might be persuaded to accept the crown. The Prussian Parliament and even the ministry urged Frederick William to seize the God-given opportunity to assume the leadership of Germany, and in other German states, too, the parliaments and public opinion staunchly backed the Frankfurt program. On April 14 many of the German states (though not the four kingdoms) approved the Frankfurt constitution and recognized the election of Frederick

William as emperor. But all to no avail. The Austrian government advertised its uncompromising opposition and recalled the Austrian deputies from Frankfurt. Frederick William, in turn, was further deterred by the attitude of the Vienna government and may have feared war with Austria and possibly Russia in the event of his accepting the crown. However, these considerations were only ancillary to his deeply felt aversion to the revolution and its objectives. On April 27 the Prussian government informed Frankfurt of the king's rejection of both the constitution and the crown. The Archduke John promptly resigned the post of vicar-general (May 8) and two days later Gagern, too, laid down his office. The final move came when, on May 14, the Berlin government recalled the Prussian deputies and the governments of Saxony, Hanover and other states followed suit.

The Parliament now had no alternative to proclaiming a federal republic and electing a president. This had been the radical program right along, but even now the moderates still hoped that federal reform could somehow be worked out in collaboration with the governments. To this end the Parliament called for new elections and the meeting of the new assembly in August. However, many of the members, now quite disillusioned, left for home. Those who remained voted (May 30) to move to Stuttgart, to be further removed from the federal troops stationed at Mainz. Before they could reassemble, all South Germany was in the turmoil of a new revolution. Only a meager rump gathered at Stuttgart and this was easily dispersed by local troops on June 18. Thus ingloriously ended the Parliament which had brought together so much ability and good will and had embarked a year before with so much confidence and enthusiasm upon the task of national unification.

6. GERMANY: THE RADICAL REVOLUTIONS

Germany, like France, Italy and Hungary, was to experience an outburst of radicalism in the spring and early summer of 1849, the last desperate protest of the revolutionary forces before being overwhelmed by the tide of reaction. The radicals, drawing their strength chiefly from the lesser *bourgeoisie* of southwest Germany and from the artisans, journeymen and factory workers of the industrialized Rhineland, Westphalia and Saxony, were a distinct minority in the Frankfurt Parliament, but were well represented by intellectuals such as teachers and writers. They had been critical of the Frankfurt constitution, which they regarded as not sufficiently democratic and as far too considerate of governments and vested rights. But now that the revolution was threatened with shipwreck, they rallied in support of the constitution, which was approved by many of the state governments under pressure from democratic societies and workers' clubs. The popular movement was, on the whole, political rather than social. In fact, many of the radical leaders were troubled by the extremism of the socialists and communists, whose objectives were suspect. Thus, when Engels attempted to exploit the insurrection in the Rhineland, the revolutionary committee of Elberfeld requested him to leave, lest he create an erroneous impression of the nature of the movement. In the Palatinate and Baden, too, the *élan* seems to have gone out of the revolution as socialists and communists came flocking from all over Europe and started to give the insurrection an unwanted turn.[53]

In the Rhineland the disorders began early in May when the militia regiments refused to obey orders and proclaimed their readiness to defend the Frankfurt constitution. For some days Elberfeld was in the hands of a revolutionary government, of which the Communists tried to secure control. The propertied classes, even the shopkeepers and craftsmen, actively opposed the extremists and the Civic Guard intervened to restore order until regular troops were brought in. The revolution was suppressed. Marx, Engels and other Communists were expelled, and the last number of the Communist organ, the *New Rhenish Gazette,* appeared on May 19.[54]

Dresden was one of the chief centers of insurgency. There the king had defied the popular will by dissolving his Parliament for urging acceptance of the Frankfurt constitution. Great meetings of protest thereupon led to the formation of a Committee of Public Safety (May 3). The king fled the city and appealed to the Prussian government for military aid. When the troops marched in, the barricades went up and some 10,000 insurgents fought desperately for four days and nights.

[53] Rudolf Stadelmann: *Soziale und politische Geschichte der Revolution von 1848* (Munich, 1948), 180 ff.; Karl Obermann: *Die deutschen Arbeiter in der ersten bürgerlichen Revolution* (Berlin, 1950), 256 ff.

[54] Marx and Engels have left their own account in their *Germany: Revolution and Counterrevolution* (1852), chap. xvii, conveniently reprinted with an introduction by Leonard Krieger as Engels: *The German Revolution* (Chicago, 1967). See also Auguste Cornu: "Karl Marx et la révolution de 1848 en Allemagne" (*Europe,* XXVI, 1948, 238–252); Hermann Meyer: "Karl Marx und die deutsche Revolution von 1848" (*Historische Zeitschrift,* CLXXII, 1951, 517–537).

The Dresden rising was noteworthy not only for the ferocity of the struggle but for the participation of several figures of world repute. Bakunin's role is still somewhat obscure, as he seems to have been more interested in stimulating a revolt in Bohemia than in defending the Frankfurt constitution. Without much confidence in the success of the rising, he enjoyed the fighting for its own sake. Another name to become famous throughout the world was Richard Wagner, at that time music director of the Dresden Opera. He had been consorting with Bakunin and other radicals for some time and had become a republican. His radicalism, however, was more cultural than political, and his objective a new and better world for art and artists than for the downtrodden and disfranchised. When finally the Prussian troops had beaten down the rebellion, Wagner managed to escape to Switzerland, but Bakunin was captured, convicted and eventually turned over to the Russian government, which sent him to exile in Siberia.[55]

In southwest Germany, the traditional center of radicalism, where there had already been two serious upheavals, the revolution was first successful in the Bavarian Palatinate, where again some of the troops rallied to the support of a provisional government. For a brief spell the Palatinate was an independent democratic republic. The Bavarian government, faced by the threat of insurgence elsewhere, lacked the forces needed to suppress the revolution and hesitated, as a matter of pride, to call upon the Prussians for aid. But presently Prussian forces, coming from the Rhineland, intervened in the Palatinate without being asked. By mid-June they had snuffed out the insurrection and driven the provisional government into flight.

In Baden the revolution, though last to materialize, proved to be the most formidable. In mid-May the troops of the Rastatt garrison revolted and a huge popular assembly at Offenburg led to the formation of a provisional government, followed by the flight of the grand duke. Radicals of every stripe and every nationality quickly flocked to Baden from every part of Germany and indeed from all over Europe. The

[55] Josef Pfitzner: *Bakuninstudien* (Prague, 1932); Edward H. Carr: *Michael Bakunin* (New York, 1937, 1961), 196; Frederick Barghoorn: "Russian Radicals and the West European Revolutions of 1848" (*Review of Politics*, III, 1949, 338–354). On Wagner, see Ernest Newman: *The Life of Richard Wagner* (New York, 1933–1945), II, chaps. iv and v; K. R. Ganzer: *Richard Wagner, der Revolutionär gegen das 19 Jahrhundert* (Munich, 1934); Maurice Boucher: *The Political Concepts of Richard Wagner* (New York, 1950).

Poles and Hungarians formed separate legions and the well-known Polish revolutionary, Mieroslawski, was given command of the insurgent forces. The Communists, too, appeared on the scene. Marx, for example, badgered the provisional government to march on Frankfurt to defend the Parliament. But once again the Prussian regulars were to give the radical revolt short shrift. At the grand duke's request they invaded Baden as soon as they had suppressed the revolution in the Palatinate. Mieroslawski, with 40,000 men, mostly untrained and poorly equipped, fought valiantly but was soon defeated at Waghäusel (June 20). The insurgents were obliged to abandon Karlsruhe and the provisional government took flight as the Prussian forces occupied the entire duchy. But only on July 23 did the beleaguered Rastatt garrison finally surrender. Prussian courts-martial then went into action, showing themselves no less ruthless than their Austrian counterparts in Hungary. About a thousand persons were convicted, of whom twenty-seven died before firing squads. Most of the insurgents, however, managed to escape. Over 10,000 of them reached Switzerland, among them Carl Schurz, who at the age of twenty had taken a prominent part in the fight and was presently to emigrate to the United States, there to make for himself a distinguished career as soldier, diplomat and statesman.[56]

The insurrections of May–June, 1849, sometimes called the Second German Revolution, revealed widespread popular support for the work of the Frankfurt Parliament, but they were the expressions only of forlorn hopes, partly because of their internal weaknesses and partly because of the forces now marshaled against them. There was, in the first place, no unity to the radical movement. The radical leaders could rarely see eye to eye and the provisional governments were usually so taken up with internal conflicts that they could not concentrate on the task of defense. At the same time the liberals had become so disheartened and so averse to further disorder and violence that they either stood aloof or else supported the governments in the work of repression. In any event, the hastily organized insurrections had no chance of survival now that the Prussian government had re-estab-

---

[56] *The Reminiscences of Carl Schurz* (New York, 1906–1908), I. Of the many books on Schurz, the following are particularly full on his early, German period: Otto Dannehl: *Carl Schurz, ein deutscher Kämpfer* (Berlin, 1929); Hanns Höwing: *Carl Schurz, Rebell, Kämpfer, Staatsman* (Wiesbaden, 1948).

lished its position at home and was willing if not eager to act as gendarme for all Germany. The fighters of 1849 were, for all their heroism, champions of a lost cause.

7. POSTLUDE: THE AUSTRO-PRUSSIAN CONFLICT

Frederick William of Prussia rejected the imperial crown offered him by the Frankfurt Parliament not because he was opposed to German unification but because he wanted to carry it through according to his own ideas, that is, along traditional lines of agreement between the German princes. The details of his program had been worked out by his friend Radowitz, whose knowledge of the German problem was derived from years of experience as Prussian military representative at the federal Diet, followed by service as deputy in the Frankfurt Parliament. Radowitz was convinced that German unity was the best antidote to revolution and that the Frankfurt constitution, revamped in a conservative direction and approved by the German princes, might well serve the purpose. According to the plan which he worked out for the king, membership in the projected empire was to be entirely voluntary. The king of Prussia was to be the head, and was to have an absolute veto on legislation enacted by the Parliament. The emperor was to be assisted by a college of six princes, as well as by a two-chamber Parliament: an upper chamber representing the member states, and a lower chamber elected on the three-class system of government just being introduced in Prussia. This German Empire was, however, to be a component part of a larger federation to include the entire Hapsburg Monarchy, under Austrian leadership. The larger federation would be governed by a directory of four, two members of which would be Austrian. It would have control of foreign affairs and trade for the entire federation, comprising all of Central Europe.[57]

This program, submitted to the German governments on May 9, 1849, was politely rejected by Schwarzenberg on May 25, for even though it met his demand of March 7 that the entire Austrian empire

---

[57] Friedrich Meinecke: *Radowitz und die deutsche Revolution* (Berlin, 1913) provides the basic account, but see also Erich Brandenburg: *Die Reichsgründung* (Leipzig, 1916), I; Erick Marcks: *Der Aufstieg des Reiches* (Stuttgart, 1936), I, 334 ff.; and the excellent, succinct treatment by Egmont Zechlin: *Die deutsche Einheitsbewegung* (Frankfurt, 1967), 157 ff. On the Austrian side, see Heinrich von Srbik: *Deutsche Einheit* (3 ed., Munich, 1940), II; Kiszling: *Fürst Felix zu Schwarzenberg*, 107 ff.

be included in the new Germany, its provision for a well-integrated inner German empire under Prussian leadership was highly objectionable. For the time being, however, the position of Austria, obliged to call on Russia for aid against the Hungarians, was exceedingly weak, while that of Prussia, called upon to suppress the revolutionary movements in South Germany, was strong. The Austrian chancellor was unable, for the moment, to do much more than encourage Bavaria and other important states to resist the Prussian proposals, baiting them with hopes of eventually being allowed to absorb the smaller states and so form a third unit on a par with Austria and Prussia.

Prussia, meanwhile, seemed to make real strides forward. On May 26 Hanover and Saxony agreed to an alliance with Prussia, on condition that Bavaria and Württemberg do likewise. These two states, under Austrian influence, declined, but in all, twenty-eight German states accepted, under varying degrees of dependence on Prussian support and with varying degrees of enthusiasm. In June, 148 members of the Frankfurt Parliament (most of them liberals) convened at Gotha and voted to support the Prussian program, on the theory that the objectives of the Frankfurt Parliament were more important than the exact means by which they were to be attained.

Within a few months, however, storm clouds began to gather. Once the Hungarians had surrendered, Schwarzenberg went over to the offensive. On August 27 he protested that the constitution envisaged by the Prussian program would be incompatible with the treaties of 1815, by which all German states were still bound. The Prussian government, never very much enamored of the schemes of the "outsider" Radowitz, drew back to the extent of accepting the establishment of a provisional federal executive, on which both Austria and Prussia were to have two members, this to continue until May 1, 1850. The agreement on this point meant that Prussia recognized the continued validity of the old Confederation and by implication expressed readiness to abandon what had become known as the "Prussian Union." Nonetheless, the Berlin government went on with its plans for elections to a Parliament that was to meet on March 20, 1850. Schwarzenberg, in turn, threatened in veiled terms that war might result if the Prussian government persisted on this course. The chancellor had by this time adopted the plan worked out by his minister of commerce, Karl Ludwig Bruck, for a vast Middle European customs union which would comprise a population of seventy million and give German industry access to the Mediterranean and the entire lower Danube Basin. This was reminiscent of the program advanced some years earlier by the famous economist, Friedrich List.[58]

For the Austrian chancellor this progressive economic concept provided a useful instrument of power politics, for he proposed that the projected customs union be given extensive jurisdiction under the federal authority at Frankfurt. He also induced Hanover and Saxony to abandon their alliance with Prussia and join with Austria in a new alliance envisaging the absorption of the smaller German states and the reorganization of Central Europe on the triune basis.[59] Much of this was undoubtedly tactical maneuvering and need not be traced in detail. The point is that the Prussian Union was under increasingly frequent and heavy attack. Yet neither Frederick William nor Radowitz would yield. They felt in honor bound to stand by their program, to which twenty-six governments still subscribed, and to protect the smaller states from the victimization that threatened them. They therefore opened the Union Parliament on March 20, 1850. Since the radicals had boycotted the elections, the membership was safely conservative or moderately liberal. It soon accepted the modifications in the draft constitution proposed by the Prussian government, subject to eventual approval also by the member governments. It then adjourned (April 29).

But on the very eve of the Erfurt meeting the federal Diet, inspired by Schwarzenberg, had invited the German states to send delegates to Frankfurt to discuss the resurrection of the old Germanic Confederation. The Prussian government insisted on prior recognition of the Union, but the Middle States stood by Austria. When the delegates assembled at Frankfurt on May 10, only ten out of the thirty-five German states were represented, but they were all the important ones, save Prussia. The two great powers were now deadlocked. Each of them appealed to Czar Nicholas for support. Since the Russian interest was to keep Central Europe only loosely federated and therefore weak,

[58] Franz J. Schoeningh: "Bruck und der grossdeutsche Zollverein" (*Hochland*, XXXI (1), 1933–1934, 325–332), and "Karl Ludwig Bruck und die Idee Mitteleuropas" (*Historisches Jahrbuch*, LVI, 1936); Henry C. Meyer: *Mitteleuropa in German Thought and Action* (The Hague, 1955), 11 ff.; Jacques Droz: *L'Europe centrale: évolution de l'idée de "Mitteleuropa"* (Paris, 1960), chap. ii.

[59] Michael Doberl: *Bayern und das preussische Unionsprojekt* (Munich, 1926).

the czar had no sympathy for the Prussian Union and hardly more for the vast Mitteleuropa scheme. He had been greatly relieved when Frederick William declined the "revolutionary" crown offered him by the Frankfurt Parliament, and was irritated when Radowitz, whom the Russian ambassador in Berlin described as "a charlatan and phrase-maker," advanced a new scheme which borrowed substantially from the Frankfurt constitution. As between the Prussian and the Austrian schemes, the latter was far less advanced and less likely to materialize. Nicholas was therefore disposed to support Vienna and bring pressure on Berlin to abandon the Union.[60]

This was the more so as the Prussian policy in the troublesome Schleswig-Holstein affair continued to estrange not only the Russian but also the British and French governments. Efforts to reconcile German and Danish views during the Malmö armistice having failed, the Danish government had in March, 1849, denounced the armistice. In the ensuing hostilities Prussian and federal troops advanced to the point of invading Jutland (July) when the powers again intervened. Russia, supported by Britain and France, obliged the Prussian govern-ment to agree to another armistice, under which matters continued to simmer for another year, until the Berlin government, fearful of losing Russian support in the German question, agreed to the Treaty of Berlin and withdrew its troops entirely from Schleswig (July 2, 1850). The Schleswigers, who refused to join in this abject surrender, kept on fighting, only to be defeated by the Danes at Idstedt (July 25). As for Holstein, which was part of the Germanic Confederation, the Danish king appealed to the revived ederal Diet for aid in restoring his control. Thus the fate of the duchies, which so influenced the attitude of the European powers toward Prussia, became a key issue also in the duel between Prussia and Austria.[61]

Matters came to a head in September, 1850, when the electoral prince of

[60] Eduard Heller: *Mitteleuropas Vorkämpfer: Fürst Felix zu Schwarzenberg* (Vienna, 1933), 102 ff.

[61] W. E. Mosse: *The European Powers and the German Question, 1848–1871* (Cambridge, 1958), 28 ff.; W. Carr: *Schleswig-Holstein, 1815–1848* (Manchester, 1963), 294 ff.; Willy Andreas: "Die russische Diplomatie und die Politik Friedrich Wilhelms IV" (*Abhandlungen der Preussischen Akademie der Wissenschaften: Phil.-Hist.* Klasse, 1926, 1–64); Ernst G. Lange: *Frankreichs Preussenpolitik in den Jahren 1849 und 1850* (Berlin, 1930); Günther Gillesen: *Lord Palmerston und die Einigung Deutschlands* (Lübeck, 1961), 77 ff.; Holger Hjelholt: *British Mediation in the Danish-German Conflict, 1848–1850* (Copenhagen, 1965–1966), II, chaps. viii, ix, xiv.

Hesse turned to the federal Diet for aid against his Parliament, which, supported by the people and the army was in revolt against his violation of the constitution. The Prussian government protested against federal action either in Holstein or in Hesse. It denied the competence of the rump federal Diet and furthermore insisted that since Hesse was still a member of the Union its case should be referred to the court of arbitration of that body. The situation was further complicated by the fact that Hesse lay between the two parts of the Prussian Monarchy and that the Prussian government had rights of military transit on two of the main roads. In Berlin the decision was made to occupy Hesse if federal troops were sent in. Schwarzenberg, relying on Russian support against the "revolution" in Hesse, resolved on his part to accept the challenge. On October 12 Austria concluded military agreements with Bavaria and Württemberg by which those states agreed to employ military force in Hesse if the federal Diet so ordered.

At this juncture the Prussian minister-president, Count Brandenburg, hurried off to Warsaw to plead with the czar, only to be followed by Schwarzenberg on the same errand. After long discussions the Prussian minister, long since soured on the Union scheme, agreed to recognize the resurrection of the old Confederation and its enlargement by inclusion of the entire Hapsburg Empire. This was tantamount to abandonment of the Union. In return Schwarzenberg would agree only that the reorganization of Germany should be decided upon by a conference of state ministers. Neither on the Holstein nor the Hesse problem was any progress made.

Meanwhile the federal Diet voted to send a commissioner to Holstein to take charge of affairs and report on the need for intervention. On October 16 it voted to send Bavarian and Hanoverian troops into Hesse. When on November 1 Bavarian forces crossed the frontier, Prussian troops at once occupied the military routes and the territory between them. Radowitz, who had been appointed Prussian minister of foreign affairs, felt that the challenge must be accepted and the federal troops be resisted even at the cost of war. He seems to have hoped that, in a showdown, if Russia supported Austria, Britain and France would stand by Prussia.[62] But the king was unwilling to contemplate a German civil war and the majority of the cabinet was also opposed to a trial of strength which they feared might have a disastrous outcome.

[62] Lange: *Frankreichs Preussenpolitik.*

Radowitz was obliged to resign (November 2) and the Prussian Union was doomed.

As for Holstein and Hesse, Schwarzenberg would not even discuss these issues until the Prussians had evacuated Hesse. This the Berlin government felt would be too great a blow at its prestige. Full mobilization was ordered (November 5). On the following day Count Brandenburg died quite unexpectedly. His successor, Count Otto von Manteuffel, had even less use for the Union and was ready to make whatever settlement was possible. How dangerous the situation had become was revealed by a minor clash between Prussian and federal (Bavarian) troops in Hesse on November 8. So close did war appear that some of the Middle States were already looking forward to an Austrian victory that would end the threat of Prussian domination.[63] Schwarzenberg might quite possibly have welcomed a military decision, but was naturally anxious to avoid further dependence on Russian good will. Furthermore, he had to reckon with the hostility of France and Britain. The French had begun to concentrate large forces on the Rhine and were clearly determined to participate in any readjustment of the balance of power. The British, while they were much irritated by the Prussian policy in the duchies and regarded the Union as a half-baked project which was endangering the peace, were nonetheless unwilling to see Prussia defeated. And finally, in all this welter of conflicting interests, Czar Nicholas was constantly urging a peaceful solution, the reflection of his conviction that war between the two German powers could result only in renewed revolution.[64]

The crisis came to a head when, on November 24, Schwarzenberg sent an ultimatum to Berlin demanding the evacuation of the Hessian fortress of Cassel within forty-eight hours. The Prussian government, hopeless of success and unwilling to invoke French aid, made no resistance. Manteuffel journeyed all the way to Olmütz to confer with the Austrian chancellor, who, after first taking a hard line, showed himself fairly conciliatory, evidently so as to strengthen the conservative elements in the Berlin government. The result of long discussion was the Convention (*Punktation*) of Olmütz (November 29), by which the

---

[63] Heller: *Mitteleuropas Vorkämpfer*, 125 ff.

[64] Andreas: "Die russische Diplomatie," 42 ff.; Lange: *Frankreichs Preussenpolitik;* Hans Precht: *Englands Stellung zur deutschen Einheit* (Berlin, 1925), 158 ff.; Gillesen: *Lord Palmerston,* 95 ff.

two powers agreed to send commissioners to Holstein as agents of the Germanic Confederation. As for the Hessian issue, Prussia agreed to permit federal forces to cross the military roads and to admit Austrian forces to share in the garrisoning of Cassel. Austria dropped the demand for complete evacuation of Hesse by the Prussians. As for the reorganization of Germany, Prussia was to abandon the Union plan, while Austria agreed that the foreign ministers of all German states should meet immediately at Dresden to study the problem. In a secret protocol Manteuffel agreed that Prussia should demobilize completely before the Dresden meeting, though Austria was obliged to demobilize only partially and the Middle States not at all.[65]

In German histories the Punctation of Olmütz is usually referred to as the "humiliation" of Olmütz. It certainly was humiliating for Prussia to sacrifice the Union and yield on both the Holstein and Hesssian issues. In the Prussian Parliament the vote of approval (January 8, 1851) was exceedingly close (146–142), despite the brilliant, realistic defense of the government's policy by Otto von Bismarck, who was now rising to prominence. The widespread feeling of frustration and defeat was further enhanced by the outcome of the Dresden conferences, which lasted from December 3, 1850, to May 15, 1851. Schwarzenberg again pressed for the inclusion of the entire Hapsburg Monarchy in the revamped Germanic Confederation, while the Prussian delegates insisted on complete equality with Austria in the leadership of the new Germany. Once more agreement proved impossible and there remained no alternative but to return to the arrangements of 1815, that is, to the reconstitution of the Germanic Confederation, with all its faults and weaknesses. "A threadbare, shabby coat is still better than none at all," the Austrian chancellor is reputed to have said.[66]

Thus liberal hopes for the unification of the German states on the basis of popular, constitutional government went up in smoke. As a result of the Dresden conferences Schwarzenberg's program for a great Middle Europe went the way of the Prussian Union. In short, all

---

[65] For an excellent analysis of the convention, see Huber: *Deutsche Verfassungsgeschichte*, II, 919 ff. Joachim Hoffmann: "Russland und die Olmützer Punktation" (*Forschungen zur osteuropäischen Geschichte*, VII, 1959, 59–71) has disposed of the story that it was the intervention of the Russian ambassador to Vienna that induced Schwarzenberg to relent.

[66] Friedrich Engel-Janosi: "Ein Kampf um Oesterreich in Berlin und Frankfurt, 1849–1855" (in his *Geschichte auf dem Ballhausplatz*, Graz, 1963, 65–102).

projects for an integrated national state were wrecked in one way or another. At the root of the failure lay the strong particularism of the German states. Prussia refused to be dissolved in a new Germany, and the Austrians were equally unwilling to have the historic Hapsburg Empire disrupted. The small German states, in turn, were in terror of being devoured by the Middle States. For that reason they were willing to join the Prussian Union, which was exactly what the Middle States refused to contemplate. And to these fundamental obstacles must be added the fact that neither Frederick William of Prussia nor Francis Joseph of Austria would have any truck with revolution or the revolutionary Frankfurt Parliament. Yet the Frankfurt constitution was probably the most practicable and forward-looking of all the projects advanced at that time and the liberal forces that created the Frankfurt Parliament were the forces of the future. If the princes and their governments were obtuse in their refusal to adopt much-needed reforms before 1848, they were even more benighted in their determination to overrule the forces making for a progressive program of national unification. It was fear and hate of popular forces that led the ruling classes to defend the old regime by armed power, which to them still seemed more important than the dictates of reason.

BIBLIOGRAPHICAL NOTE

Most writings on the revolutions of 1848–1849 deal exclusively with the events and issues of specific countries. However, Priscilla Robertson's *Revolutions of 1848: a Social Study* (Princeton, 1952) provides an overall narrative, with emphasis on nonpolitical, nonmilitary aspects, and Arnold Whitridge: *Men in Crisis: the Revolutions of 1848* (New York, 1949) reviews the European upheavals through the biographies of their leaders. The centenary of the revolutions, in 1948, produced a number of collaborative works, in which specialists reviewed developments in various counties. *The Opening of an Era, 1848,* edited by François Fetjto (2 vols. London, 1948) is a most useful work of this sort. In the same general category are *Actes du Congrès Historique du Centenaire de la Révolution de 1848* (Paris, 1948); the Italian *Il 1848 nella Storia d'Europa* (Rome, 1949); and the Soviet Academy of Sciences' *Revolutsii, 1848–1849* (2 vols., Moscow, 1952). Lewis B. Namier: *1848: the Revolution of the Intellectuals* (London, 1944), is a stimulating and provocative essay by an outstanding British historian.

France. *1848: le Livre du Centenaire,* edited by Charles Moulin (Paris, 1948) and *1848,* edited by Georges Bourgin and Max Terrier (Paris, 1948) provide impressive collections of essays and and much unique pictorial material. Among the numerous monographic studies the best are Jean Dautry: *1848 et la Deuxième République* (Paris, 1957); and Louis Girard: *La Deuxième République, 1848–1851* (Paris, 1968), the work of an eminent French historian. Albert Crémieux: *La Révolution de Février* (Paris, 1912), a microscopic, archival study of the events of a few days, is still basic. For a shorter and more readable account, there is Jean Bruhat: *Les Journées de Février, 1848* (Paris, 1948). For the period from February to June there is an admirable book, translated from the French, by Georges Duveau: *1848: the Making of a Revolution* (New York, 1966). Other monographs worth mentioning are Gaston Martin: *La Révolution de 1848* (2 ed., Paris, 1959), excellent on the social side; Emile Tersen: *Quarante-huit* (Paris, 1958), written from a moderate Marxist standpoint. René Gossez: *Les Ouvriers de Paris* (Paris, 1966) is a valuable analysis of the role of the working classes, and Donald C. McKay: *The National Workshops* (2 ed., Cambridge, Mass., 1965) is a definitive study of this crucial institution and its suppression. Frederick A. de Luna: *The French Republic under Cavaignac, 1848* (Princeton, 1969) examines the second, somewhat neglected period of the revolution. Among biographical studies H. Remsen Whitehouse: *The Life of Lamartine* (2 vols., Boston, 1918) ; Paul Keller: *Louis Blanc und die Revolution von 1848* (Zurich, 1926) ; and Alvin R. Calman: *Ledru-Rollin and the Second French Republic* (New York, 1922) are still worth consulting.

The career of Louis Napoleon Bonaparte and the prelude to the Second Empire have called forth a mass of literature. F. A. Simpson: *Louis Napoleon and the Recovery of France* (3 ed., London, 1951) is still outstanding, but the following more recent studies are all commendable: James E. Thompson: *Louis Napoleon and the Second Empire* (New York, 1955) ; J. P. T. Bury: *Napoleon III and the Second Empire* (London, 1964). Among French works one of the most up-to-date and most readable is Adrien Dansette: *Louis-Napoléon à la Conquête du Pouvoir, 1808–1851* (2 vols., Paris, 1961). Pierre Dominique: *Louis-Napoléon et le Coup d'Etat du décembre 2* (Paris, 1957) is actually a useful review of the entire presidency of Louis Napoleon. Henri Guillemin: *Le Coup d'Etat du 2 décembre* (Paris, 1951), is one of the best studies of the coup d'état and its background.

The German States. Still the classic account, based on wide archival study, is Veit Valentin: *Geschichte der deutschen Revolution, 1848–1849* (2 vols., Berlin, 1930), but there is an excellent more recent study by Jacques Droz: *Les Révolutions Allemandes de 1848* (Paris, 1957). Friedrich Meinecke: *1848, eine Sakularbetrachtung* (Bonn, 1948) is a noteworthy reflective essay by the leading German historian of his day. Rudolf Stadelmann: *Soziale und politische Geschichte de Revolution von 1848* (Munich, 1956) is the broadest and best of the shorter treatments, though Paul Wentzke: *1848: die unvollendete deutsche Revolution* (Munich, 1938) and Wilhelm Mommsen: *Grosse und Versagen des deutschen Burgertums* (Stuttgart, 1949) are both noteworthy as reflecting the liberal viewpoint. Hermann Meyer: *1848: Studien zur Geschichte der deutschen Revolution* (Darmstadt, 1949) is important for its analysis of radicalism in Berlin and Vienna. The well-documented monograph by Frank Eyck: *The Frankfurt Parliament, 1848–1849* (New York, 1968) covers that important subject in an objective, scholarly way. Much attention has of late been paid to the role of the workers and of socialism in the German revolution. Among many socialist or communist studies mention may be made of the Soviet monograph edited by Fedor V. Potemkin and A. I. Molok, translated into German under the title *Die Revolution in Deutschland, 1848–1849* (Berlin, 1956) ; the very competent study of Karl Obermann: *Die deutschen Arbeiter in der Revolution von 1848* (2 ed., Berlin, 1953) ; and Gerhard Becker's *Karl Marx und Friedrich Engels in Koln, 1848–1849* (Berlin, 1963). As antidotes to the Marxist literature one should read the solid, critical account of Paul Noyes: *Organization and Revolution: Working-Class Associations in the German Revolution of 1848–1849* (Princeton, 1966), and the recent study by Oscar J. Hammen: *The Red 48'ers: Karl Marx and Friedrich Engels* (New York, 1969).

The Habsburg Empire. The revolution in Austria is commonly treated in the histories of the German Revolution, but for the interrelationship of the revolutionary movements in the entire empire one should consult Rudolf Kiszling and others: *Die Revolution im Kaisertum Oesterreich, 1848–1849* (2 vols., Vienna, 1948, 1952). R. John Rath: *The Viennese Revolution of 1848* (Austin, Texas, 1957) is an excellent systematic account. Useful, too, are the biographies of Schwarzenberg by Rudolf Kiszling and by Jacques Droz. The solid Marxist study of the revolution in Bohemia: *Aufzeichnungen uber die Geschichte des nationalen und politischen Kampfes in Bohmen im Jahre 1848* (Berlin, 1953) may now be supplemented by Stanley I. Pech: *The Czech Revolution of 1848* (Chapel Hill, 1969).

The Italian Revolution. A number of books in English are of interest and value, among them the well-known works of George M. Trevelyan, written with Romantic fervor: *Garibaldi's Defence of the Roman Republic* (new ed., London, 1908) ; *Manin and the Venetian Republic of 1848* (New York, 1923). In addition there are the books on Garibaldi by Denis Mack Smith: *Garibaldi* (New York, 1956) and Christopher Hibbert: *Garibaldi and his Enemies* (London, 1965). For Mazzini, Gwilyn O. Griffith: *Mazzini* (New York, 1932) is still the best general study in English.

Most of the literature on the Italian Revolution is, of course, in Italian. Only a select list need be given here. Pietro Silva: *Il 1848* (Rome, 1948) is a competent, succinct review. On the military events there are useful studies by Guido Porzio: *La Guerra Regia in Italia nel 1848–1849* (Rome, 1955) and Pietro Pieri: *Storia Militare del Risorgimento* (Turin, 1962). Antonio Monti: *Il 1848 e le Cinque Giornate di Milano* (Milan, 1948) is authoritative for the Lombard revolution. The same author has an excellent book on *Pio IX nel Risorgimento* (Bari, 1928). On the revolution and the republic in Rome Domenico Demarco: *Pio IX e la*

Rivoluzione Romana de 1848 (Modena, 1947) and Luigi Rodelli: *La Repubblica Romana del 1849* (Pisa, 1955) are outstanding. The revolution in Sicily is admirably treated in Federico Curato: *La Rivoluzione Siciliana del 1848–1849* (Milan, 1940), and the history of the Venetian Republic in Vincenzo Marchesi: *Storia Documentata della Rivoluzione e della Difensa di Venezia negli anni 1848–1849* (Venice, 1913).

International Aspects Of The Revolutions. Eugène de Guichen: *Les Grandes Questions Européennes et la Diplomatie des Puissances sous la Seconde République* (2 vols., Paris, 1925, 1929) rests upon extensive archival study and is still valuable. The same is true of Donald M. Greer: *L'Angleterre, la France et la Révolution de 1848* (Paris, 1925). More recently Emile Tersen: *Le Gouvernement Provisoire et l'Europe* (Paris, 1948) has done for French policy what Greer did for the British. The diplomacy of the German problem has been studied in great detail. W. E. Mosse: *The European Powers and the German Question, 1848–1871* (Cambridge, 1958) provides an excellent introduction, while G. Gillesen: *Lord Palmerston und die Einigung Deutschlands, 1848–1851* (Berlin, 1961) incorporates earlier studies and concentrates on the revolutionary period. Holger Hjelholt: *British Mediation in the Danish-German Conflict, 1848–1850* (2 vols., Copenhagen, 1965) is a truly exhaustive monograph. Charles Sproxton: *Palmerston and the Hungarian Revolution* (Cambridge, 1919) is still valuable. Italian problems are analyzed in A. J. P. Taylor: *The Italian Problem in European Diplomacy, 1847–1849* (Manchester, 1934), which deals largely with the Austrian-Piedmontese conflict, and more recently in the comprehensive monograph of Ruggero Moscati: *La Diplomazia Europea e il Problema Italiano nel 1848* (Florence, 1947). Ferdinand Boyer: *La Seconde République et Charles-Albert en 1848* (Paris, 1967) is a detailed archival study of the crucial problem of French intervention in northern Italy. Emile Bourgeois and Emile Clermont: *Rome et Napoléon III* (Paris, 1907) is still indispensable for the study of the French intervention in Rome, though a more comprehensive as well as a more recent treatment of the complex problem of the temporal power of the Papacy is Guido Quazza: *La Questione Romana nel 1848–1849* (Modena, 1947). The Russian intervention against the Hungarian Republic has been analyzed at great length in Erzsebet Andics: *Das Bundnis Habsburg-Romanow* (Budapest, 1963), and in Revekka A. Averbukh: *Revolutsiia i Nationalno-Osvoboditelnaia Borba v Vengrii, 1848–1849* (Moscow, 1965).

INDEX

Academic Legion (Austrian), 36 ff.
Albert, Archduke, 34–35
Ancona, 130
Anti-Corn Law League, influence of, abroad, 2
Antonelli, Cardinal, 117–118
Arago, François Dominique, 14, 26
aristocracy, 18
armies, Austrian, 35, 95; Hungarian, 43, 45; Piedmontese, 120; Prussian, 74 f., 95
Arnim-Suckow, Baron von, 83 f.
Augusta, princess of Prussia, 78
Austria and German unity, 90–91, 94; and the Roman Republic, 119; revolution in, 33 ff.
Austro-Slavism, 46

Bach, Alexander, 165, 175
Baden, 69 f., 185 f.
Bagehot, Walter, 146
Bakunin, Michael, 49 ff., 185
Balcercu, Nicolas, 149 ff.
Balta Liman, Convention of, 150
"Banquet of the People," 29–30
banquets, political, in France, 7
Barbès, Armand, 25
Barrot, Odilon, 2, 11 ff., 107, 126, 132–134
Bastide, Jules, 65–66, 150
Batthyány, Count Louis, 40, 46, 154, 174
Bavaria, 1848 revolution in, 70
Belgium, 6, 19
Bem, General Joseph, 157 f., 170, 172
Berends, Julius, 73
Berlin, revolution in, 73 ff., 159 ff., 162, Treaty of, 190
Berryer, Pierre Antoine, 107
Bismarck, Otto von, 77–78, 193
Blanc, Louis, 2, 14 ff., 26, 108
Blanqui, Auguste, 18, 21, 23, 25
Blum, Robert, 85, 158, 178
Bologna, 115

Bonaparte, Carlo, prince of Canino, 115
Born, Stefan, 79 ff., 97 ff., 159
Brandenburg, General Friedrich Wilhelm von, 161 ff., 191
Brofferio, Angelo, 112
Bruck, Karl Ludwig, 165, 188
Brunetti, Angelo, 114 ff.
Budapest, 167, 171, 174
Bugeaud, General Robert, 11–12

Cabet, Etienne, 22
Camarilla, Court, Austrian, 43 ff., 51, 165, Prussian, 77 f., 159, 162
Camphausen, Ludolf, 77 ff.
Capucines, Boulevard des, "massacre" of, 11
Carnot, Hippolyte, 135
Casati, Count Gabrio, 53
Catholic Church, Roman, in France, 18, 136–137; See also, Papacy
Cattaneo, Carlo, 54–55
Caussidière, Marc, 14
Cavaignac, General Eugène, 30, 65, 103 ff., 110 f., 118
Cavour, Count Camillo Benso di, 56, 111
Central Republican Committee (in Paris), 17
Changarnier, General Nicolas, 134–139
Charles Albert, King of Sardinia, 55 ff., 112 ff., 120 ff.
cholera, 134, 172
Chrzanowski, General Joseph, 120–121
Circolo Populare (Roman), 114 f.
citizen guard (Burgerwehr), Austrian, 34 f.; Prussian, 76 f., 160; Tuscan, 113; Roman, 117
civic guard, see citizen guard
classes, social, 67
Cobden, Richard; influence of, on the Continent, 2 f., 173

199